Lecture Notes in Computer Science 12585

More information about this subseries at http://www.springer.com/series/7409

Thoralf Reis · Marco X. Bornschlegl ·
Marco Angelini · Matthias L. Hemmje (Eds.)

Advanced Visual Interfaces

Supporting Artificial Intelligence and Big Data Applications

AVI 2020 Workshops, AVI-BDA and ITAVIS
Ischia, Italy, June 9, 2020 and September 29, 2020
Revised Selected Papers

Editors
Thoralf Reis
University of Hagen
Hagen, Germany

Marco Angelini
Sapienza University of Rome
Rome, Italy

Marco X. Bornschlegl
University of Hagen
Hagen, Germany

Matthias L. Hemmje
University of Hagen
Hagen, Germany

ISSN 0302-9743 ISSN 1611-3349 (electronic)
Lecture Notes in Computer Science
ISBN 978-3-030-68006-0 ISBN 978-3-030-68007-7 (eBook)
https://doi.org/10.1007/978-3-030-68007-7

LNCS Sublibrary: SL3 – Information Systems and Applications, incl. Internet/Web, and HCI

This Springer imprint is published by the registered company Springer Nature Switzerland AG
The registered company address is: Gewerbestrasse 11, 6330 Cham, Switzerland

Preface of AVI-BDA Workshop

First of all, this volume contains the full papers presented, discussed, extended, and revised in the context of the 15th Conference on Advanced Visual Interfaces (AVI) within the Workshop on Road Mapping Infrastructures for Artificial Intelligence Supporting Advanced Visual Big Data Analysis (AVI-BDA), held on June 9th, 2020. The workshop initializing the work was organized by us in our capacity as PhD student, as postdoc, and as Chair of Multimedia and Internet Applications at the Faculty of Mathematics and Computer Science at the University of Hagen, Germany. The workshop was curated by an international Program Committee of fourteen scientists from nine different universities in six different countries.

Handling the complexity of Big Data requires new visualization techniques in regards to data access, perception, and interaction. Employing Artificial Intelligence can help to lower the entry barriers for different types of Big Data Analysis users and ease their journeys from data integration to data transformation and data exploration. Then again it introduces further challenges for human-computer interaction and interoperability. Therefore, this workshop addressed these issues with a special focus on supporting AI-based intelligent advanced visual user interfaces for Big Data Analysis. In this way, the purpose of this research road-mapping workshop was threefold. Firstly, it aimed at consolidating information, technical details, and research directions from the diverse range of academic R&D projects currently available. Secondly, based on visions of future infrastructures and gaps in the current state of the art, a new reference model was presented, and thirdly, this reference model was validated by the workshop participants. To achieve these aims the workshop brought together researchers and practitioners who are able to contribute and to aid in the research road-mapping, in the validation of a novel reference model, and in providing publications based on their own work in correspondence to the derived reference model. The results of this validation and the corresponding reference model can be used to inform, influence, and disseminate ideas to the wider research community. In consequence, the Call for Papers of the workshop invited contributions from academic researchers and practitioners working in the areas of Big Data Analysis, Visualization, and Artificial Intelligence. The nine initial submissions of position papers from six different countries were each carefully reviewed by three Program Committee members.

Based on submitted position papers and existing research, the workshop outlined the current baseline of infrastructures for AI-based intelligent advanced visual user interfaces for Big Data Analysis. Furthermore, it outlined research gaps that need to be filled to achieve the targeted research and development ambitions. Realizing these ambitions was supported by the presentation and discussion of research aiming at delivering Artificial Intelligence and Big Data Analysis application scenarios, e.g. through intelligent advanced visual user interfaces, supporting researchers and organizations in applying and maintaining distributed (spatially, physically, as well as potentially cross-domain) research resources. These application scenarios served to validate a reference model that utilizes open standards and that can be materialized through an open architecture and components derived from state-of-the-art research results and which is able to deal with Big Data Analysis, Visualization, and Artificial Intelligence resources and services at scale. In this way, the validated reference model can pave the way towards collaboration on the development of an AI-based Big Data Analysis and Visualization tool suite that adopts common existing open standards for access, analysis, and visualization. Thereby, it helps to realize a ubiquitous collaborative workspace for researchers which is able to facilitate the research process and its Big Data Analysis and Artificial Intelligence applications.

The workshop took place during a full day and was structured in four sessions to provide maximum time for group discussion and brainstorming. In the first session the participants introduced themselves together with their accepted paper. Following this, the workshop presented a novel reference model for Artificial Intelligence supporting Big Data Analysis and Visualization. In the third session, a gap analysis and validation was completed on the basis of each presented research domain perspective and on the basis of the derived reference model. In the fourth session the group summarized the gaps and set out a timeline and areas for completing their corresponding full publications in order to reflect the gaps and fully validate the derived reference model.

We would like to thank all the authors for contributing high-quality research position papers to the workshop and full papers as well as revisions of these full papers after an additional review to establish the content for these proceedings. We would also like to express our sincere thanks to the Organizing and Program Committees, to the members of our Editorial Board, as well as to all the additional external reviewers for reviewing the papers within a very short period of time. Finally, we thank Springer for publishing the proceedings in the Lecture Notes in Computer Science series.

November 2020

Thoralf Reis
Marco X. Bornschlegl
Matthias L. Hemmje

Preface of ITAVIS Workshop

In addition, this volume also contains the proceedings of the 2nd edition of the ITAVIS workshop. The second edition of the ITAVIS workshop consolidated and expanded the encouraging results obtained from the first edition (ITA.WA.- Italian Visualization & Visual Analytics workshop). The goal was to make an additional step toward the creation of an Italian research community on the topics of Visualization, Visual Analytics, HCI and Design, allowing identification of research directions, joining forces in achieving them, linking researchers and practitioners and developing common guidelines and programs for teaching activities in the fields of Visualization and Visual Analytics. The workshop accepted for the first time five contributions, split into two full research papers, one position paper and two activity presentation reports. The workshop took place during a half-day and was structured in 3 sessions: a keynote speaker session, a research paper session and an activity presentation session. This program fostered a lively discussion and helped in the formation of new connections between research institutions on the topics of Visualization and Visual Analytics. Finally, the ITAVIS workshop produced a future road-map to strengthen the effort of creating an Italian community on these subjects. I would like to thank all the authors for contributing high-quality papers. My thanks go to the Organizing and Program Committees for helping to create an interesting program. I thank Springer for publishing the proceedings in the Lecture Notes in Computer Science series.

November 2020 Marco Angelini

Organization of AVI-BDA Workshop

Organizing Committee

Thoralf Reis	University of Hagen, Germany
Marco X. Bornschlegl	University of Hagen, Germany
Matthias L. Hemmje	University of Hagen, Germany

Program Committee

Haithem Afli	Munster Technological University, Ireland
Marco X. Bornschlegl	University of Hagen, Germany
Paolo Buono	University of Bari Aldo Moro, Italy
Tiziana Catarci	Sapienza University of Rome, Italy
Abbas Cheddad	Blekinge Institute of Technology, Sweden
Felix C. Engel	University of Hagen, Germany
Anna Esposito	University of Campania Luigi Vanvitelli, Italy
Matthias L. Hemmje	University of Hagen, Germany
Massimo Mecella	Sapienza University of Rome, Italy
Andrea Molinari	Università di Trentino, Italy
Thoralf Reis	University of Hagen, Germany
María Inés Torres	University of the Basque Country, Spain
Haiying Wang	Ulster University, UK
Huiru Zheng	Ulster University, UK

Organization of ITAVIS Workshop

Organizing Committee

Marco Angelini	Sapienza University of Rome, Italy
Giuseppe Santucci	Sapienza University of Rome, Italy

Program Committee

Paolo Buono	University of Bari Aldo Moro, Italy
Tiziana Catarci	Sapienza University of Rome, Italy
Antonina Dattolo	University of Udine, Italy
Giuseppe Desolda	University of Bari Aldo Moro, Italy
Sara Di Bartolomeo	Northeastern University, Boston, USA
Giuseppe Di Battista	Roma Tre University, Italy
Paolo Federico	Vienna University of Technology, Austria
Beatrice Gobbo	Politecnico di Milano, Italy
Simone Lenti	Sapienza University of Rome, Italy
Giuseppe Liotta	University of Perugia, Italy
Fabrizio Montecchiani	University of Perugia, Italy
Maurizio Patrignani	Roma Tre University, Italy
Laura Tarantino	Università dell'Aquila, Italy

Contents

AI2VIS4BigData: A Reference Model for AI-Based Big Data Analysis and Visualization

Thoralf Reis(✉), Marco X. Bornschlegl, and Matthias L. Hemmje

Faculty of Mathematics and Computer Science, University of Hagen, 58097 Hagen, Germany
{thoralf.reis,marco-xaver.bornschlegl,matthias.hemmje}@fernuni-hagen.de

Abstract. Public interest in the combined application domain of Artificial Intelligence (AI) - based Big Data Analysis and Visualization is currently peaking. Yet until recently, there was no reference model that provided common ground for information exchange in bigger projects or collaboration scenarios, that prevented scientists and private companies from reinventing the wheel. The introduction of AI2VIS4BigData Reference Model recently filled this gap. This paper targets to introduce the AI2VIS4BigData Reference Model, its elements and all interconnections between them in very detail. It provides an overview of example reference models, their general history and objectives and introduces the reference models that were utilized to derive AI2VIS4BigData.

Keywords: Reference model · Big Data · AI · Visualization · AI2VIS4BigData

1 Introduction and Motivation

The development of comprehensive software systems can be a challenging task. It becomes even more challenging in collaboration scenarios of many people, multiple organizations or companies. Precise information exchange [1] e.g. through unambiguous interface and entity definitions are a key to master this complexity and achieve the objectives of the software project. Reference models are an instrument of software engineering [2] that provide common baselines and entity-relationship definitions. They enable precise exchange of information [1] even in collaboration scenarios. Reference models empower architects and developers to develop comprehensive software systems through reusing established concepts and employing refined specifications and guidelines [2].

Growing volume of data, enhanced analysis capabilities through elaborated algorithms and hardware drive progress in various application domains which emphasizes the importance of Big Data research. To define the trending yet vague term of Big Data, a popular definition approach is to utilize the data management challenges summarized as the *"three v's"* of Gartner analyst Doug

T. Reis et al. (Eds.): AVI-BDA 2020/ITAVIS 2020, LNCS 12585, pp. 1–18, 2021.
https://doi.org/10.1007/978-3-030-68007-7_1

Laney [3]. These challenges are relevant, if the amount of data is very big (volume), the frequency of data inflow is very high (velocity) or there is a great number of different data manifestations like, e.g., data format, data structure or data semantics (variety) [4]. If one of these challenges is present, this data can be considered to be Big Data. Another trending topic is Artificial Intelligence (AI): Following today's media coverage, there seems to be hardly an industry which does not apply AI to enhance or to revolutionize their value chain. This trend is backed by a recent study: according to a Gartner Inc. research, 85% of CIOs will launch or have ongoing AI projects by 2020 [5]. According to ISO/IEC JTC 1/SC 42 standard, AI is a form of intelligence displayed by machines in contrast to natural intelligence that is displayed by humans and animals [6]. Even though AI is a trending topic, ideas of intelligent objects and creatures have a long history [7] in which Alan Turing's accomplishments in the 1950s can be summarized as the beginning of the modern AI [8]. AI's big industrial relevance consequently leads to more focus on this topic in science while progress in technology reinforces this trend. Popular application areas of this trending topic cover trading [9], health care [7,10], driverless cars and humanoid robots [7]. Further applications on shopping websites to recommend products, video streaming providers to recommend films and social media platforms to individually decide upon content relevance for each user [9] has become part of everyday life. Visualization enables connecting the two research domains Big Data Analysis and AI. It offers the chance to meet the increasing demand for explainability and transparency [11]. Especially for AI, in-transparent decision paths make trust and comprehension for humans difficult and raise questions regarding debugging, fairness, accountability [8], and even data-driven discrimination [12]. The demand for transparency in industrial applications of AI is supported by a Gartner Inc. research which predicts the probability of funding for AI projects through a company's CIO to be 100% higher, if they offer built-in transparency [5].

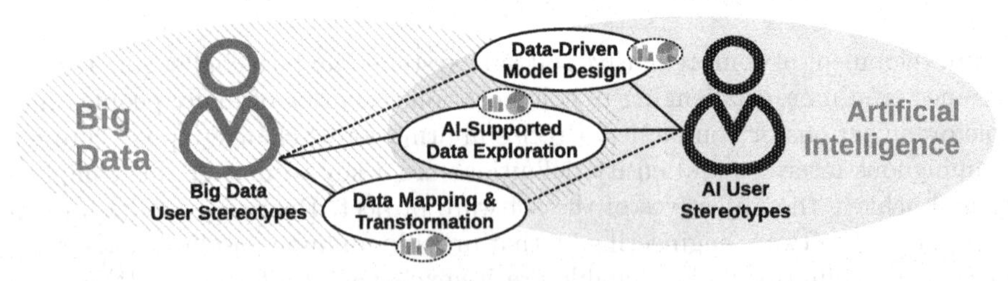

Fig. 1. Use cases interconnecting big data analysis and artificial intelligence [11]

According to [6], the application scenarios and research areas of Big Data and AI are closely connected. Common use cases that link both terms together are introduced in [11] and visualized in Fig. 1. They comprise the process of deriving and designing AI models in which Big Data is utilized to derive patterns and rules (*"Data-Driven Model Design"* [11]), the process of exploring the data in order to gain insight supported by AI models that ease this exploration journey e.g. through providing hints to the human data analyst (*"AI-supported Data Exploration"* [11]) as well as the process of transforming and mapping the data itself through e.g. clustering it (*"Data Mapping & Transformation"* [11]).

[1]An approach to quantify the relevance and growing popularity of the combined application domain of AI-based Big Data Analysis and Visualization is to evaluate search query topics of an internet search engine. Figure 2 therefore shows the normalized frequency of occurrence of worldwide search queries for Big Data, AI, Visualization, a combination of all three as well as the reference baseline topic of Computer Science for the most-popular search engine. The graph covers the years from 2004 to 2020. The y scale is normalized with 100 % being the number of search queries for Computer Science in 2004. The baseline topic of Computer Science lost popularity (or at least fewer users searched for it) starting from its peak in 2004 until 2011 when it reached a constant level of approximately 30%. In the same year, 2011, Big Data started to become a relevant topic: From almost zero search queries until then, it reached approximately 5% in 2014 which it kept since then. The search queries for AI back the statement of continuous relevance of this topic: between 2004 and 2016, AI's relevance oscillated between 30 and 40% where it matched the reference baseline topic of computer science between 2011 and 2015. Since 2016, the importance of AI is rising (hence exceeding the reference baseline term) with reaching an all-time high in 2020. Although the topic of Visualization is not as often subject to search queries as Big Data Analysis or AI, it is the only term that keeps a constant level of relevance from 2004 to 2020 (between 5 and 10%). When combining the three application domains (adding their number of search queries), one can clearly state that the combined application domain of AI-based Big Data Analysis and Visualization is getting more and more important with almost being twice as much searched for in 2020 than the reference topic of computer science.

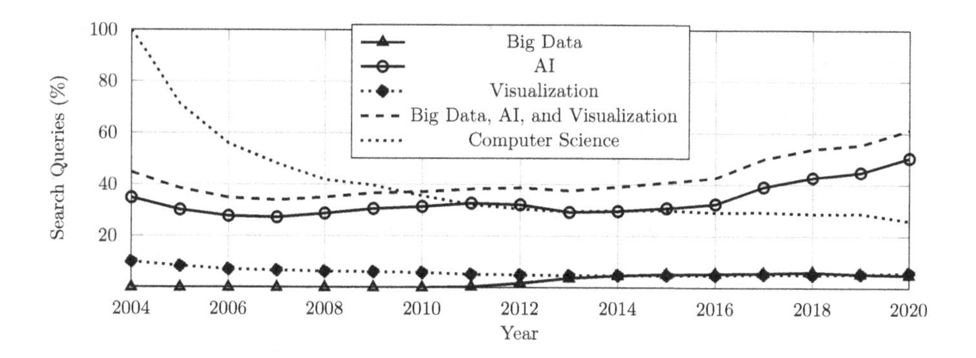

Fig. 2. Search query popularity comparison using google trends

[1] Data source: Google Trends (https://www.google.com/trends).

Although the popularity of the combined application domain of AI-based Big Data Analysis and Visualization for both industry and science clearly is growing, there was no reference model covering it until [11] systematically derived and introduced the first reference model AI2VIS4BigData to the public. The detailed introduction and explanation of this reference model, its purpose and its elements is the objective of this publication.

The remainder of this paper introduces the state of the art for reference models using practical examples (Sect. 2), explains the approach that was taken to derive the AI2VIS4BigData Reference Model, the reference model itself and its elements in every detail (Sect. 3), provides an outlook to future AI2VIS4BigData research (Sect. 4) and summarizes the contributions of this work (Sect. 5).

2 State of the Art

Comprehension of the history and definition of reference models is a key to understanding the motivation for the creation of AI2VIS4BigData. With the support of example reference models, this section targets to make this motivation clear.

2.1 Reference Models

The history of reference models in information systems is difficult to be traced [13]. One potential starting point is the Kln Integration Model (KIM), a *"universal model for an integrated data processing system"* [13]. Although the authors of the KIM never used the term reference model, the terms *"universal model"* and *"basic model"* imply similar intentions [13]. The first usage of the term reference model might go back to Scheer's publication on business process engineering which introduces a data model [13]. Referring to this data model, the publication's second edition was subtitled *"Reference Models for Industrial Enterprises"* [13]. While Scheer defined reference models to enable the *"development of solutions based on concrete problems"* [13], Thomas defined reference models in 2005 to be models that support the construction of other models [13]. Nevertheless it remains a subjective decision, to call or not to call a model a reference model [13]. The depth and extent of reference model descriptions can vary drastically depending on their purpose and application domain. The later in this section introduced examples of the ISO OSI layer model, the IVIS4BigData Reference Model, and AIGO's AI System Lifecycle make this clear. Therefore the success of reference models doesn't depend on the depth and extent of key artifacts (e.g. exchanged information) descriptions, rather on the ability to describe these key artifacts as specific as necessary yet as generalizable as possible [1].

The International Standards Organization (ISO) introduced in 1978 the Open Systems Interconnection (OSI) Reference Model [14], probably the most-famous reference model. Its purpose is to establish a standard that once being followed, enables communication between two computers that might be located anywhere in the world [14]. As illustrated in Fig. 3, its description and specifications consist

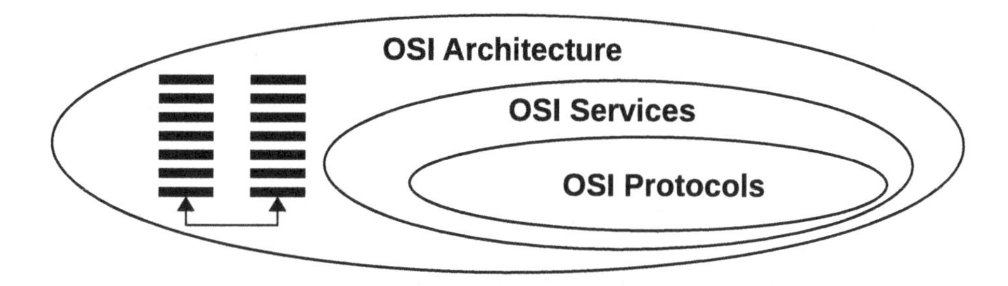

Fig. 3. The different levels of abstraction of the ISO OSI reference model [14]

of three levels of abstraction: the OSI architecture, the OSI services and the OSI protocols [14]. The architecture, which is standardized in ISO 7498, defines a seven-layer communication model (from physical layer to application layer) as well as *"objects, relations, and constraints"* [14]. The OSI services defines *"tighter constraints"* [14] for protocol-independent services as well as abstract interfaces for communication between consecutive layers of the seven-layer model [14]. The lowest abstraction level (and hence the most specific description) are the OSI protocols. These protocols are precise, specific definitions of the interfaces for consecutive layers that describe, *"what control information is to be sent and what procedures are to be used to interpret this control information"* [14].

2.2 IVIS4BigData Reference Model

Another reference model example is the Information Visualization for Big Data (IVIS4BigData) Reference Model introduced by Bornschlegl et al. in 2016 [15]. This theoretical reference model targets to *"close the gap in research with regard to Information Visualization challenges of Big Data Analysis as well as context awareness"* [3]. It was derived through combination of two other reference models: the information flow and key artifacts of Kaufmann's Big Data Management (BDM) Reference Model were projected onto the Information Visualization (IVIS) Reference Model and complemented with Big Data Analysis user stereotypes [15]. According to Bornschlegl et al., there are clearly distinguishable user stereotypes with different technical and organizational knowledge levels [15]: from technical users like, e.g., domain experts and data engineers, data analysts, specialists for data visualization to management-level end user stereotypes [15]. Since human interaction, perception, and information visualization are pivotal elements for Big Data Analysis, these user stereotypes are defined as integral parts of this reference model. Further reference model elements are the description of the information workflow for Big Data Analysis from raw data over integrated data into views that enable the different user stereotypes involved into Big Data Analysis to benefit through insight [15]. Besides the user stereotype definition and the workflow, this reference model provides a description of all data artifacts relevant to Big Data Analysis together with an IVIS4BigData architecture [15].

2.3 AIGO's AI System Lifecycle Reference Model

The AI Group of Experts at the OECD (AIGO) System Lifecycle for AI systems is a reference model that isn't labeled as such. Yet it fulfills Thomas' definition of a model that supports the creation of other models (in this case a reference model that supports the creation of AI models). It was introduced in 2019 and consists of 4 phases. The phases are visualized in Fig. 4. They are often passed through in an iterative manner [8]. The first phase covers the design of the model itself and marks the starting point. It consists of planning and designing of all, data collection, data processing as well as model building and interpretation [8]. The models that are designed within the first phase are verified and validated by users with special domain knowledge in phase two before they are deployed into a production environment for execution in phase three [8]. To assure that the productive AI system is working properly and its *"recommendations and impacts"* [8] are valid, it is assessed to maintain and if necessary to adapt the system within the fourth phase called *"operation and monitoring"* [8].

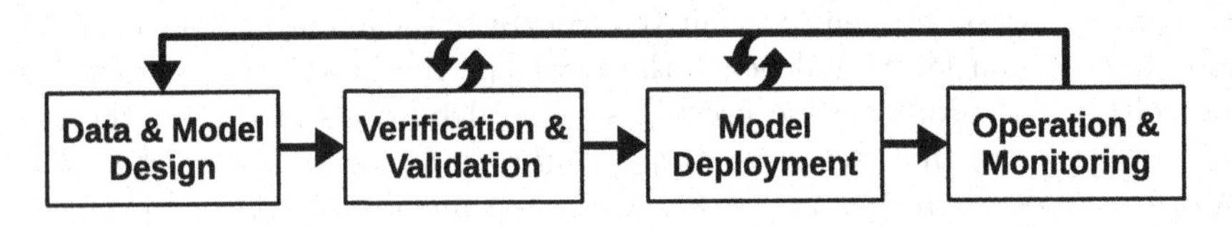

Fig. 4. AIGO's AI system lifecycle [8]

3 Conceptual Modeling

The conducted approach in [11] to derive the AI2VIS4BigData Reference Model combines the IVIS4BigData Reference Model for Big Data Analysis and Visualization with AIGO's AI System Lifecycle, the formerly introduced AI reference model [11]. Further key elements that were considered are the different existing types of AI models, the data that is necessary to apply AI models as well as the different user stereotypes that are involved in the application of these AI models [11]. A visualization of the conduced approach is shown in Fig. 5.

The following sections describe with the AI model types (Sect. 3.1), AI data (Sect. 3.2), and AI user stereotypes (Sect. 3.3) the key elements and artifacts of the AI2VIS4BigData Reference Model. The reference model itself will be introduced in Sect. 3.4 The detailed derivation of the different elements and artifacts is introduced in [11]. In a nutshell, the AI model types were derived though combining existing AI taxonomies from state of the art in science with the use cases displayed in Fig. 1, the AI data was derived through assessing necessary input and output data of each AI system lifecycle phase, and the AI user stereotypes were derived through examination of the maturing process of AI models and the therein relevant activities [11].

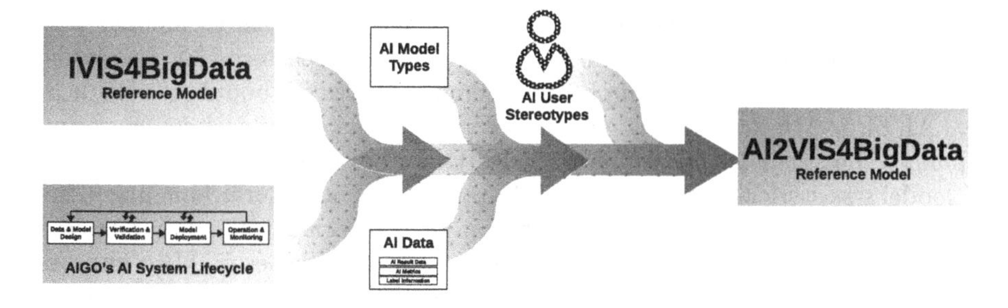

Fig. 5. Visualization of the reference model derivation approach followed in [11]

3.1 AI Model Types

There are various ways to classify the different aspects of AI models and AI model research. Examples are the conducted approach, the application areas, ML techniques and algorithms, optimization strategies, contextualization [8] or the degree of explainability [16]. Since there is no AI taxonomy that is widely agreed-upon [8], this paper focuses on the first two aspects. For the design of a reference model for AI-based Big Data Analysis and Visualization this means that the possible AI model approaches as well as the different use cases existing in this research area are analyzed.

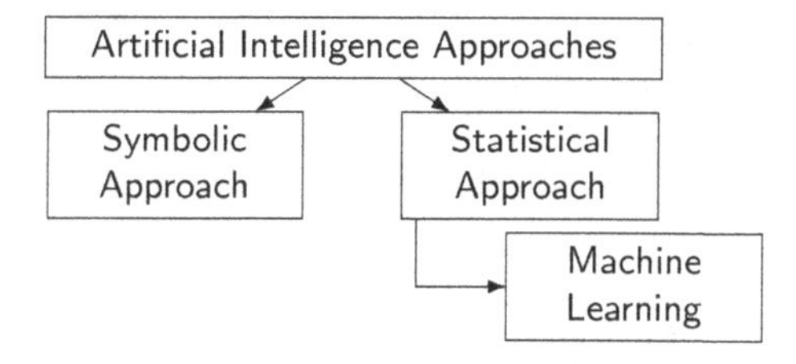

Fig. 6. Taxonomy of approaches to AI according to MIT's IPRI [8]

Model Approaches. A taxonomy provided by the Internet Policy Research Initiative at MIT (IPRI) [8] divides the different existing approaches into two categories: symbolic and statistical approaches [8]. Symbolic AI strongly depends on model designers with a deep domain knowledge. The reason for this requirement is the approach of trying to formalize intelligent behavior and decision paths within a knowledge base. This knowledge base (or *"logical representations"* [8]) is then provided to machines and computers which apply them on input data in order to deduce conclusions as output [8]. Symbolic AI enjoys popularity for application domains for which formal rules exist like, e.g., *"optimisation and planning tools"* [8]. In contrast to these *"human-understandable decision structures"* [8] of symbolic AI, the second category of AI model approaches, statistical AI, utilizes data as foundation for intelligent behavior: statistical techniques and algorithms are implemented by machines and computers to identify patterns within the data and to induce trends from these patterns [8]. Increasing amounts of data in almost all application domains drives the popularity of statistical AI. Since ML *"algorithms are characterized by the ability to learn over time without being explicitly programmed"* [6], ML can be sorted as a subcategory of AI model's statistical approach. The AI applications of Natural Language Processing (NLP) is an example, how both major categories can collaborate in a symbiotic relationship: NLP utilizes the statistical approaches of AI to improve through learning from data while it uses symbolic AI approaches to align the learned results with existing grammar rules [6]. The introduced taxonomy is visualized in Fig. 6.

AI Model Application Areas. At a first glance, the application areas of AI model within AI-based Big Data Analysis and Visualization can be summarized with the three use cases in Fig. 1. However, a closer look shows that these use cases' application domains are not clearly distinguishable. To take this into account, [11] utilized these use cases as starting points for the derivation of three different AI models: analytics models, automation models, and UI models [11]. The latter two were motivated through the necessity of bridging the knowledge gap between involved users from different scientific backgrounds (data science as well as AI users) [11]. A task that can be fulfilled with automation (e.g. referring to a Gartner Inc. research according to which *"more than 40% of data science tasks will be automated"* by 2020 [5]) and intelligent UI (in which AI supports the user in dealing with underconstrained UI situations, where the user is overcharged with *"a variety of choices"* [17]).

- **Analytics Models:** These AI model's main purpose is to process data in order to carve out the required insights. Most AI application scenarios in the combined application domains of AI-based Big Data Analysis and Visualization map to this AI model type. An example is data clustering.
- **Automation Models:** Automation AI models target to reduce the occurrence of repetitive or foreseeable user behavior and system calculations by carrying out these activities automatically, calculate automatically, and thereby save time for the system's users [11]. A further benefit that automation provides is using the enhanced knowledge of future system activities to optimize the utilization of existing resource constraints and reduce infrastructure peak load probabilities [11]. Statistical AI scenarios utilize historic user interaction and system activity data for this purpose while an expert user provides the required insight for symbolic AI models.
- **UI Models:** Intelligent User Interfaces (IUIs) support users in *"managing the complexity of information"* that is being displayed, especially in *"time-critical"* scenarios [17]. These IUIs can be provided by both symbolic and statistical AI models. These AI models offer the chance to individualize the

UI to the capabilities and requirements of each user. As data is key to statistical AI, a common approach is to record the different user's interaction with a system and utilize this data to identify patterns to predict user-specific manner while expert users might define rules that model intelligent UI adaptations.

Utilizing the AI model approaches and the AI model application areas to determine the different AI model types, that the AI2VIS4BigData Reference Model needs to take into account, results in overall six different AI model types: two different AI approaches combined with three different AI model application areas.

3.2 AI Data

According to the Generic Abstract Intelligence Model (GAIM) by Wang et al., intelligence is the transformation of stimuli and enquiries into information, knowledge, and behaviors [18]. This model can be applied to all forms of intelligence including natural and artificial intelligence [18]. Consequently the application of AI can be summarized as the transformation of input data to output data. The systematically derived AI data presented in [11] shows that these input and output data can look very differently (e.g. different formats, origins, and purposes). As a common baseline, these AI data are introduced as follows:

- **Raw Data Sources:** Raw data sources already existed in IVIS4BigData [15]. The term summarizes raw input data that is subject to analysis in a Big Data system as well as the origin of that data from which it has to be integrated. The input data can be used by an AI model that targets to analyze or to transform it. In that case, selected elements of this input data can be considered to be a *"feature"* [8]. As mentioned before, the raw data sources have to be integrated into the system before they are able to be utilized. Bornschlegl et al. propose for this a Semantic Integration (SI) based on a Mediator-Wrapper Architecture (MWA) [15]. Following this approach, each different raw data source requires its own wrapper to query the differently formatted data [15]. A mediator assures uniform access to all raw data sources. Examples for raw data that is integrated from raw data sources for the introduced AI application examples from Sect. 1 are stock data (trading), ecg sensor data (health care), radar sensor data (driverless cars), or camera sensor data (humanoid robots).
- **Label Annotation:** Further input data for AI models are label annotations. In statistical AI approaches like, e.g., ML this data accompanies raw input data during training of an AI model. AI models use these label annotations to induce trends within the raw input data that enable them to predict the same labels as good as possible. Besides model training, label annotation data can be utilized in model testing where it empowers evaluators to determine how well an AI model is performing. The source of the label annotation can either be algorithms (e.g. for synthetic data or programmable classification

tasks), historic data (e.g. stock performance data) or be of human origin. The process of creating man-made label annotation data is referred to as labeling while an example for this data in driverless cars AI use cases are the labeling of objects like, e.g., cars, sidewalks, and pedestrians within a camera picture recorded from a vehicle.

- **System/User Activities:** Considering the AI model types for automation and UI (refer to Sect. 3.1), necessary input data for these AI models to fulfill their objectives are system activities as well as user activities. In the case of the combined application domains of AI-based Big Data Analysis and Visualization, system activity data comprises documentation of the performed tasks of the corresponding system (e.g. timestamped system log data of activities together with information on the execution environment). An example application for an automation AI model is to utilize the information regarding performed tasks within the system activities as label annotation data and the timestamps and environment information as input data to train the AI models to predict when to execute a certain task while taking environmental conditions into account. User activity data comprises actions triggered through the different users of the corresponding systems. It can be utilized to either automatize likely user activities or to adapt the user interface and visualizations in a way that supports the users through explanation or user empowerment. An example for the utilization of user activities within AI models for UI are intelligent tool-tips that steer the users attention to a tool that might help the user but that is not used by the user by then.
- **AI Results/Labels:** The primary output data of AI models and their application is AI result data. Depending on the utilized AI approach, semantics, and data format of this AI result data varies. Within the statistical AI approach of regression, AI result data can be coefficient values that describe the course of a graph that either separates two or multiple data clusters or that visualizes a mathematical formula. The materialization of AI result data in ML are labels and therefore the association data to categories or clusters. The labels are either explicit outputs of a model or derived indirectly through the output of confidence values (the confidence of the algorithm to assign a data sample to a class where the label is derived through association to the class with the highest confidence) or distance measures (the distance data samples to cluster centers within a coordination system where the label is derived through association to the nearest cluster). In symbolic AI, a documentation of the decisions taken by following the explicit rules and algorithms (e.g. a path through a graph) can be considered its result data.
- **AI Metrics:** Besides AI result data like, e.g., labels, a secondary output of AI models are AI metrics. These metrics can either be directly calculated by the models itself or be determined afterwards. AI metrics are any form of information that indicates how a model performs in terms of resource consumption,

time consumption or quality of its output. The latter is described using Key Performance Indicators (KPIs) like, e.g., accuracy rates, confusion matrices, or the concept of true and false positive rates [19]. In order to determine these KPIs, an AI model's result data has to be compared to a ground truth. This ground truth is provided by the introduced label annotation data. A typical scenario of KPI creation during model design and validation is splitting a data set consisting of pairs of a data sample and the corresponding label into a training and a testing data set. While the model is trained using the data samples of the training data set, the KPIs are determined applying the trained model on the data samples of the testing data set and comparing its AI result data with the existing labels [20].

- **AI Model Meta Information:** Another output of AI models is AI model meta information data. This meta information's purpose is to describe how a model was created. Content, coverage size, and format of this meta information strongly depends on the application domain of the AI model itself: While data privacy is a very important aspect not only in medical AI applications, the application of an AI based hiring process in companies requires measures to prevent data-driven discrimination [12], and military AI applications need to pay special attention to ethics. This meta information is key to enable audits of AI applications in these sensitive areas and thereby to either comply with existing law like, e.g., the EU General Data Protection Regulation (GDPR) or to prevent legislators from creating new obstacles for innovation [21]. An example content for this meta information is a documentation of the data origin and patient consent for medical applications and of the data and feature selection in model training for human resources hiring as well as military applications.
- **Model Configuration:** The model configuration for ML and statistical AI models is neither AI model input nor output data. It comprises all technical specifications and descriptions that are required to deploy the AI model into a productive environment and apply it for the intended purpose. Therefore this data contains information about the AI model's algorithm, parameter values, input data, and data preparation. Further information are AI result data content, format, application schedules, triggers as well as relevant environmental conditions.
- **Knowledge Representation:** The equivalent to a model configuration in symbolic AI is the knowledge representation. While model configuration data contains no information about how the determined algorithm performs its calculation and classification tasks (black-box), knowledge representation data specifically describes the rules, relationships, and algorithms that are modeling the decision structures of symbolic AI [8]. Further required information for symbolic AI applications like, e.g., a formal description of input data and preparation, application schedules or triggers and relevant environmental conditions are identical to model configuration data.

3.3 AI User Stereotypes

Partitioning the different activities that are being performed during the application of AI as well as the necessary skills required for them into different user stereotypes does not necessarily mean that there have to be multiple persons involved in every AI application. Multiple user stereotypes can easily be implemented by a single human being, especially in smaller AI projects. These user stereotypes rather target to identify activities that need to be conducted and skills that need to be incorporated by the same person. They provide clearly distinguishable skill sets that are required in every AI project which can be utilized e.g. for project planning and staffing decisions. Figure 7 visualizes the different AI user stereotypes that have been introduced in [11] alongside AIGO's AI System Lifecycle and its maturing process.

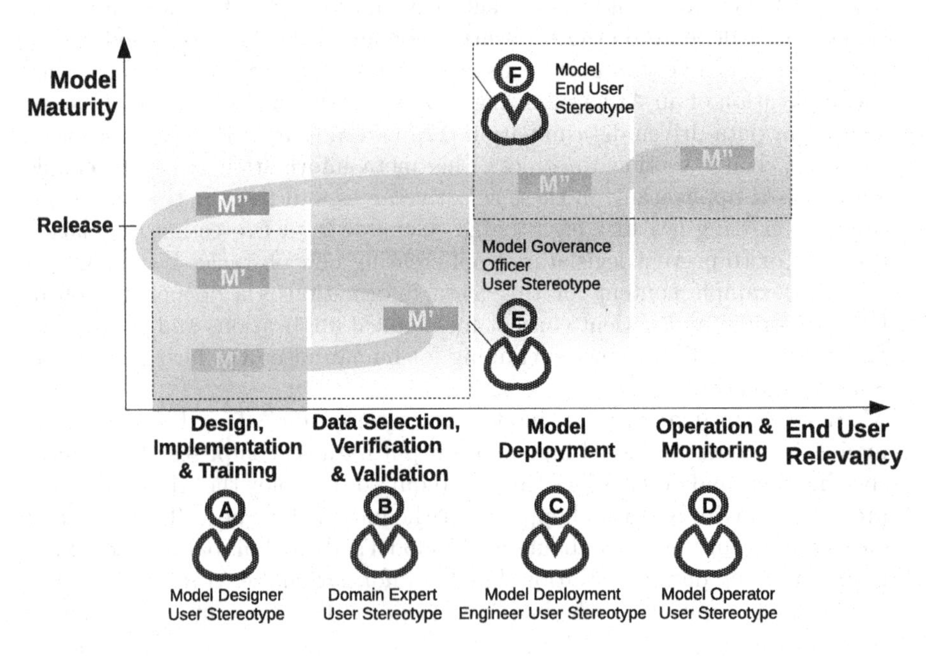

Fig. 7. AI user Stereotypes alongside model lifecycle and maturing process [11]

- **Model Designer User Stereotype (A):** The model designer user stereotype is closely connected to the first AI lifecycle phase of designing, implementing, and training AI models [11]. Hence, the performed activities cover planning and designing the data and feature preparation, selecting suitable AI model types for a certain objective, accordingly designing these AI models as well as training them in case of ML [8]. As Fig. 7 shows, the activities allocated to this user stereotype mainly take place before an AI model is released. Besides deep knowledge about AI models and algorithms, the skills that are required for this user stereotype comprise a good abstraction capability and analytic thinking in order to translate practical problems into AI applications.

- **Domain Expert User Stereotype (B):** Selecting appropriate data, verifying AI models, and validating their results are the main activities of the second AI lifecycle phase [11]. These activities are mostly conducted prior to release of an AI model yet once the model itself is developed further on, verification and validation is obligatory. It requires deep domain expertise in the application domain of the specific AI problem and also good analytic skills to investigate whether an AI model that looks well designed at a first glance is really well prepared even for rarely occurring cases. Further required skills are a good knowledge of AI evaluation methods.
- **Model Deployment Engineer User Stereotype (C):** The user stereotype that is closest connected to the third AI lifecycle phase is the model deployment engineer. This user stereotype receives designed and verified AI models and is responsible to transfer them into a productive environment and start their execution. Especially in cases of resource consumption intensive application scenarios, cloud technologies can play a major role as a target of model deployment. These activities are directly linked to the release milestone of AI model maturity. The required skills cover a deep knowledge about deployment configuration and automation (e.g. deployment scripting), as well as cloud technologies and infrastructure constraints.
- **Model Operator User Stereotype (D):** The model operator user stereotype is directly linked to the last AI lifecycle phase of model operation. Activities within this user stereotype's responsibility comprise all tasks related to the steady monitoring of correct AI model execution within the productive environment. These tasks include supervising all, input data quality, AI model output data quality, resource consumption as well as further environmental conditions. As Fig. 7 shows, all activities are chronologically located after model release. Required skills comprise a profound knowledge of deployment environments, AI models as well as AI evaluation capabilities.
- **Model Governance Officer User Stereotype (E):** This user stereotype is not directly linked to a certain AI lifecycle phase. It was introduced in [11] and motivated with the growing public (and thus legislator) interest in AI applications. The main activity of this user stereotype is the documentation of sensitive aspects in course of all tasks involved in AI model design, verification, validation, and deployment. Sensitive in terms of ethical standards, data privacy [22], data security, and all topics that are relevant to provide as much transparency through audits or public explanations as necessary to comply with all laws and to establish trust with authorities and the target audience.
- **Model End User Stereotype (F):** The last user stereotype involved in AI applications is the target audience itself: the model end user [11]. This heterogeneous user group interacts with a system utilizing AI models and consumes its AI result data. This consumption can either be on purpose (e.g. a data scientist that uses a classification of a data set generated by a

statistical analytics AI model) or without explicit knowledge of the user (e.g. suggestions of a suitable video by a video streaming service). Consequently no specific skills are required to be incorporated by users of this user stereotype.

3.4 AI2VIS4BigData Reference Model

Following the introduced approach, [11] arrived with the AI2VIS4BigData Reference Model [11] at a framework, that connects the different existing types of AI models, the multiple manifestations of data involved in AI application as well as the various different AI user stereotypes with each other and links them to the core elements of the underlying reference models IVIS4BigData as well as AIGO's AI System Lifecycle. The resulting reference model not only reveals relationships and interconnections between the different elements but also illustrates chronological orders and logical sequences (e.g. flow of data and causal chains between the elements). AI2VIS4BigData offers applications in the areas of AI-based Big Data Analysis and Visualization the opportunity to reuse established concepts and software and targets to prevent developers from overseeing important aspects and relationships in early project stages (that can only be integrated with high effort in later projects stages).

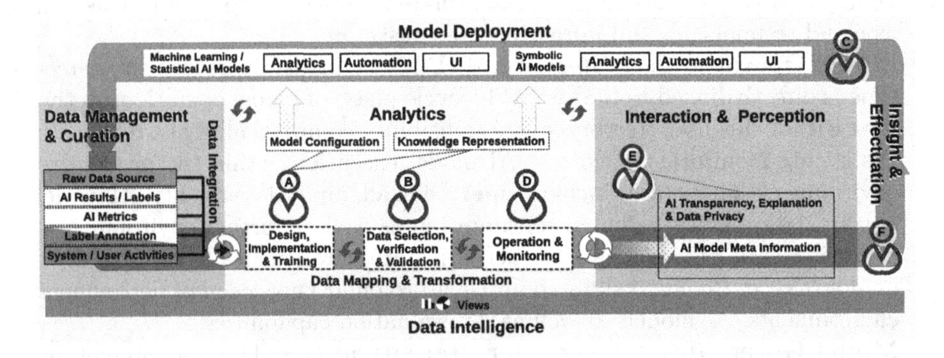

Fig. 8. AI2VIS4BigData - a reference model for AI-based big data analysis and visualization [11]

The AI2VIS4BigData Reference Model is visualized in Fig. 8. It consists of overall 6 layers: A data intelligence layer (originally from IVIS4BigData [15]) visualized at the bottom that provides all involved user stereotypes the possibility to observe all activities and data within the system which empowers them through comprehension to influence and manipulate the system. The four layers *"Data Management & Curation"*, *"Analytics"*, *"Interaction & Perception"* as well as *"Insight & Effectuation"* are displayed within the center of the reference model. These layers represent the original data transformation pipeline of the reference model for Visualization and Big Data Analysis applications IVIS4BigData [15]. The sixth layer is the model deployment layer which originates from the corresponding AI System Lifecycle phase of AIGO's reference model [8]. It is displayed on top of all other layers emphasizing the often cloud-located model deployment. It spreads over the whole data transformation pipeline. It contains all six AI model types that were introduced in Sect. 3.1 as well as the AI user stereotype of the model deployment engineer (C). All six layers are interconnected through a big blue data and information loop which all data artifacts run through one or many times.

The center layer *"Data Management & Curation"* marks the starting point of the data transformation pipeline. Consequently most of the data artifacts introduced in Sect. 3.2 are visualized within this layer: raw data sources, AI results/labels, AI metrics, label annotation as well as system/user activities. With the aid of three colors, the data artifacts are associated with Big Data (blue), AI (white), and Visualization respectively user interaction (green). This layer concludes with a data integration that passes the data artifacts through to the *"Analytics"* layer. This second layer in the data transformation pipeline hosts the three remaining AI lifecycle phases [8] as *"design, implementation and training"*, *"data selection, verification and validation"* and *"operation and monitoring"*. All three phases are modeled directly within the data and information loop, are closely linked and iteratively passed through (visualized through bidirectional arrows). The related user stereotypes model designer (A), domain expert (B) and model operator (D) are visualized directly above these three phases. The *"Analytics"* layer and its three AI lifecycle phases are connected with the model deployment layer and its AI models through two data artifacts: the model configuration data that is designed and created by the model designer user stereotype (A) connects the *"Analytics"* layer with the ML and statistical AI models as well as the knowledge representation data, which is created in close collaboration between model designer (A) and domain expert (B) user stereotypes and connects the *"Analytics"* layer with the symbolic AI models. The third center layer *"Interaction & Perception"* is connected with the *"Analytics"* layer via the data and information loop. This connection is reinforced by the data artifact AI model meta information that is located within this layer: this data is produced within *"Analytics"* layer yet employed within the *"Interaction & Perception"* layer (Fig. 8 visualizes this through a connecting arrow) in order to emphasize its effect of disclosure and documentation for AI transparency, AI explanation as well data privacy. The corresponding model governance officer user stereotype (E) is consequently located within this layer as well. The last center layer, *"Insight & Effectuation"*, contains the AI end user stereotype (E). Since this user stereotype consumes the AI result data as well as further information and insight that was prepared and created within the system, it is located directly within the data and information loop.

4 Remaining Challenges and Outlook

Several subjective decisions were included in the derivation of AI2VIS4BigData [11] or the arrangement of the reference model's elements. Furthermore, the reference model's completeness strongly depends on the completeness of the ingredients it was derived from: existing AI model types, AI data as well as AI user stereotypes. The most-pressing challenge is therefore to validate whether the taken decisions during derivation were correct and if the ingredients were complete. Further remaining challenges can be derived from general reference model objectives: One target of a reference model is to enable overcoming of relevant challenges in its application domain (refer to Sect. 3.4). Hence another remaining challenge is to systematically derive all relevant challenges and verify, whether the introduced reference model already provides sufficient measures or not. Another reference model objective is to provide guidelines and refined specifications like, e.g., entity relationship definitions. As this publication represents just the beginning towards these guidelines and specifications, a further challenge is to continue conceptual modeling and create use case diagrams, detailed data specifications as well as a reference model architecture. A further benefit of reference models is that they enable the reusing of established concepts and existing implementations. As there exists no implementation of the AI2VIS4BigData Reference Model that could be reused by practical applications, these implementations remain a challenge.

The immediate next steps in AI2VIS4BigData research are a comprehensive workshop and survey analysis based on the feedback of an international group of researchers that are experts in different application domains that involve AI, Big Data Analysis as well as Visualization. This workshop and survey was conducted in June, 2020 and targeted to evaluate all decisions taken in reference model derivation, the completeness of AI model types, AI data and AI user stereotypes as well as the retrieval of existing challenges in the researchers' projects. The results of this evaluation need to be analyzed and necessary changes to the AI2VIS4BigData Reference Model need to be identified. Further research targets to assess three AI-based Big Data Analysis and Visualization use cases in the bioinformatics area of metagenomics research in order to derive a conceptual AI2VIS4BigData architecture. The medium-term outlook contains detailed specifications (e.g. use case diagrams, entity relationship diagrams) and an implementation of the reference model for application of practical use cases.

5 Conclusion

This paper introduces a detailed description of the AI2VIS4BigData Reference Model, a specialized reference model for the combined application domains of AI-based Big Data Analysis and Visualization, together with a presentation of its components. In more detail, it provides an overview of the existing use cases in the combined application domain and conducts a search engine trend analysis to motivate the increasing relevance. Using the interest of search engine users in the combined application domain as a benchmark, the relevance is continuously growing since 2013 and peaking recently with an all-time high. A further contribution of this paper is a detailed summary of origin, definition, and advantages of reference models through introduction of, inter alia, the ISO OSI layer

Reference Model. The conceptual modeling within the paper starts with an explanation of the approach that was followed in [11] to derive the reference model: In a nutshell, the two reference models IVIS4BigData (application domains Big Data Analysis, and Visualization) and AIGO's AI System Lifecycle (application domain AI) were merged under consideration of AI model types, AI data as well as AI user stereotypes. The major contribution of this paper is a detailed description and introduction of the latter three reference model ingredients and their relationships within AI2VIS4BigData itself: a explanation of the overall six different AI model types, eight different AI data artifacts and six different AI user stereotypes followed by a comprehensive description of the AI2VIS4BigData Reference Model. This description explains the reference model's six layer concept which is interconnected via a data and information loop. It clarifies logical relationships and causal chains. This paper concludes with an overview of the remaining challenges in AI2VIS4BigData research and an outlook how they shall be solved: Through identification of necessary reference model adaptions based on the result of an expert round table workshop and survey as well as through the development of an architecture and reference use case implementations.

References

1. Gunter, C., Gunter, E., Jackson, M., Zave, P.: A reference model for requirements and specifications. IEEE Softw. **17**(3), 37–43 (2000)
2. Engels, G., Heckel, R., Taentzer, G., Ehrig, H.: A combined reference model- and view-based approach to system specification. Int. J. Softw. Eng. Knowl. Eng. **7**(4), 457–477 (1997)
3. Bornschlegl, M.X.: Advanced Visual Interfaces Supporting Distributed Cloud-Based Big Data Analysis, Dissertation, University of Hagen (2019)
4. Laney, D.: 3D Data Management: Controlling Data Volume, Velocity, and Variety. Technical Report, META Group (2001)
5. Krensky, P., et al.: Critical Capabilities for Data Science and Machine Learning Platforms, Gartner Inc., vol. G00391146 (2020)
6. ISO, ISO/IEC JTC 1/SC 42 Artificial Intelligence (2018). https://isotc.iso.org/livelink/livelink/open/jtc1sc42
7. Bond, R., et al.: Digital empathy secures Frankenstein's monster. CEUR Workshop Proc. **2348**, 335–349 (2019)
8. OECD, Artificial Intelligence in Society (2019)
9. Roehrig, P., Malcolm, F., Pring, B.: What To Do When Machines Do Everything: How to Get Ahead in a World of AI, Algorithms, Bots, and Big Data. John Wiley & Sons, Hoboken (2017)
10. Healy, M.: A machine learning emotion detection platform to support affective well being, pp. 2694–2700 (2018)
11. Reis, T., Bornschlegl, M.X., Hemmje, M.L.: Towards a reference model for artificial intelligence supporting big data analysis, To appear. In: Proceedings of the 2020 International Conference on Data Science (ICDATA 2020) (2020)
12. Buxmann, P.: Ein neuer Hype? Zur Ökonomie der künstlichen Intelligenz, Forschung & Lehre, pp. 22–23, January 2020

13. Thomas, O.: Understanding the term reference model in information systems research: history, literature analysis and explanation. In: Bussler, C.J., Haller, A. (eds.) BPM 2005. LNCS, vol. 3812, pp. 484–496. Springer, Heidelberg (2006). https://doi.org/10.1007/11678564_45
14. Day, J.D., Zimmermann, H.: The OSI reference model. Proc. IEEE **71**(12), 1334–1340 (1983)
15. Bornschlegl, M.X.: *IVIS4BigData*: a reference model for advanced visual interfaces supporting big data analysis in virtual research environments. In: Bornschlegl, M.X., Engel, F.C., Bond, R., Hemmje, M.L. (eds.) AVI-BDA 2016. LNCS, vol. 10084, pp. 1–18. Springer, Cham (2016). https://doi.org/10.1007/978-3-319-50070-6_1
16. Barredo Arrieta, A., et al.: Explainable Artificial Intelligence (XAI): concepts, taxonomies, opportunities and challenges toward responsible AI. Inf. Fusion **58**, 82–115 (2020)
17. Birnbaum, L., Lieberman, H., Horvitz, E., Marks, J., Kurlander, D., Roth, S.: Compelling intelligent user interfaces - how much AI? In: Proceedings IUI International Conference on Intelligent User Interfaces, pp. 173–175 (1997)
18. Wang, Y.: On abstract intelligence: toward a unifying theory of natural, artificial, machinable, and computational intelligence. Int. J. Softw. Sci. Comput. Intell. **1**(1), 1–17 (2009)
19. Davis, J., Goadrich, M.: The relationship between precision-recall and roc curves. In: Proceedings of the 23rd International Conference on Machine Learning, pp. 233–240. ACM (2006)
20. Kohavi, R., et al.: A study of cross-validation and bootstrap for accuracy estimation and model selection. In: Ijcai, Montreal, Canada, vol. 14, no. 2, pp. 1137–1145 (1995)
21. Wendehorst, C.: Ist der Roboter haftbar? Künstliche Intelligenz und gültige Rechtsnormen, Forschung & Lehre, pp. 24–25, January 2020
22. Woopen, C., Lohaus, I.: Grundlegende Rechte und Freiheiten Schützen: Ethische Implikation der künstlichen Intelligenz, Forschung & Lehre, pp. 18–20, January 2020

A Visual Analytics Technique to Compare the Performance of Predictive Models

Paolo Buono(✉) and Alessandra Legretto

University of Bari Aldo Moro, Via E. Orabona, 4, 70127 Bari, Italy
{paolo.buono,alessandra.legretto}@uniba.it

Abstract. Decisions that people make every day are affected by the information available in a given moment. Predictive models are used to estimate future values. For a given set of data and an analysis goal, the results of the models can vary, so it is important to select the most accurate model for the set of data. This paper proposes a Visual Analytics technique for comparing the performance of predictive models. It consists of four main components that support the tasks of the Keim's Visual Analytics Mantra: "*analyze first, show the important, zoom, filter and analyze further, details on demand*". The first component, *analyze data*, by building predictive models using various machine learning algorithms; the other three components are interactive visualizations that *show* the important results found by the models, *zoom and filter* on results of interest and finally, *further analyze* the selected results by showing *details* on the data.

Keywords: Comparison Matrix · Pie Chart Matrix · Instance Level Explanation · Visual workflow

1 Introduction

The increasing use of machine learning models to address several important problems, like predicting cancerous cells, presses researchers in understanding how models are trained and evaluated, in order to discover possible incorrect correlations and wrong generalizations.

Different models applied on a same dataset may have the same accuracy but produce different outcomes. Understanding how models preform becomes very important in order to avoid wrong decisions. This issue is known as model interpretability (e.g. see [2]). The literature reports the difficulties in selecting the model that provides correct predictions [3].

The research work reported in this document provides a contribution towards the creation of a Visual Analytics (VA) Technique capable to support the analyst in exploring and comparing a wider range of models, so that the model that best fits the data, i.e. that provides the most correct predictions on the specific data, can be selected. The proposed VA technique supports the tasks of the Keim's Visual Analytics Mantra: *analyze first, show the important, zoom, filter and analyze further, details on demand* [4].

Specifically, the technique has four main components that perform activities of the VA mantra: a) a component that uses classical data mining methods on a dataset and

T. Reis et al. (Eds.): AVI-BDA 2020/ITAVIS 2020, LNCS 12585, pp. 19–27, 2021.
https://doi.org/10.1007/978-3-030-68007-7_2

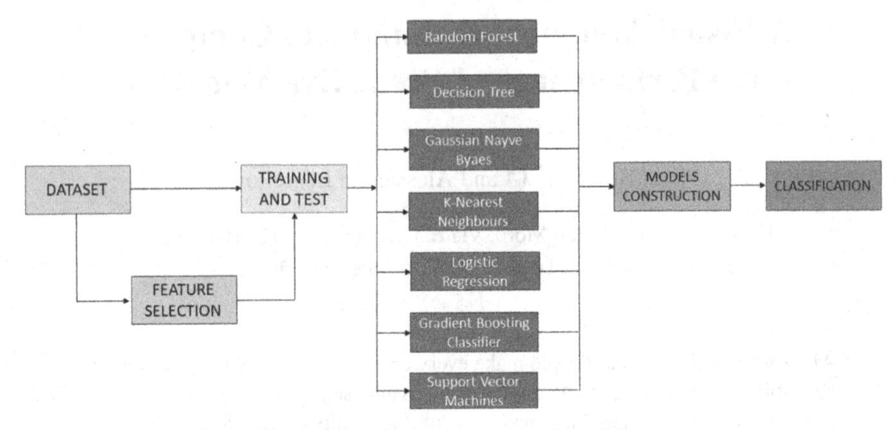

Fig. 1. Diagram of the proposed workflow

builds the corresponding predictive models (analyze first); b) a component that shows the important results (show the important) found by component "a"; c) a component that permits to zoom and filter on results of interest and further analyze the selected results (zoom filter and analyze further); d) a components that should provide details on the data (details on demand), if required by the analyst. Figure 1 briefly describes the proposed workflow for the construction of models. After the choice of the dataset, if possible, a feature selection technique is applied, then the dataset is divided into training and test data. Subsequently, all the available algorithms are applied. Figure 1 shows a selection of seven techniques. The model construction enables the tool to predict new instances having the same features as those of learning, on the base of the training instances. Finally, the classification selects the class made by each model for each instance.

It is important to remark that component a) can be further modified and integrated according to the analyst's needs. The contribution of this paper is in the creation of three different visualizations that have been developed according to the User-Centred Design (UCD) approach. The three visualizations support the activities b), c), and d) and are called Predictive Models Comparison Matrix, Two Models Pie-Chart Matrix and Instance Level Explanation, respectively.

This workflow fits the AI2VIS4BigData model [16]. Specifically, in Data Management & Curation it starts from the raw data source and exploits Machine Learning techniques to annotate data and present them to the users, which can interact with the tool. In the Model Deployment it fits in the Analytics and User Interface components. It also involves the data mapping & transformation because data must be selected and verified. During operation and monitoring, the user may decide to go back to the beginning or to the previous phases.

2 Background and Related Work

The research work refers to machine learning supervised classification problems. The dataset used to present the result of the project reports the Genetic Variant Classification (Clinvar in the rest of this document). It is a public resource containing annotations about human genetic variants. This kind of dataset is very important and the problem of classification is relevant in many contexts. Some authors faced the problem using the recent convolutional neural network approach (e.g. [15]), but in many situations (such as domains with unlabeled data) the more traditional classification algorithms are used. First, these variants are (usually manually) classified by clinical laboratories on a categorical spectrum of 5 values: benign, likely benign, uncertain significance, likely pathogenic, and pathogenic. Not all laboratories provide the same classification; variants that get conflicting classifications by the laboratories can cause confusion when clinicians or researchers try to interpret whether the variant has an impact on the disease of a given patient [1]. Thus, the variants are classified in two main classes: Class 1 includes variants that were classified consistent, i.e., they got the same value (of the 5 values above) by all laboratories; Class 2 includes variants that were classified conflicting, i.e., they got different values by laboratories. It is a binary classification problem where each record in the dataset is a genetic variant assigned to Class 1 or Class 2.

After the selection of the dataset, it is divided into training set (usually 70%) and test set (usually 30%). The model learns on the training set and then it is evaluated on the test set, where values of the target variable (the GT) are a priori known but hidden to the model. To evaluate a model, the prediction values are compared to the GT.

A common metric to evaluate predictive models is the accuracy score. It is defined as the ratio between the number of correctly predicted instances of the test set and the total number of instances in the test set; more precisely the number of correctly predicted instances TP (true positive) and TN (true negative) is the numerator, while the denominator is the sum of TP, TN and the wrong predictions FP (false positive) and FN (false negative). Thus, the accuracy score formula is:

$$accuracy\ score = \frac{TP + TN}{TP + TN + FP + FN}$$

But the accuracy is not enough to be able to select the model that best fits the data. The three visualizations described in this document suggest other metrics and information to compare models and help the user to identify the most interesting ones. The construction of the predictive models is the first component of the developed VA technique.

VA combines automated analysis techniques with interactive visualizations for an effective understanding, reasoning and decision making on the basis of very large and complex data sets [4].

Researchers working in VA have developed several interactive visualizations techniques. In order to give some examples, we briefly mention some works that use interactive visualizations to support the analysis of predictive models.

Several visualizations support the analysis of the features of a model. For instance, in [5] visualizations help the analyst to understand how the features are ranked by different algorithms, and the analyst may improve a model by selecting the most significant features. Krause et al. [6] propose a visual analytic workflow to help data scientists and domain experts exploring, diagnosing, and understanding the outcome of a binary classifier. The workflow identifies a set of features that tend to influence the model outcome. However, support for model comparison is not provided.

FeatureInsight is a tool that permits a feature-level comparison between the wrongly predicted instances and the correctly predicted instances, recommending features that could potentially be used to reduce erroneous predictions [7]. In Prospect [8], interactive visualizations are used to address two problems: detecting classification errors and providing insights for generating new features. The user can investigate regions in which instances are equally predicted by the models in order to detect errors in instance classifications and provide insights for generating new features.

EnsembeMatrix [9] is an interactive visualization system for exploring the space of combinations of classifiers. It presents a visualization of the confusion matrices that help the user to improve the accuracy score of a model. The work by Zhang et al. presents various interactive visualizations to support the comparison of predictive models [10]. Models are compared primarily through a scatterplot-based visual summary that overviews the models' outcome. However, there are some difficulties in interpreting these scatterplots. In our work, we are trying to provide users with easy to understand visualizations. This is remarked in the literature; for instance, Russell says that decision-makers "prefer visualizations that are easy to understand and to use for immediate data insights" [11].

3 The Three Visualizations

This section describes the three visualizations, namely Predictive Models Comparison Matrix, Two Models Pie-Chart Matrix and Instance Level Explanation. A previous version of the first two visualizations is presented in detail in [14]. These visualizations are the three main components of the VA technique that we created using a User-Centred Design (UCD) protocol to support the Keim's Visual Analytics Mantra. In particular, according to Buono et al. [13], various tests were performed with users according to the thinking aloud protocol, using prototypes of increasing complexity.

3.1 Predictive Models Comparison Matrix

The interactive visualization called Predictive Model Comparison Matrix (PMCM) shows the results of the application on a dataset of some classical data mining methods and the construction of the correspondent predictive models. The generated visualization uses a triangular matrix where the models are reported on both, rows and columns; a cell of the matrix refers to a pair of models corresponding to the cell row and column (Fig. 2).

Each cell contains two nested boxes. The outer box represents the prediction difference between the two models corresponding to the cell row and column. This value is computed as the ratio between the number of instances of the test set that the two models predict differently and the total number of instances in the test set. The inner box shows the accuracy difference, i.e., the difference between the accuracy scores of the two correspondent models. These two metrics are represented using two different gray scales. As reported in the legend, a greater prediction difference corresponds to a darker gray level; while a lower accuracy difference corresponds to a darker gray level. This choice allows the analyst to quickly identify the most significant pairs of models to be later analyzed in more details. Thus, the analyst is interested in identifying cells with darker inner and outer box; i.e., the pairs of models that mostly differ in their prediction of instances, still being similar in their accuracy.

In order to make more evident the inner box with respect to the outer box, the inner box is visualized with a black border.

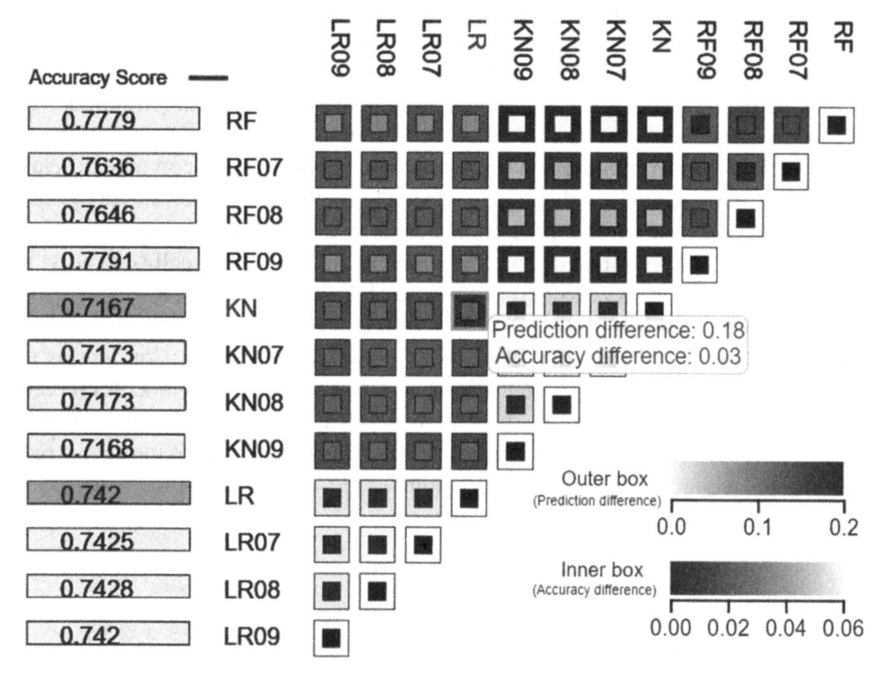

Fig. 2. Predictive models comparison matrix. Since the user has moved the cursor on the cell comparing KN and LR models, the values of prediction difference and accuracy difference of the two models are shown in the tooltip.

According to the User-Centred Design, formative tests have been performed with three data analysts with medium experience on predicting models. In these tests, some users observed also that they would expect the possibility to reorder the models according to the accuracy score. This is possible by clicking on the "Accuracy score" label. Moreover, in order to provide the analyst with some details about data, the interactive visualization in Fig. 2 provides a mouse-over feature that, when the mouse is on the cell, highlights the cell, the name of the models of the cell row and column and their accuracy scores in the horizontal histogram on the left of the figure; furthermore, the values of prediction difference and accuracy difference of the two models are shown in a tooltip near the cell.

The analyst is now interested in knowing more about such models. To this aim, the second visualization, based on pie charts, is used once the analyst clicks on a cell of interest, as described in the next section. Of course, the cells on the diagonal are not clickable (since the correspondent cells compare each model with itself).

3.2 Two Models Pie-Chart Matrix

The analyst goal is now to further analyze what is represented in a cell of the PMCM. More specifically, the interest is to compare pairs of models in order to understand the prediction error of two models when classifying the instances in the available classes. The interactive visualization called Two Models Pie-Chart Matrix (TMPM) has been provided. It shows a matrix of Pie-Charts to compare two models selected by the analyst. Figure 3 presents the comparison between KN and LR models, whose accuracy values are 0.716 and 0.742, respectively. It is worth noticing that this visualization supports the tasks *zoom, filter and analyze further* of Keim's Mantra. Specifically, once the analyst clicks on a cell of the PM Comparison Matrix because he/she wants to compare in details the two correspondent models, the matrix generated by the TMPM technique appears. Rows and columns represent the prediction classes available in the dataset. Therefore, also this matrix is always squared. More specifically, in Fig. 3, each cell (i, j) provides information about instances classified as class i by KN and class j by LR.

Indeed, at this step of the analysis process, the analyst is primarily interested in finding out how many instances are not correctly classified by a model. Considering the cell (i, j) and looking at the legend, four situations are possible: 1) both models correctly predict a number of instances (grey, both correct); 2) KN is incorrect in predicting a number of instances (blue); 3) LR is incorrect in predicting a number of instances (red); 4) both models are incorrect in predicting a number of instances (red-blue striped).

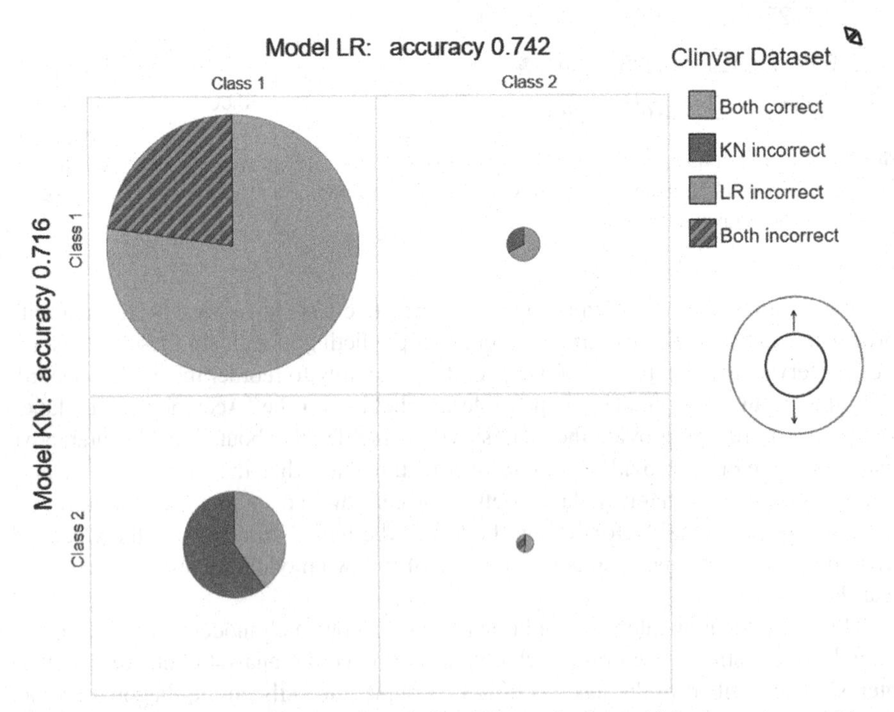

Fig. 3. Two Models Pie-Chart Matrix of the Clinvar dataset which determines a binary classification problem

The radius of each pie-chart is proportional to the number of instances predicted by the two models. In Fig. 3, it is evident that the biggest number of predicted instances is in the cell (1,1) and the smallest number is in the cell (2,2). Since the pie chart in cell (2,2) is very small and the sectors are not very visible, the button switches to a normalize view, which shows the pie charts having the same larger radius. Again, when the mouse is on the cell a tooltip shows the information about the number of instances per colour and the radius of the selected pie chart becomes larger.

It is worth remarking that the analyst is not interested on the cells along the diagonal since they refer to instances classified in the same way by both models. The analyst wants to know more about instances differently classified by the two models.

In order to identify the best predictive model for a given dataset it is important to know more about the classification of instances by the two models. This actually corresponds to the last task of the Keim's Mantra, namely *details on demand*. To this aim, the third visualization technique has been developed, which is described in the next section. With reference to the TMPM, because the analyst is interested to understand the reasons of possible classification errors and to analyze in details the features used by the two models, he/she may click on each cell of the TMPM that is not on the matrix diagonal; this triggers the third visualization technique, as described in the next section.

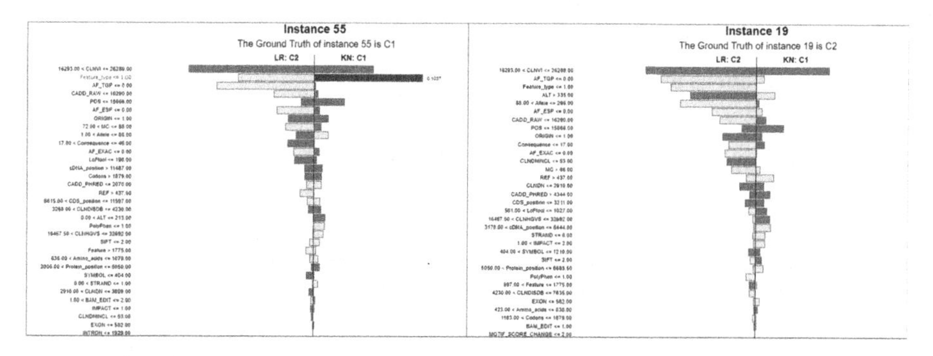

Fig. 4. Instance Level Explanation of the cell (1,2) of the TMPM in Fig. 3

3.3 Instance Level Explanation (ILE) Visualization

The Instance Level Explanation (ILE) visualization shows the features that contributed to the decision of the model. The ILE visualization appears after the user has clicked on a cell of the TMPM. It shows details of only 2 instances of the dataset in case of a binary classification problem. This because in case of a binary problem the pie-chart in each cell of the TMPM shows only 2 slices, one referring to the instances of the dataset wrongly classified by the model represented by the cell row and the other referring to the instances of the dataset wrongly classified by the model represented by the cell column. Since it is assumed that instances having the same Ground Truth (GT) but wrongly predicted (with the same class) by a model are similar and provide similar values for the features, all instances of a slice of the pie-chart can be represented by one instance. This means that the instances of the 2 slices of the pie-chart are represented by one instance each and the instance can be randomly selected.

Figure 4 shows the ILE visualization that appears when the user clicks on the cell (1,2) of the TMPM in Fig. 3. The 2 instances visualized in Fig. 4 are "Instance 55" and "Instance 19". The ILE provides, for each visualized instance, the following information, which is shown by either using text or a visual code:

- The *Ground Truth* (GT) on the top of each box.
- The *classes predicted* by the two compared models; reported under the GT. In Fig. 3, LR and KN models classify each instance as Class 2 and Class1, respectively.
- the *feature rules*, showing the range of values of each feature for that instance; reported on the left of each box.
- the *importance score* of each feature rule, i.e., a value from 0 to 1 that indicates how much the rule affects the model prediction; it is represented by the length of each bar correspondent to the feature rule.
- the *representativeness* of each feature rule for the predicted class, which indicates, for each model, if it considers the rule as representative or not of the class predicted by the model; the bar indicating the importance score is green if the rule is representative, otherwise it has no colour.

The ILE visualization is computed by using LIME, a Python library whose aim is to explain the predictions of a classifier [12].

4 Conclusion

The research work reported in this document provides a contribution towards creating a software system that supports the analyst in exploring and comparing a wider range of models, in order to investigate their behaviors. The objective is to build a tool to support domain experts in the selection of the best predictive model. The domain expert, i.e. those who are not expert of machine learning can understand which features are used to predict instances. Without showing the technical details of the models' parameters, which are difficult to understand for non-experts in machine learning and data mining, the ILE visualization gives to the user the opportunity to understand the main features on which is based the prediction of the most classic models used with the default parameters, and thus, they can select the model that best fit the available data.

All interactive visualizations were created using a User-Centred Design protocol in order to received constant feedback by the users. Formative tests with users were carried out and provided hints to improve the proposed approach.

Acknowledgments. The support of the MIUR-Ministero dell'Istruzione dell'Università e della Ricerca through the project "TALIsMan -Tecnologie di Assistenza personALizzata per il Miglioramento della quAlità della vitA" (Grant ID: ARS01\01116), funding scheme PON RI 2014–2020 is acknowledged.

References

1. KAGGLE. https://www.kaggle.com/kevinarvai/clinvar-conflicting. Accessed 20 Aug 2020
2. Gilpin, L.H., Bau, D., Yuan, B.Z., Bajwa, A., Specter, M., Kagal, L.: Explaining explanations: an overview of interpretability of machine learning. In: 5th International Conference on data science and advanced analytics (DSAA), pp. 80–89. IEEE (2018)
3. Kuhn, M., Johnson, K.: Applied predictive modeling, vol. 26. Springer, New York (2013)
4. Keim, D.A., Mansmann, F., Thomas, J.: Visual analytics: how much visualization and how much analytics? ACM SIGKDD Explor. Newsl. **11**(2), 5–8 (2010)
5. Krause, J., Perer, A., Bertini, E.: INFUSE: Interactive feature selection for predictive modeling of high dimensional data. IEEE Trans. Visual Comput. Graphics **20**(12), 1614–1623 (2014)
6. Krause, J., Dasgupta, A., Swartz, J., Aphinyanaphongs, Y., Bertini, E.: A workflow for visual diagnostics of binary classifiers using instance-level explanations. In: IEEE Conference on Visual Analytics Science and Technology (VAST), pp. 162–172. IEEE (2017)
7. Brooks, M., Amershi, S., Lee, B., Drucker, S.M., Kapoor, A., Simard, P.: FeatureInsight: visual support for error-driven feature ideation in text classification. In: IEEE Conference on Visual Analytics Science and Technology (VAST), pp. 105–112. IEEE (2015)
8. Patel, K., Drucker, S.M., Fogarty J., Kapoor, A., Tan, D.S.: Using multiple models to understand data. In: Twenty-Second International Joint Conference on Artificial Intelligence (2011)
9. Talbot, J., Lee, B., Kapoor, A., Tan, D.S.: EnsembleMatrix: interactive visualization to support machine learning with multiple classifiers. In: Proceedings of the SIGCHI conference on human factors in computing systems, pp. 1283–1292. ACM (2009)
10. Zhang, J., Wang, Y., Molino, P., Li, L., Ebert, D.S.: Manifold: a model-agnostic framework for interpretation and diagnosis of machine learning models. IEEE Trans. Visual Comput. Graphics **25**(1), 364–373 (2018)
11. Russell, D.M.: Simple is good: observations of visualization use amongst the big data digerati. In: Proceedings of the International Working Conference on Advanced Visual Interfaces, Bari, Italy, pp. 7–12. ACM (2016).
12. Ribeiro, M.T., Singh, S., Guestrin, C.: Why should i trust you?: explaining the predictions of any classifier. In: Proceedings of the 22nd ACM SIGKDD international conference on knowledge discovery and data mining, pp. 1135–1144. ACM (2016)
13. Buono, P., Costabile, M.F., Lanzillotti, R.: A circular visualization of people's activities in distributed teams. J. Vis. Lang. Comput. **25**(6), 903–911 (2014)
14. Buono, P., Legretto, A., Bertini, E., Costabile, M.F.: Visual techniques to compare predictive models. In: Proceedings of the 13th Biannual Conference of the Italian SIGCHI Chapter: Designing the next interaction, pp. 1–5, (September 2019)
15. Dimauro, G., et al.: Nasal cytology with deep learning techniques. Int. J. Med. Inform. **122**, 13–19 (2019). https://doi.org/10.1016/j.ijmedinf.2018.11.010
16. Reis, T., Bornschlegl, M.X., Hemmje, M.L.: Towards a Reference Model for Artificial Intelligence Supporting Big Data Analysis, In: Proceedings of the 2020 International Conference on Data Science (ICDATA 20) (2020)

Affective Analytics and Visualization for Ensemble Event-Driven Stock Market Forecasting

Praveen Joshi(✉) and Haithem Afli(✉)

ADAPT Centre, Cork Institute of Technology, Cork, Ireland
{praveen.joshi,haithem.afli}@adaptcentre.ie

Abstract. This study provides a comprehensive and objective valuation of factors included in the prediction of the stock market price of an organization. It examines the earlier financial-based model, machine learning-based model, and state of the art achieved deep learning model in contrast to the proposed method. The proposed model also evaluates the methodologies adapted while building the aforementioned models. For evaluation purposes, the dataset has been curated from one of the social media platforms- 'twitter', business news website- 'Financial Times', and from 'Quandl' to obtain financial indicators respectively to an organization. Big Data technologies have been deployed to accumulate and pre-process the data. An essential goal of this study is to support the visualization of such multidimensional data for exploration and analysis. Different tools and methodologies were evaluated to provide concise information at a particular instant by processing cumulative data of the organization under study. Affective analysis of news and twitter has been done with early defined models, and custom formulas derived in the research and the same have been plotted in real-time over the dashboard. Once specified pattern and transformation have been made, the transformed data curated is evaluated overall existing models and the proposed hybrid model. The model holds the ability to drive decisions after incorporating quantitative data such as stock price indicators, as well as qualitative data curated from social media platforms and business news website.

Keywords: Computer systems organization heterogeneous (hybrid) systems · Computer systems organization data flow architectures · Software and its engineering abstraction · Modeling and modularity · Theory of computation streaming models · Theory of computation data modeling · Human-centered computing scientific visualization · Computing methodologies natural language processing · Computing methodologies philosophical/theoretical foundations of artificial intelligence · Computing methodologies machine learning · Computing methodologies modeling and simulation

1 Introduction

In the artificial intelligence (AI) community, stock price prediction has always been one of the biggest challenges [51]. Starting from the initial time, professional

T. Reis et al. (Eds.): AVI-BDA 2020/ITAVIS 2020, LNCS 12585, pp. 28–55, 2021.
https://doi.org/10.1007/978-3-030-68007-7_3

traders developed lots of analytical methods to cater to this problem, in which few methods which caught the eye were fundamental analysis, quantitative analysis, and many more [56]. However, none of the earlier financial methods showed any noticeable results to determine the stock market prices. Prediction of stock prices has been seen beyond the capability of professional traders who, in general, are driven by greed and fear were not able to make rational decisions about buying and selling in the stock market [40] and traditional AI that is supposed focus on imitating human [56]. Recent days have seen the exponential growth of the artificial neural network in terms of underhood capability to approximate any complex continuous. These developments enable an artificial intelligence system to find out the more complicated relationship between the features and the target class and ability to cater lots of data with the advancement in algorithmic architecture to parallelize for a huge amount of data [23].

This research project is aimed to capture the events happening in real life, which can be a merger of a company, changes made in the hierarchy of an organization in respective company and subsidiary companies to the change in own nation's growth where that particular organization is expanded and change in the relationship amongst different countries. The study tries to captures these events in the form of sentiment scores and in-depth emotion score to measure events impact on the rise and fall of the stock price for the concerned organization.

Social media platform provides a space to every individual around the world to put up their concerns and thoughts regarding the different aspects of an organization, which can depict their likeliness towards the new launch of a product, service released by the organization or any event in association to the respective organization. These opinions and flowing thoughts have been captured concerning the organization and processed to analyze the sentiments and emotions of the general people, which is then further passed upon to the predictive models to relate such events to the rise and fall of the organization's stock price.

Business News is another platform that captures the sentiments and emotions of the people who bring in the money into the stock market. Business NEWS helps in capturing critical events as compared to the social media platform as it targets explicitly to bring insight from the event. As experts in the financial area derive the notion of the event, analysis done over Business News holds vital importance. All engineered features processed from the Business NEWS are again passed onto the predictive models to learn the correlation amongst those features to predict the stock price movement.

The financial indicators and its derived features with the existing formulated financial models have been deriving the investment in the stock market until recent years. They have been powerful to capture enough trends and movement of the stock market. With the exponential growth of other platforms now these models can be empowered with more advanced features and hybrid AI models can be introduced to capture feature relation, which is still not known to financial experts.

This study aims to assess the hybrid predictive models and their capability to make advancement in the financial model by incorporating many powerful features directly related to the response of the events from the general expert or non-expert people in finance around the world. Amid finding the best model for prediction, the study also tries to visualize the continuous stream of tweets and periodic feeds of business news to visually infer and get a notion of attachment of stock prices to the affective response of the peoples.

2 Background

This section provides a brief about the stock price and how artificial intelligence can help in inferring the prices of stocks. As Big Data streaming is captured from different sources and analyzed, thereby, this section also aids in creating a notion of Visual Analytics (VA) tools.

2.1 Stock Marketing

A stock market is a place in real or virtual, which provides "trading" facilities on corporations' stock and derivatives to the investors to trade securities and stocks of a corporation or mutual organization. The stock exchange is a regulatory body that governs the issue and redemption of securities. It also facilitates investments, income, capital events, and dividends [49]. The stock market is also known as the secondary market as it involves trading between two individuals where individuals can be organization, corporation, broker, or investor [51]. Stock prices are highly volatile, but the notion of price remains the same where if the stock is highly in demand, its price will rise, whereas on the contrary, if the market notion is against the notion of the company, there will be a dip in the prices. All companies whose stocks can be purchased over the stock exchange are known as "listed companies."

2.2 Introduction to Artificial Intelligence

Artificial Intelligence or AI as we call it is still a field of ongoing research and experiment. AI is a field in which human intelligence is replicated into machines which enhances them from simple mechanical devices to enhanced intelligent and self-sufficient machines. AI has a different sense of understanding of different people. Some think that AI should closely replicate the human behaviour and thought process while others think that it should be free from the notion of emotion and should be able to figure out the best way rationally. AI is like an umbrella which takes into consideration various fields and their respective perspectives and techniques be it from philosophy, mathematics or computer science. Many think that the notion of AI itself is a modern idea, but the vision has been there since last 50 or so years. It was Alan Turning who bought AI into trend after the introduction of Turing Machines (1937) [52] which was a model of ideal self-sufficient, intelligent computer based on which he developed the theory of AUTOMATA. After this, the first developed artificial network the MP neuron was work of Walter Pitts and McCulloch in 1943 [35]. Ever since then researchers all across the globe have been trying to imitate the process of the human brain. A simple machine qualifies as an AI machine if it can perform all the work that a human can with the help of his brain. If a machine can impersonate human behaviour is qualified to be called as an artificially intelligent machine.

1. **Machine Learning**
   Machine Learning is an Artificial Intelligence approach to enable the systems to automatically learn and refine itself from experience without providing any external code for all the features [7]. The heart of Machine Learning lies in the development of programs that retrieve the data and utilise it to learn and improve. The learning procedure involves observing the data for the patterns present and make future decisions based on the patterns and examples provided to the system. The goal is to make the system to learn and adjust on its own without any interference of human.
   In Machine Learning there two major categories of division as described underneath:
   (a) **Supervised Machine Learning Algorithms:** It utilises past learning into the new data to make predictions of future events, only when data is pre-labeled.
   (b) **Unsupervised Machine Learning Algorithms:** It is used in scenarios where the data are not labelled or classified. The data is explored to draw inferences to determine the hidden structure from unlabelled data.
   Semi-Supervised Machine Learning Algorithms: It utilises both labelled and unlabeled data for learning. It is used in cases where labelled data need resources for further training.
   Reinforcement Machine Learning Algorithms: This method produces action to interact with the environment. It involves the trial and error search and delayed reward.
2. **Deep Learning**
   Deep learning is one of the three subsets of the significant broad classification of machine learning where algorithms are inspired by the structure and the functioning of the human brain. Deep learning allows the computational models to learn multiple levels of abstraction within the data in the multiple computational layers of the composed model [27]. These methods worked astonishing well in multiple domains by improving the existing state-of-the-art.
3. **Transfer Learning**
   In today's era, even with the abundance flow of data, there are some domains where a lesser amount of work have been done. Less research and low reachability to such topics have led to significantly fewer data in those domains. Even if the problem is similar to one of the existing problem which has been tackled with the help AI, it is sporadic that new problem also follows the same distribution as to the problem already been solved. In such cases, if knowledge transfer is done correctly, it can lead to significant performance improvement

in the model, taking away the much more painful task of addressing and labelling more data. In the recent decade, transfer learning has emerged as one of the new learning frameworks to address the problem of labelled data scarcity [43]. There are two main types of Transfer Learning techniques:

(a) **Networks as feature extractors:** In this approach, features are extracted from some interim processing layer of a computational deep learning model, and the values coming out of those network at this stage are used as feature vectors. This feature vectors down the processing pipeline are used with different models for specific tasks in another domain different than on what the deep learning model was initially trained upon [21].

(b) **Fine tuning pre-trained networks:** In this approach, a pre-trained network is used as a starting point; then continuous efforts are made in order to fine-train the pre-existing weights such that they can generalise well over the new task [6].

2.3 Artificial Intelligence in Stock Market Prediction

Recent days have witnessed numerous research that was carried with the help of artificial intelligence to predict stock prices. In AI-enabled stock market prediction, it is noticeable that not only the combination of indicators but new features also came into existence and incorporated into the traditional and latest AI model. In early 2008, in order to simulate the market, a genetic algorithm (GA) in combination with a support vector machine (SVM) was introduced [13]. Where GA was able to simulate the indicator variables, but feature selection was not introduced hence made the model computationally very expensive. The subsequent year 2009, to cut down the computational cost attached to GA, proposed another 3 stage approach that bought down computational need multi-fold [28]. The three-stage approach proposed initial technical analysis over the indicator variable based on historical data, secondly selection of features amongst them, and then applying SVM. This machine learning and statistical model outperformed the earlier model. In the year 2010, with intense research over the market, new indicators were introduced, which extended the horizon for the number of factors that were included in earlier days to many more independent variables that were proven to impact the stock prices. Also, because of new predictors variables and the availability of data, new ways were exploited to build new models. One of the models was based on the artificial neural network with the given exploded indicator variables [24]. This model outperformed the existing machine learning (ML) model and financial mathematical model, giving rise to a new wave of ANN-based models for stock price prediction.

2.4 AI Stock Market Prediction with Financial Indicators

In stock market financial indicators such as open, high, low and close (OHLC) holds great importance. These trading indicators can show the captivity of the organisation in the real world. OHLC is considered to be complete in order to show the behaviour of an organisations' stock prices. In general, for an extended period, it can provide useful insights about not only the trading strength but also the price gaps. For example, if we plot low and high points for the day, it can provide insights regarding the day level volatility of the stock in stock exchange [17].

Significant data processing capabilities not only extended our horizon of finding the influences of financial factors over a long period which were not known earlier but also helped in advancing our decision making capability. With progress in the capability of harnessing the Big Data and to nurture it for a particular requirement also opened a whole new world for building more data-driven models and the ability to incorporate more number features.

In 2015, the deep learning based event-driven stock price model showed significant improvement as compared to all previously ML-based model [16]. DL based model was able to show a remarkable 6% improvement when compared to earlier model SP 500 stock historical data. With extensive data and new implementation of models also made stock predictions of stocks to reach near to the actual future price of the stocks. One of the recent research paper published in 2017, was also able to provide essential baselines when the different architecture of the ANNs was deployed to predict stock market price [11]. It was able to show that ANN as compared to the existing model was able to identify more hidden context from the data. It was also able to increase covariance estimation when it was subjected to the covariance-based market analysis.

2.5 AI Stock Market Prediction with Textual Data

Widespread adoption of technologies not only bought the world together but also enabled individuals to share their thought, ideas and experiences over the worldwide forum. These thoughts and experiences started building the sentiments amongst the people of same interest leading to favouritism and boycott of a product or organisation with a higher impact and over a global level.

In very recent years, 2009, new research was carried which showed the dependency of the financial news over the stock price prediction [47]. This paper introduced a new world of natural language processing (NLP) to qualitative financial data. Now qualitative data also came into consideration as one of the major contributing factors towards the stock price prediction. Financial news was processed using NLP to create a bag of words including only noun phrases and the named entities for the financial domain. The closeness of model prediction on the real-time financial news was very close to the receding stock price of the impacted organisation. Not only data from different forums but with a general inclination towards Twitter as a social platform also narrowed down the horizon to collect and compute the sentiments of the people regarding any organisation. With hashtag functionality and constrained length of tweets made Twitter favourable amongst the researchers to get motivated towards finding sentiments from the twitter data. In 2013, Twitter tweets and time series data of stocks formed the baseline of another research [50]. Topic-based analysis of the Twitter data and its incorporation with past historical data of stock price variation of a particular organisation showed the worth of the twitters' tweet and power that it was able to pass on to the quantitative financial data. With advancement in NLP, another paper published in 2015, was able to find a relation between the specific topics impacts on a specific organisation [41]. This method explained how data collected from different forms could be processed and cleaned to the data which is of real concern in the prediction of stocks for that particular company. Paper was able to bring the notion of defined topics for specific industries and change in sentiments for that particular topic. It was also able to bring down the cost of pre-processing needed for the data to be of any importance as suggested by the earlier research. Data used to build the model incorporated existing topic modelling approaches with newly proposed methods and historical financial data. Research not only showed the improvement which was gained over the existing approaches by 2.07% for 18 stocks over a year time but was also able to capture the sentiment analysis contribution in stock price prediction in the real world effectively.

1. **Sentiment Analysis Tasks**
   Exponential growth in an individual's power to access the internet and so for social media has led to a flood of thoughts and ideas that are shared per second across the world. Ease of curation of such thoughts and experiences of individuals for an organisation has given rise to sentiment analysis. As Zhang, Lei explained, Sentiment analysis or opinion mining is the computational study of people's opinions, sentiments, emotions, appraisals, and attitudes towards entities such as products, services, organisations, individuals, issues, events, topics, and their attributes [2,32]. Over last decade numerous research tried to capture the opinions which are individuals as customers, people of the state and far most as the human to find the influence over the organisations, countries and towards global topics. It was not only able to find the rationale of individuals belonging to a particular geographical area but all over the global level and tried to measure its impact on different higher level organisations. Sentiment analysis is broadly categorised and studied under three categories which are document level, sentence level and aspect level [55].
   (a) **Document-level** sentiment analysis task tries to classify the sentiments as neutral, positive or negative based on the overall sentiment captured in a document. The document-level analysis assumes the notion that each document will be talking about one context. One tweet can also be considered a document which can represent the opinion of an individual regarding some product or organisation.
   (b) **Sentence level** sentiment analysis task provides the capability to capture the sentiment of the document on the sentence level. In sentence level, before going for sentiment analysis, the sentence is mostly checked for the subjectivity. Subjectivity classification helps in avoiding objective opinion which is none other than facts [31]. Only sentences with high subjectivity are taken into consideration to undergo sentiment analysis task. Sentence level sentiments are also captured in three classes neutral, positive and negative respectively.

(c) **Aspect level** sentiment analysis task focuses on summarising and bringing out overall sentiments from people's opinion for any particular entity also known as targets. Aspect level sentiments express sentiments for each aspect of an entity. For example, if an organisation is considered as an entity, then the salary package can be considered as one aspect and employee perks as different aspect and so on. When aspect level sentiments are captured, one can easily find out whether salary or employee perks are useful in the organisation.

2. **Emotions Analysis Task** are closely related to the sentiment with more analysis of the inferred polarity. For example, negative sentiment can be caused by sadness or anger, while a positive sentiment can be caused by happiness or anticipation. Thus, following the way in sentiment analysis, many deep learning models are applied to detect emotions [55]. Zhou proposed an Emotional Chatting Machine (ECM) that can generate appropriate responses grammatically relevant and emotionally consistent based on GRU [55]. Their system is modelling the emotion factor, using emotion category embedding, internal emotion memory, and external memory. A bilingual attention network model was proposed by Wang [54] for code-switched emotion prediction. Abdul-Mageed and Ungar, built a large, automatically curated dataset for emotion detection using distant supervision and then used GRNNs to model fine- grained emotion [1]. They extended the classification to model by Plutchik [44], in which he proposed 8 primary emotion dimensions as shown in Fig. 1.

2.6 AI Stock Market Prediction with Twitter Data Analysis

The rising number of blogs and social media platform in the last decade provided a mean for people to put forward their opinion regarding the entities which can be an organisation or individuals'. This massive amount of opinionated data mining has provided a mean by which we can quickly capture the sentiments of targeted individuals regarding any product, organisation or government institution. In social media, Twitter gained favouritism from the world-wide community in terms of its use and became one of the dominant platforms to convey opinions. With the limit in tweet length and worldwide acceptance also grabbed attention from the AI community. Many research papers were published to establish the tweets sentiments relations to the stock market prediction in the last decade. In 2010, A.Pak proposed twitter corpus for sentiment analysis. In that particular corpus tweets where tagged to specific emotions manually, such that happy emoticons signified positive sentiment and sad emoticons signified negative sentiments [42]. In 2013, Twitter tweets with the time series data were able to provide significant results in stock market prediction [50].

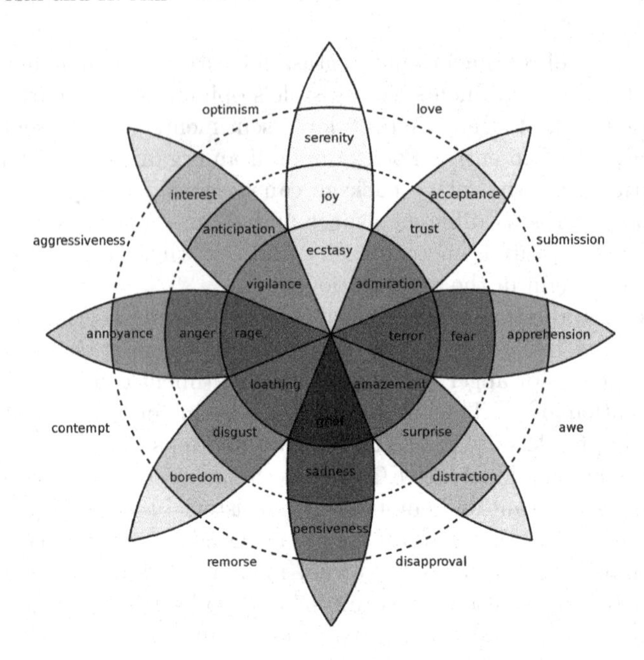

Fig. 1. Plutchik's wheel of emotion

2.7 AI Stock Market Prediction with News Data Analysis

While in last decade there were plenty of articles and research paper were published in data mining and time series to predict stock market prices, but there is very handful of papers which covered text mining in stock market prediction. Some of the earliest research paper who started using business news for financial forecasting [10,26], did a remarkable job but still due to the absence of news and public opinion about the particular organisation and nature of high volatility of stock price there was still scope to enhance the model. Most of the sentiment classification involves the training of the system based on the labelled documents by the experts or generated by the system. In 2004, Mittermayere proposed NewsCATS engine which was able to classify the news into three classes namely Good, Bad and No-movers. In this based on the category of the News movement of the stocks was predicted [38]. The AZFinText system proposed in 2010 is a regression system which also tried to predict the stock market prediction based on the news [48].

2.8 Big Data Visualisation of Streaming Data

Big Data poses a computing challenge because of its rapid velocity, immense volume, and a wide variety of [25]. With ever-increasing, human-centered systems are creating enormous amounts of data. As this enormous high volume of a wide variety of information can easily be generated and collected at a very high speed; Have created a necessity of Big Data visualization and visual analytics in a diverse real-world application.

In the last few years, there has been the development of various tools and techniques to visualize patterns in the textual data. Which most popular ones try to find the co-occurrences of the entities [9,18]. Also, there has been a multi-fold increment in the software to visualize such data [4]. Tableau is one of the most commonly used software for the analysis; It's the ability to hook with different ingestion system make its favorable choice amongst the developers and higher managers to crunch data quickly into multiple axis [14]. Alongside different systems were built to not only visualize the Big Data but to provide end to end solution to the Big Data visualization problem. ELK stack is one of the commonly used stacks which is used in the industry [20].

2.9 Contribution

The main contribution of this work is to analyze and develop the architecture to provide visualization aid to the prediction of the stock market prices. In prior research, most of the time, groups were mainly focused upon either the qualitative or the quantitative data, which have concentrated upon the more modest algorithms to solve that task without any practical validation. As the state of the art algorithms comprises the machine learning models which made this research novel in the financial domain but at the same time deployment of deep learning (DL), model made it to lose the explainability aspect of it. The visualization aid was aggregated to the framework to make it more explainable to mitigate the drawback of using deep learning algorithms.

Our approach extends the existing framework described in Sect. 2.8. In addition to developing together with the components that worked best in abstract design, we also created a pipeline that can ingest from multiple platforms in parallel without any concerns of qualitative or qualitative data. Framework in integrated with state of the art machine learning models of the finance domain and at the same time, the ingested data was represented in real-time over the tableau dashboard to comprehend the model's prediction.

Our findings are that model prediction does not need to come at the expense of the explainability. For the approaches to building the framework, we have developed components extension to integrate seamlessly, which provided the necessary aid of visualization to the financial model prediction. Although the data ingestion requires unique formulation and filtering, the process itself is straight forward and easily accessible.

3 Big Data Pre-processing and Visualization of Tweets, Business NEWS and Financial Indicators

This section defines the end-to-end pipeline that has been utilized in this study for analysis of qualitative as well as quantitative data flowing in from the different platforms. Although data is scrapped based on the scrapping policies and API utilized to connect to the different platform, but once we have a data stream, the ingestion, processing tunnel and storage space remains the same for the project.

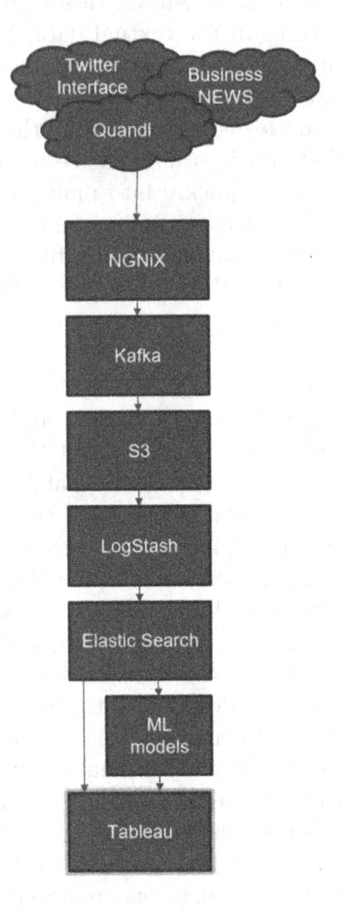

Fig. 2. Proposed architecture

Figure 2 describes the proposed architecture that has been used in the project for creating a visualization pipeline and also used for the data modeling part. In an initial study, all the platforms for the study were evaluated based on scrapping policies and availability of API, and three different platforms were found best for the study. Twitter interface API has been used to collect the twitter data from the social media perspective, Financial times feed was consumed to gather the business NEWS, and Quandl API was consumed to collect the financial indicators of the Microsoft stocks. Based on API and feed, Kafka streaming tunnel with NGNiX was created for continuous monitoring and streaming of data from the different platforms. S3 has been consumed to create a data lake for the data getting ingested from the Kafka pipeline. Over S3, the logstash component was built whose primary aim was to provide server-side processing pipeline, and output was served to elasticsearch. In elastic search, data can be found in a much more meaningful way as it forms a definite structure. This processed and ready to use data is then consumed by the machine learning models to predict the stock price as well as same data was consumed by tableau for intermediary visualization and analysis to get a notion of how the model should behave and then the model was tweaked if any discrepancies in the visual and inference from machine learning model are found.

Data set curated from different platforms for the Microsoft organization is from the 4th of April 2015 till the 28th of March 2019. Whereas due to less number of data points, no development set have been taken out from the data set, and training and the testing split is based on the dates. Training data points are taken from the 4th of April 2015 till the 1st of January 2019, and testing data is the point is from the 2nd of January 2019 till the 28th of March 2019. Data set Overview is provided in the Table 1

Table 1. Dataset overview - train and test split

Company	Start date	End date	No. of days	Train	Test	f	'f (VIF)'
Microsoft News	4/4/2015	3/28/2019	1027	961	66	25	23
Microsoft Twitter	4/4/2015	3/28/2019	1419	1332	87	26	16
Microsoft Finance	4/4/2015	3/28/2019	983	923	60	32	9
Microsoft News BERT	4/4/2015	3/28/2019	1027	961	66	768	–
Microsoft Twitter BERT	4/4/2015	3/28/2019	1419	1332	87	768	–
Combine	4/4/2015	3/28/2019	1423	1336	87	79	16

In the Table 1, 'f'- refers to the number of features in the data set and 'f(VIF)'- represents the number of features after removing the correlated features from the data frame. Also, the table 'f(VIF)' is null for Microsoft finance and NEWS BERT because features arrangement holds a semantic representation of each textual document, and hence the relation can break if the correlation feature removal is implemented in the data set.

3.1 Data Pre-processing

The need for data pre-processing is only required by the raw textual data curated from the Twitter platform and financial times website.

Pre-processing of Scrapped Textual Data

The textual dialogues are processed using *ekphrasis*[1] tool [5] in which series of operation are performed. A brief visual description of this tool is described in Fig. 3 as well as components are explained underneath:

[1] https://github.com/cbaziotis/ekphrasis.

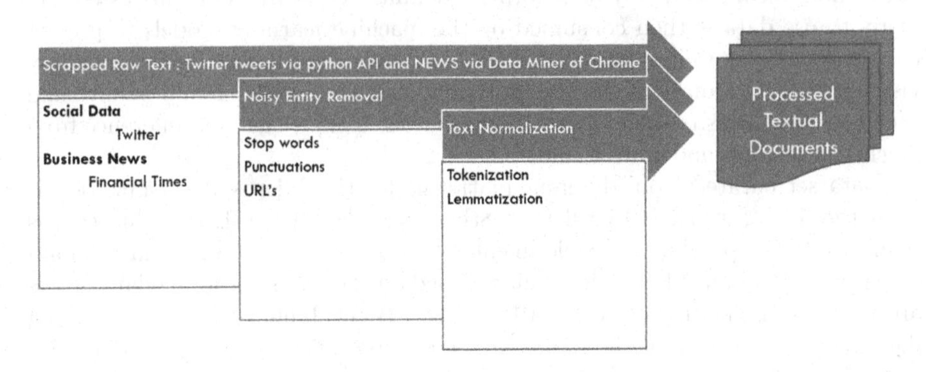

Fig. 3. Pre-proessing pipeline for textual data

1. Noisy Entity Removal: Twitter being a social networking platform on the global level, which makes tokenisation of twitter data most complicated task. It is essential to keep the words intact with the corresponding emotions attached to it. Also, creative writing use for new emotion generations and hashtag should be considered. Textual data curated from the Business NEWS platform are much more formal hence requires fewer efforts for cleaning. The goal here is to remove any stop words, punctuation's, URLs with censored words, and not to remove complex emoticons.
2. Text Normalization: This step involves tokenising the processed data coming after the above-stated stage. Tokenised words are then lemmatised so that each word can be visualised as root words.

3.2 Feature Extraction Techniques

Feature Extraction from Textual Data

1. **Sentiment Analysis.** For capturing sentiment analysis different libraries and ontology have been used:
   (a) **TextBlob**
   TextBlob is a library supporting Python 2 and 3 for the original processing data. It provides a simple application interface which helps in efficiently leveraging everyday natural language tasks such as part-of-speech (POS) tagging, extraction of entities based on the POS tags, sentiment analysis and more [33]. TextBlob under the hood utilises NLTK and pattern library which are widely used and accepted in natural language processing NLP community. In recent years, TextBlob gained wide acceptance in AI community which can be readily determined by the number of a research paper using it as a tool for sentiment analysis [3,34,53].

(b) **Pysentiment**
Pysentiment is the library for sentiment analysis which is built on top of the dictionaries. Two dictionaries which are used by this library is namely Harvard iv-4 by Harvard University and Loughran and McDonald Financial Sentiment Dictionary.
i. Harvard Institute provides **HIV4** dictionary. This dictionary provides 185 features for each of the 11789 words. One hundred eighty-five features in this dictionary represent the different aspects of the word ranging from sentiment, affiliation, psychological, emotions and many more.
ii. In 2012, **Loughran and McDonald Financial Sentiment Dictionary (LM)** consisted of 84330 financial words with their sentiments was published [36]. This dictionary after its release in public domain assisted much research to captures sentiments from financial articles, business news and much more

2. **Emotion Analysis:** "Words are associated with emotions," as quoted in the research paper NRC emotion Lexicon [39]. In order to capture the emotions from the tweets and business news, there are different deep learning models available [8], but to make the architecture lightweight, tokenized processed documents are mapped against the NRC emotion lexicon. Eight emotions are captured in the process. As tweets posted over the twitter platform for a day is more than ten thousand, hence more advanced emotion normalization score system is used to compute the emotions.
Score Formation for Emotions:

$$\frac{\sum_{i=1}^{l} \frac{\sum_{i=1}^{d} emotion_i \ appearing \ in \ a \ tweet}{length \, of \, the \, tweet}}{number \ of \ tweets \ per \ day} \tag{1}$$

In Eq. 1, 'i' refers to the single tweet of the day 'd' refers to total number of tweets for a day. 'i' refers to the total number of days.

3. **Bidirectional Encoder Representations from Transformers (BERT): State-Of-The-Art Textual Representation of Textual Documents.** BERT provides the pre-trained vectors representation of the words, which can be used further with the various AI models. BERT architecture is a frame to provide representations by joint conditional probabilities both from the left and right context for all the processing layers [15]. BERT vectors are used in the experiment to utilise the shallow transfer learning models to enhance the capabilities of the current predictive models. BERT is used as a service, to convert processed text both for twitter and business NEWS to its corresponding vector. As there are multiple models in BERT, current experiment utilises **BERT-Base-Uncased** which holds the capability to represent the word in the 768 dimensions.

Feature Extraction from Financial Indicators. As platform 'Quandl' provides the financial indicators such as OPEN, CLOSE, Adj CLOSE, VOLUME

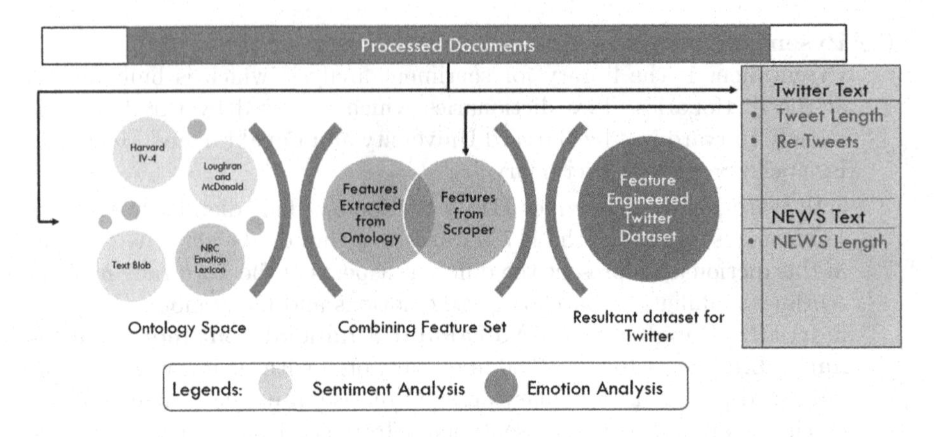

Fig. 4. Textual: feature engineered data set preparation

and DATE for a range of specific duration. Existing research in the area of stock market prediction can help the system to derive out a significant number of derivative features from the information provided by the Quandl platform. As for generating a label for the dataset, as explained in Sect. 3.3, the system is using the open price of the stock of the current and successive day. Hence all derived features are built upon the OPEN financial indicator. From OPEN financial indicator corresponding Fourier transformation have been derived based upon the wavelet research [30], the moving average is computed as a feature with a lag of 2, 7 and 21 days [22], Moving Average Convergence Divergence MACD [12,46], Upper and lower bounds [29], exponential moving average [37] with lag of 12 and 21 days, momentum and log momentum [19].

3.3 Formulation of the Feature Engineered Data Set and Label

Feature extraction techniques Sect. 3.2 are used to build overall feature engineered dataset for the current experiment. Qualitative textual data is converted into quantitative data with the help of the feature extraction techniques, and the custom score mechanism explained in Sect. 3.2. In parallel derivative financial indicators have bee developed based on the prior research in the field of finance.

Formulation of Target Labels. As the system tries to predict the rise or fall for particular days under test for the current organisation. Hence, opening stock price is taken as a measure to compute the label for the particular day. The formula for computing the target label is provided underneath:

$$TargetLabel_t := if\ (OpenIndex_t \leq OpenIdex_{t+1})\ then 1 else 0 \tag{2}$$

In this equation, t depicts the day under evaluation or for which label is to be assigned and t + 1 represents the next day. According to the equation, if the market is going up, one is assigned as label whereas on the contrary 0 will be assigned as a label for the fall of the stock price.

Formulation of the Textual Feature Engineered Data Set. Feature extraction techniques provided a way to extract the features and to give quantitative meaning to them. All the features from the analysers are combined to formulate the overall data-set. In addition to features coming from the analyser twitter also have one more feature provided by the Twitter API, which is also taken into consideration. Architecture for textual feature engineered data set is visualised in Fig. 4.

Formulation of the Financial Indicators Based Feature Engineered Data Set and Label. As described in the previous section, all the derivatives of the OPEN indicator formulated the new engineered feature. Visualisation of data set formulation of the financial indicator is provided in the Fig. 5.

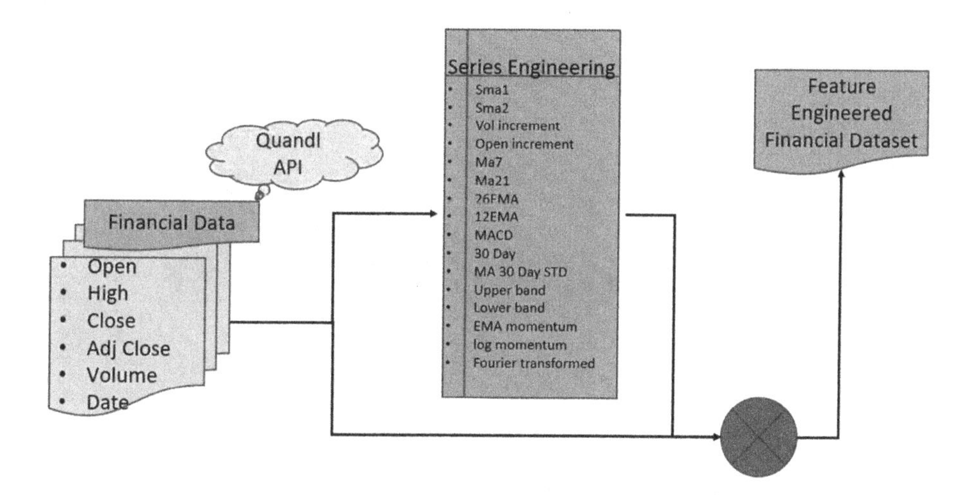

Fig. 5. Financial indicator: feature engineered data set preparation

3.4 Twitter Data Accumulation and Visualization

Once we formulate the definite dataset as described in Table 1. Emotion analysis over the tweets is done with the help NRC [2] lexicons, and individual emotion score is further amplified with the custom score Eq. 1. Two positive emotions, namely- 'trust' and 'joy' are evaluated against the OPEN index of the stock market and visualised in Fig. 6. Two negative emotions namely- 'anger and 'sadness' are evaluated against the OPEN index of the stock market and visualised in Fig. 7.

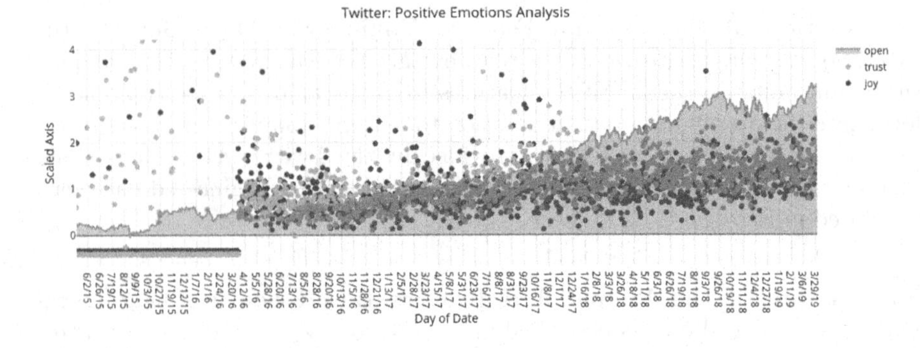

Fig. 6. Positive emotions in Tweets

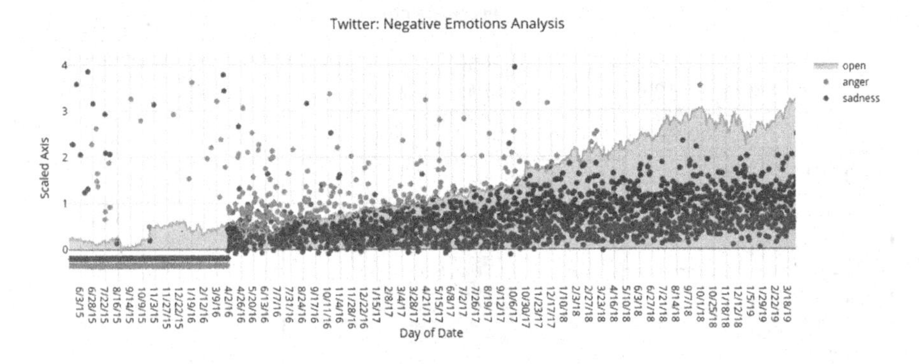

Fig. 7. Negative emotions in Tweets

Sentiment Analysis of tweets is done with the help of TextBlob 1a library and pysentiment 1b library. In the pysentiment library, two libraries are used, Harvard Institute dictionary and Loughran and McDonald Financial Sentiment Dictionary to capture the sentiments flowing in the tweets concerning the organisation. All the sentiments are averaged out and visualised in Fig. 8.

3.5 Business NEWS Data Accumulation and Visualization

Emotion analysis over the Business NEWS is done with the help NRC 2 lexicons, and individual emotion score is further amplified with the custom score Eq. 1. Two positive emotions, namely- 'trust' and 'joy' are evaluated against the OPEN index of the stock market and visualised in Fig. 9. Two negative emotions namely- 'anger and 'sadness' are evaluated against the OPEN index of the stock market and visualised in Fig. 10.

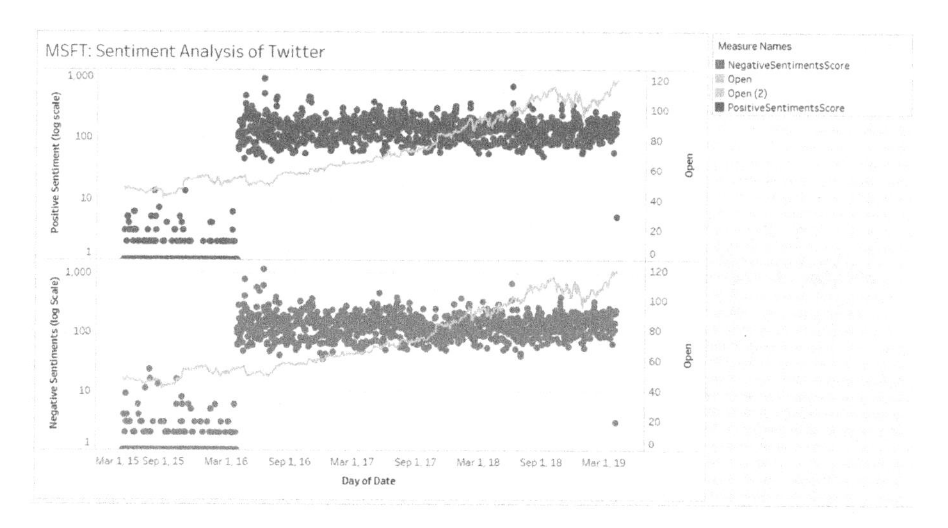

Fig. 8. Sentiments vs opening price for Microsoft stocks based on Tweets

Sentiment Analysis of Business NEWS is done with the help of TextBlob 1a library and pysentiment 1b library. In the pysentiment library, two libraries are used, Harvard Institute dictionary and Loughran and McDonald Financial Sentiment Dictionary to capture the sentiments flowing in the tweets concerning the organisation. All the sentiments are averaged out and visualised in Fig. 11.

4 Architecture for Stock Market Prediction

As experiment evaluates data gathered from the social platform, business NEWS, and financial indicators with the state-of-the-art models. Hence two strategy has carried forward to build the hybrid architecture to improve the performance of the earlier existing systems.

4.1 Hybrid Architecture Based on Best Model Selection Strategy

The first strategy followed is to build an Architecture that can incorporate quantitative as well as qualitative data. Hence prediction from the best performance models for each of the platforms is taken together and given to the voting classifier. The voting classifier then uses the soft voting technique to assign a weight to different models based on the classifier, which are housed in the voting classifier, as visualized in the Fig. 12.

4.2 Hybrid Architecture Based on Shallow Transfer Learning Model

The second strategy is the formulation of the effectiveness of the state-of-the-art shallow networking based transfer learning technique in the form of BERT

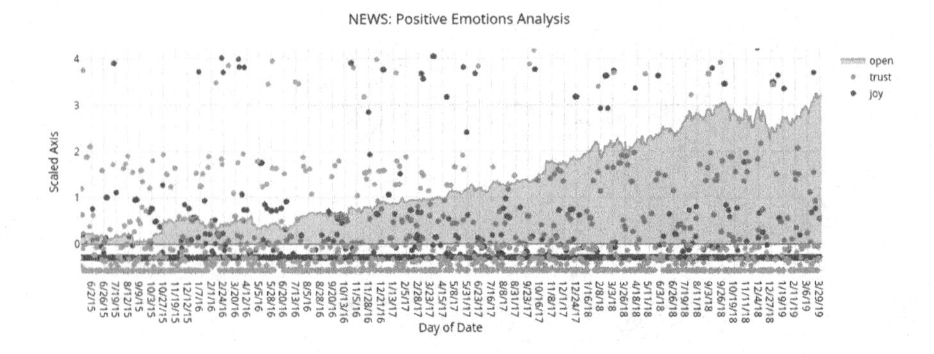

Fig. 9. Positive emotions in business NEWS

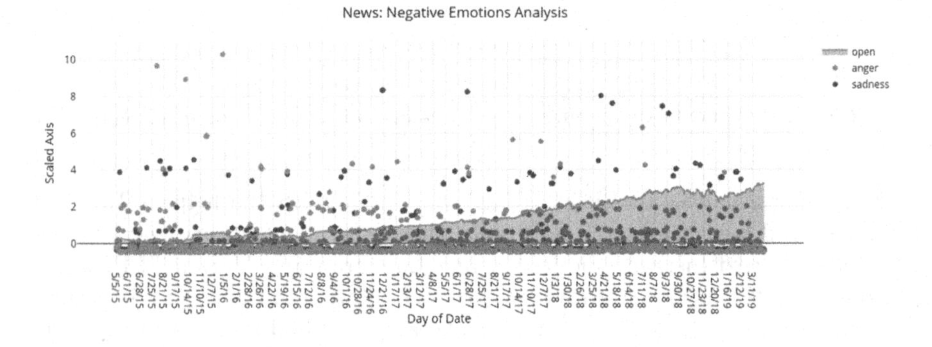

Fig. 10. Negative emotions in business NEWS

vectorization. A tweet and an abstract of NEWS formed an independent document of variable length. Each of the documents then goes through the BERT vectorization service, where it gets converted into the fixed-length vector. The fixed-length vector of tweets and news are independent of each other. Once all the fixed-length vector for the whole day is identified, then the average fixed-length vector is formed for that particular day, which then merges (twitter and news) to create a day data point. A high context level diagram is provided in Fig. 13.

4.3 Hybrid Architecture Based on Engineered Feature Dataset

The third strategy is the formulation of the dataset. The dataset preparation is done by combining all the features extracted from twitter, business news, and Quandl collected financial data. Once data is formulated, it is then subjected to the machine learning models for the training and inference purpose. A high context level diagram is provided in Fig. 14.

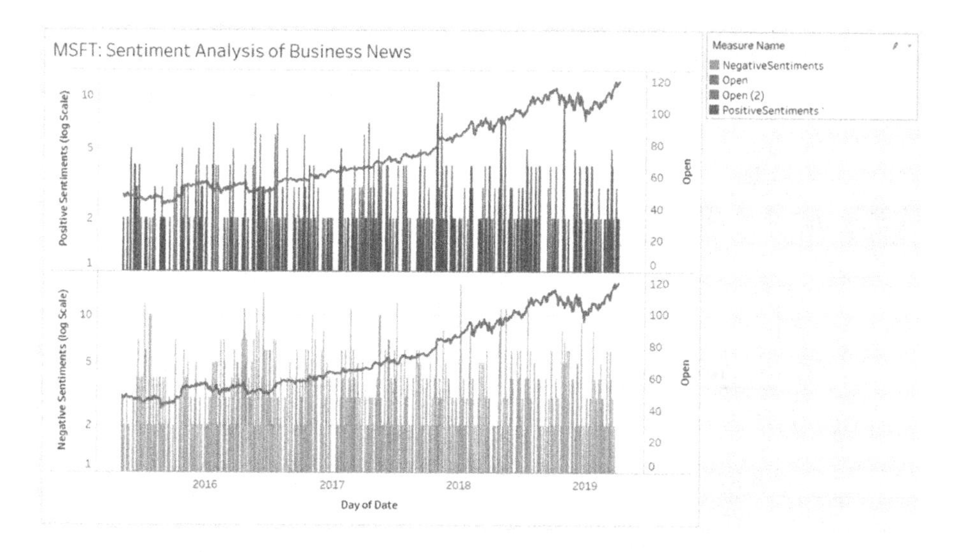

Fig. 11. Sentiments vs opening price for Microsoft stocks based on business NEWS

5 Evaluation Metrics

As current experiment carried out is a supervised problem, hence matrics evaluated for the comparison of the results from the different machine learning model and the deep earning models has been done based on accuracy, precision, recall and F1-Score.

1. Accuracy:
   Accuracy is the ratio of total correct predictions that have been made in all the classes in the classification problem. Mathematically it can be visualised as the ratio of true positive and true negative with all the data points present in the data-set. Mathematical formula of accuracy is given underneath:
   $$\frac{\sum_{i=1}^{l} \frac{tp_i+tn_i}{tp_i+fn_i+fp_i+tn_i}}{l} \tag{3}$$
   In Eq. 3, 'tp' represents the true positive from the model. 'tn' represent the true negative from the model. 'fn' represents the false negative from the model. 'fp' represents the false positive from the model.
2. Precision:
   Precision defines the exactness of the system. It is defined as the ratio of true positives identified by the model over actual number of positive marked by the model. Mathematical formula of the precision is given underneath:
   $$\frac{\sum_{i=1}^{l} \frac{tp_i}{tp_i+fp_i}}{l} \tag{4}$$

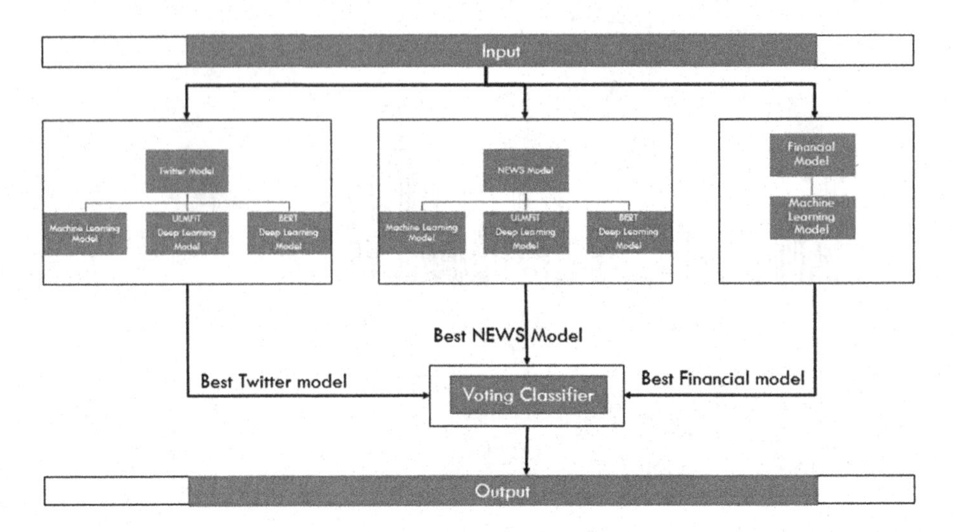

Fig. 12. Hybrid architecture based on best model selection strategy

In Eq. 4, 'tp' represents the true positive from the model. 'tn' represent the true negative from the model. 'fp' represents the false positive from the model.

3. Recall:
   Recall helps in evaluating the completeness of the model. It is the ratio of predicted positive over the ground truth positive classes. Mathematical formula of recall is given underneath:

$$\frac{\sum_{i=1}^{l} \frac{tp_i}{tp_i+fn_i}}{l} \tag{5}$$

   In Eq. 5, 'tp' represents the true positive from the model. 'tn' represent the true negative from the model. 'fn' represents the false negative from the model.

4. F1-Score:
   F1-Score is computed by evaluating the harmonic mean of the precision and recall. Mathematical formula of F1-score is given underneath:

$$\frac{(\beta^2+1)\, Precision_M\, Recall_M}{\beta^2(Precision + Recall)} \tag{6}$$

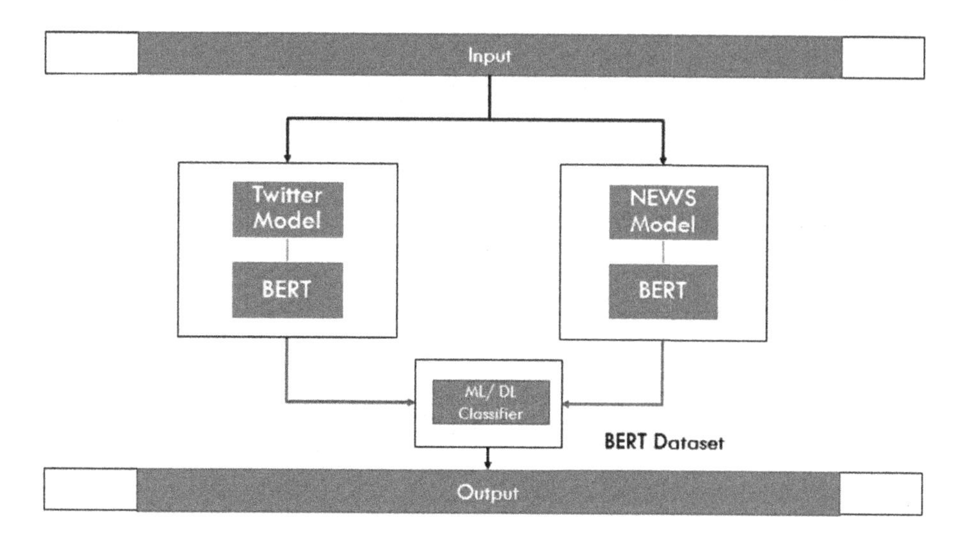

Fig. 13. Hybrid architecture based on shallow transfer learning model

6 Results

As current experiment carried out is a supervised problem, hence matrics evaluated for the comparison of the results from the different machine learning model and the deep earning models has been done based on accuracy, precision, recall, and F1-Score.

6.1 Hybrid Architecture Based on Best Model Selection Strategy

Best model from the different platforms has been selected. From Twitter models the dense, deep neural network has been taken, from Business NEWS models Naive Bayes model has been taken and from financial indicator models Random Forest has been taken; Individual output coming from each of the best models will be given to Voting Classifier to make the prediction. Results obtained from the architecture is described in Table 2.

Table 2. Evaluation metric for hybrid architecture based on best model selection strategy

Model	Accuracy	Precision	Recall	F1-score
VotingClassifier	0.5714	0.63	0.57	0.59

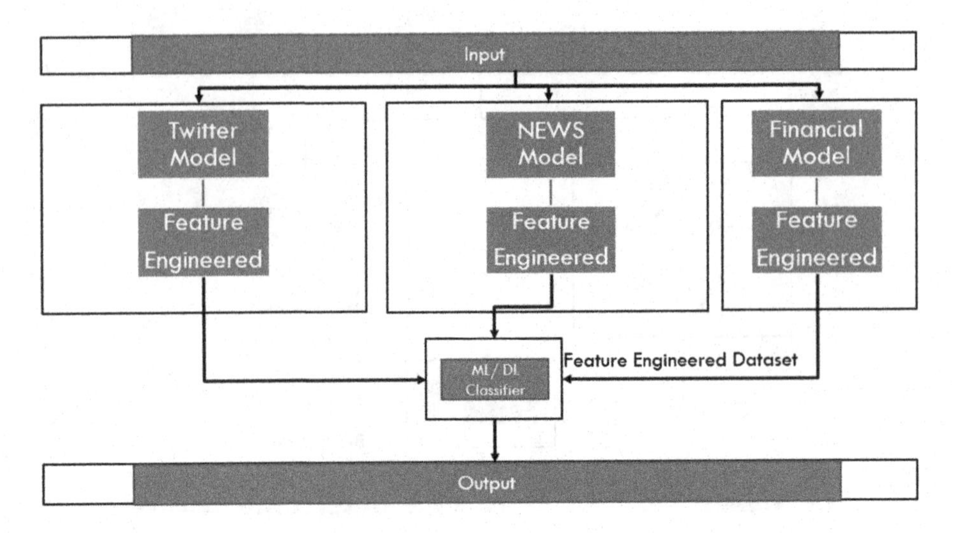

Fig. 14. Hybrid architecture based on engineered feature dataset

6.2 Hybrid Architecture Based on Shallow Transfer Learning Model

Dataset evaluated in this section is a resultant dataset obtained after the merger of the BERT vector of Twitter documents and Business NEWS articles on a daily basis. The evaluation result over machine learning model is provided in Table 3 and evaluation on deep learning model is provided in Table 4.

Table 3. Evaluation metric for hybrid architecture based on shallow transfer learning ML model

Model	Accuracy	Precision	Recall	F1-score
Naive Bayes	0.4827	0.53	0.48	0.49
RandomForest	0.6091	0.98	0.61	0.74
xGBoosting	0.592	0.6	0.6	0.49

6.3 Hybrid Architecture Based on Engineered Feature Dataset

Accumulated feature engineered datasets, from multiple platforms, are taken and evaluated with the machine learning and deep learning models. The evaluation result of Machine Learning models on the framed dataset is provided in Table 5 and deep learning-based models evaluation is provided in Table 6

7 Validation of the AI2VIS4BigData Reference Model

Section confirms and maps the proposed architecture of the study to the AI2VIS4BigData reference model [45], as shown in Fig. 15. This mapping is

Table 4. Evaluation metric for hybrid architecture based on shallow transfer learning DL model

Model	Accuracy	Precision	Recall	F1-score
Naive Bayes	0.4827	0.53	0.48	0.49
DenseNetwork	0.4367	0.43	0.44	0.44
CLSTMNetwork	0.5402	0.6	0.54	0.56
CBiLSTMNetwork	0.5172	0.69	0.52	0.58
CGRUNetwork	0.5517	0.66	0.55	0.59
CRNNNetwork	0.5747	0.82	0.57	0.66

Table 5. Evaluation metric for hybrid architecture based on engineered features dataset ML model

Model	Accuracy	Precision	Recall	F1-score
Naive Bayes	0.4367	0.84	0.44	0.54
RandomForest	0.7241	0.72	0.72	0.72
xGBoosting	0.69	0.69	0.69	0.69

necessary to validate the proposed system but also to provide a useful gateway to extend this research and possible collaboration in the future. As in the AI2VIS4BigData reference model for processing step 'Data Management & Curation,' our data ingestion pipeline, as proposed in Sect. 3, can directly be used. In other processing steps, as mentioned in the AI2VIS4BigData reference model, 'Interaction & Perception' tableau can facilitate the meaningful visualization needed for explanation of the inference made by the AI model.

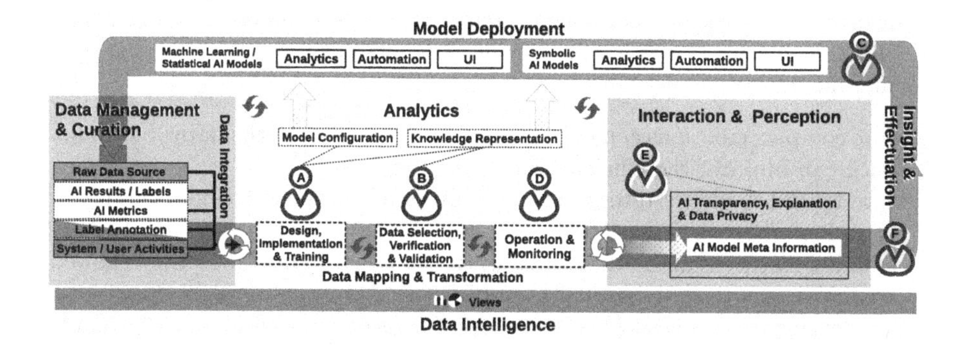

Fig. 15. AI2VIS4BigData reference model

Table 6. Evaluation metric for hybrid architecture based on engineered features dataset DL model

Model	Accuracy	Precision	Recall	F1-score
Naive Bayes	0.4367	0.84	0.44	0.54
DenseNetwork	0.6896	0.7	0.69	0.69
CNN_LSTMNetwork	0.5632	0.57	0.56	0.56
CNN_Bi-LSTMNetwork	0.5057	0.52	0.51	0.5
CNN_GRUNetwork	0.6206	0.62	0.62	0.62
CNN_RNNNetwork	0.5862	0.59	0.59	0.59

8 Conclusion and Future Work

Amongst all the Hybrid architecture, the Random Forest model was able to outperform all the other machine learning and deep learning model by the significant margin. Accuracy of **72.41%** and weighted average precision of **72.00%** shows the balanced inclination of the model towards the respective two classes, which are rise and fall of the stock price for the subsequent day.

The present research has been carried out to provide the feasibility study of the social media platform and Business NEWS over the stock market prediction. The findings in terms of affective analysis visualization and model building showed a significant correlation amongst the social media platform and Business NEWS for stock price prediction. It also captured the results obtained from the state-of-the-art methodologies over the research problem. As a remark, even though there is high volatility in the stock market but with the amount of data flowing in different social media platforms and righteous Business NEWS, in coming future, it will be very much possible to capture the stock price movement with multiple such platforms efficiently.

In future, underneath mentioned directions can be explored to build better visualization platform which can provide explainability to black-box machine learning model:

- More complex emotions can be captured with a correct mathematical formula, which can improve the efficiency of the system.
- More hybrid models strategy can be evolved and evaluated, and deep neural network on most the cases underperformed in the current experimental setup.
- Complex features can be developed in the financial indicator as they showed prominent results as individual models.
- Parallel research on multiple different platforms demands scalability. Scalable modules can be developed to capture the events in real-time.

Acknowledgments. This research was conducted with the financial support of ADVANCE CRT PHD Cohort under Grant Agreement No. 18/CRT/6222 and at the ADAPT SFI Research Centre at Cork Institute Of Technology. The ADAPT SFI Centre for Digital Media Technology is funded by Science Foundation Ireland through the SFI Research Centres Programme and is co-funded under the European Regional Development Fund (ERDF) through Grant # 13/RC/2106.

We want to thank Johnson Controls for contributing the idea of moves, which helped in accomplishing the research with significant results.

References

1. Abdul-Mageed, M., Ungar, L.: EmoNet: fine-grained emotion detection with gated recurrent neural networks. In: Proceedings of the 55th Annual Meeting of the Association for Computational Linguistics (Volume 1: Long Papers), vol. 1, pp. 718–728 (2017)
2. Afli, H., Maguire, S., Way, A.: Sentiment translation for low resourced languages: experiments on Irish general election Tweets (2017)
3. Arai, K., Tolle, H.: Method for real time text extraction of digital manga comic. Int. J. Image Process. (IJIP) **4**(6), 669–676 (2011)
4. Bassil, S., Keller, R.K.: Software visualization tools: survey and analysis. In: Proceedings of the 9th International Workshop on Program Comprehension, IWPC 2001, pp. 7–17. IEEE (2001)
5. Baziotis, C., Pelekis, N., Doulkeridis, C.: DataStories at SemEval-2017 task 6: siamese LSTM with attention for humorous text comparison. In: Proceedings of the 11th International Workshop on Semantic Evaluation, SemEval@ACL 2017, Vancouver, Canada (2017)
6. Bengio, Y., Lamblin, P., Popovici, D., Larochelle, H.: Greedy layer-wise training of deep networks. In: Advances in Neural Information Processing Systems, pp. 153–160 (2007)
7. Bishop, C.M.: Pattern Recognition and Machine Learning. Springer, New York (2006)
8. Bouchekif, A., Joshi, P., Bouchekif, L., Afli, H.: EPITA-ADAPT at SemEval-2019 task 3: detecting emotions in textual conversations using deep learning models combination. In: Proceedings of the 13th International Workshop on Semantic Evaluation, pp. 215–219 (2019)
9. Braun, P., Cuzzocrea, A., Keding, T.D., Leung, C.K., Padzor, A.G., Sayson, D.: Game data mining: clustering and visualization of online game data in cyber-physical worlds. Procedia Comput. Sci. **112**, 2259–2268 (2017)
10. Bushee, B.J.: The influence of institutional investors on myopic R&D investment behavior. Account. Rev. **73**(3), 305–333 (1998)
11. Chong, E., Han, C., Park, F.C.: Deep learning networks for stock market analysis and prediction: methodology, data representations, and case studies. Expert Syst. Appl. **83**, 187–205 (2017)
12. Chong, T.T.L., Ng, W.K.: Technical analysis and the London stock exchange: testing the MACD and RSI rules using the FT30. Appl. Econ. Lett. **15**(14), 1111–1114 (2008)
13. Choudhry, R., Garg, K.: A hybrid machine learning system for stock market forecasting. World Acad. Sci. Eng. Technol. **39**(3), 315–318 (2008)
14. D'Agostino, M., Gabbay, D.M., Hähnle, R., Posegga, J.: Handbook of Tableau Methods. Springer, Heidelberg (2013)
15. Devlin, J., Chang, M.W., Lee, K., Toutanova, K.: BERT: pre-training of deep bidirectional transformers for language understanding. arXiv preprint arXiv:1810.04805 (2018)

16. Ding, X., Zhang, Y., Liu, T., Duan, J.: Deep learning for event-driven stock prediction. In: IJCAI, pp. 2327–2333 (2015)
17. Duarte, J.: Trading Options for Dummies. Wiley, Hoboken (2017)
18. Dubois, P.M., Han, Z., Jiang, F., Leung, C.K.: An interactive circular visual analytic tool for visualization of web data. In: 2016 IEEE/WIC/ACM International Conference on Web Intelligence (WI), pp. 709–712. IEEE (2016)
19. Fama, E.F., French, K.R.: Size, value, and momentum in international stock returns. J. Financ. Econ. **105**(3), 457–472 (2012)
20. Fuente, A.D.D., Andreassen, O., Charrondière, C.: Monitoring mixed-language applications with elastic search logstash and kibana (ELK). In: Proceedings of ICALEPCS, pp. 9–12 (2015)
21. Kim, Y.: Convolutional neural networks for sentence classification. arXiv preprint arXiv:1408.5882 (2014)
22. Kimoto, T., Asakawa, K., Yoda, M., Takeoka, M.: Stock market prediction system with modular neural networks. In: 1990 IJCNN International Joint Conference on Neural Networks, pp. 1–6. IEEE (1990)
23. Kordonis, J., Symeonidis, S., Arampatzis, A.: Stock price forecasting via sentiment analysis on Twitter. In: Proceedings of the 20th Pan-Hellenic Conference on Informatics, p. 36. ACM (2016)
24. Krollner, B., Vanstone, B., Finnie, G.: Financial time series forecasting with machine learning techniques: a survey (2010)
25. Laney, D.: 3D data management: controlling data volume, velocity and variety. META Group Res. Note **6**(70), 1 (2001)
26. Lavrenko, V., Schmill, M., Lawrie, D., Ogilvie, P., Jensen, D., Allan, J.: Language models for financial news recommendation. In: Proceedings of the Ninth International Conference on Information and Knowledge Management, pp. 389–396. ACM (2000)
27. LeCun, Y., Bengio, Y., Hinton, G.: Deep learning. Nature **521**(7553), 436 (2015)
28. Lee, M.C.: Using support vector machine with a hybrid feature selection method to the stock trend prediction. Expert Syst. Appl. **36**(8), 10896–10904 (2009)
29. Levy, H.: Upper and lower bounds of put and call option value: stochastic dominance approach. J. Finance **40**(4), 1197–1217 (1985)
30. Li, J., Shi, Z., Li, X.: Genetic programming with wavelet-based indicators for financial forecasting. Trans. Inst. Measur. Control **28**(3), 285–297 (2006)
31. Liu, B., et al.: Sentiment analysis and subjectivity. In: Handbook of Natural Language Processing, vol. 2, pp. 627–666 (2010)
32. Lohar, P., Dutta Chowdhury, K., Afli, H., Mohammad, H., Way, A.: ADAPT at IJCNLP-2017 task 4: a multinomial Naive Bayes classification approach for customer feedback analysis task (2017)
33. Loria, S.: TextBlob documentation (2018)
34. Loria, S., Keen, P., Honnibal, M., Yankovsky, R., Karesh, D., Dempsey, E., et al.: TextBlob: simplified text processing. Secondary TextBlob: simplified text processing (2014)
35. McCulloch, W.S., Pitts, W.: A logical calculus of the ideas immanent in nervous activity. Bull. Math. Biophys. **5**(4), 115–133 (1943). https://doi.org/10.1007/BF02478259
36. McDonald, B.: Loughran and McDonald financial sentiment dictionary (2012)
37. Melvin, M., Taylor, M.P.: The crisis in the foreign exchange market. J. Int. Money Finance **28**(8), 1317–1330 (2009)

38. Mittermayer, M.A.: Forecasting intraday stock price trends with text mining techniques. In: 2004 Proceedings of the 37th Annual Hawaii International Conference on System Sciences, p. 10. IEEE (2004)
39. Mohammad, S.M., Turney, P.D.: NRC emotion lexicon. National Research Council, Canada (2013)
40. Naresh, G., Thiyagarajan, S., Mahalakshmi, S.: Is there any real market indicator to predict stock index returns? A sem approach (2016)
41. Nguyen, T.H., Shirai, K., Velcin, J.: Sentiment analysis on social media for stock movement prediction. Expert Syst. Appl. **42**(24), 9603–9611 (2015)
42. Pak, A., Paroubek, P.: Twitter as a corpus for sentiment analysis and opinion mining. In: LREc, vol. 10, pp. 1320–1326 (2010)
43. Pan, S.J., Yang, Q.: A survey on transfer learning. IEEE Trans. Knowl. Data Eng. **22**(10), 1345–1359 (2009)
44. Plutchik, R.: The nature of emotions: human emotions have deep evolutionary roots, a fact that may explain their complexity and provide tools for clinical practice. Am. Sci. **89**(4), 344–350 (2001)
45. Reis, T., Bornschlegl, M.X., Hemmje, M.L.: Towards a reference model for artificial intelligence supporting big data analysis. In: Proceedings of the 2020 International Conference on Data Science (ICDATA 2020) (2020, to appear)
46. Rosillo, R., De la Fuente, D., Brugos, J.A.L.: Technical analysis and the Spanish stock exchange: testing the RSI, MACD, momentum and stochastic rules using Spanish market companies. Appl. Econ. **45**(12), 1541–1550 (2013)
47. Schumaker, R.P., Chen, H.: Textual analysis of stock market prediction using breaking financial news: the AZFin text system. ACM Trans. Inf. Syst. (TOIS) **27**(2), 12 (2009)
48. Schumaker, R.P., Chen, H.: A discrete stock price prediction engine based on financial news. Computer **43**(1), 51–56 (2010)
49. Setty, D.V., Rangaswamy, T., Subramanya, K.: A review on data mining applications to the performance of stock marketing. Int. J. Comput. Appl. **1**(3), 33–43 (2010)
50. Si, J., Mukherjee, A., Liu, B., Li, Q., Li, H., Deng, X.: Exploiting topic based Twitter sentiment for stock prediction. In: Proceedings of the 51st Annual Meeting of the Association for Computational Linguistics (Volume 2: Short Papers), vol. 2, pp. 24–29 (2013)
51. Soni, S.: Applications of ANNs in stock market prediction: a survey. Int. J. Comput. Sci. Eng. Technol. **2**(3), 71–83 (2011)
52. Turing, A.M.: On computable numbers, with an application to the Entscheidungsproblem. Proc. Lond. Math. Soc. **2**(1), 230–265 (1937)
53. Upadhyaya, B., Khomh, F., Zou, Y.: Extracting restful services from web applications. In: 2012 Fifth IEEE International Conference on Service-Oriented Computing and Applications (SOCA), pp. 1–4. IEEE (2012)
54. Wang, Z., Zhang, Y., Lee, S.Y.M., Li, S., Zhou, G.: A bilingual attention network for code-switched emotion. In: Proceedings of the International Conference on Computational Linguistics (COLING 2016) (2016)
55. Zhang, L., Wang, S., Liu, B.: Deep learning for sentiment analysis: a survey. Wiley Interdisc. Rev. Data Min. Knowl. Discov. **8**(4), e1253 (2018)
56. Zheng, A., Jin, J.: Using AI to make predictions on stock market

Understanding the Role of (Advanced) Machine Learning in Metagenomic Workflows

Thomas Krause[1](✉), Bruno G. N. Andrade[2], Haithem Afli[2], Haiying Wang[3], Huiru Zheng[3], and Matthias L. Hemmje[4]

[1] University of Hagen, Hagen, Germany
thomas.krause@fernuni-hagen.de
[2] ADAPT Centre, Munster Technological University, Cork, Ireland
bruno.andrade@cit.ie, haithem.afli@cit.ie
[3] Ulster University, Belfast, Northern Ireland
{hy.wang,h.zheng}@ulster.ac.uk
[4] Research Institute for Telecommunication and Cooperation (FTK), Dortmund, Germany
mhemmje@ftk.de

Abstract. With the rapid decrease in sequencing costs there is an increased research interest in metagenomics, the study of the genomic content of microbial communities. Machine learning has also seen a revolution with regards to versatility and performance in the last decade using techniques like "Deep Learning". Classical as well as modern machine learning (ML) techniques are already used in key areas within metagenomics. There are however several challenges that may impede broader use of ML and especially deep learning.

This paper provides an overview of machine learning in metagenomics, its challenges and its relationship to biomedical pipelines. Special focus is put on modern techniques such as deep learning. The results are then discussed again in the context of the AI2VIS4BigData reference model to validate its relevancy in this research area.

Keywords: Machine learning · Deep learning · Metagenomics · Big data · AI2VIS4BigData

1 Introduction

1.1 Importance of Microbiome Analysis

Metagenomics studies try to explain the role of communities of microorganisms ("microbiomes") in their respective environment by analyzing their genomic content [4,44]. Many studies have demonstrated the importance of these microbiomes—like in the development and health status of human or animal

T. Reis et al. (Eds.): AVI-BDA 2020/ITAVIS 2020, LNCS 12585, pp. 56–82, 2021.
https://doi.org/10.1007/978-3-030-68007-7_4

hosts [5,24,61]. The exact mechanisms and role of the individual microorganisms and how they work together is however still largely unknown. A practical example is the analysis of methane production in ruminant livestock. Methane is a powerful greenhouse gas that is produced by microorganisms in the rumen [51]. Understanding the interactions responsible for methane production could be a first step in reducing these emissions [33,54].

Traditionally, microbiomes would be studied by culturing samples in a lab. Nowadays, their genomes can be decoded using high-throughput sequencing machines, providing previously impossible insights. Since the first human genome was sequenced and published by the human genome project in 2001, the sequencing cost has decreased a millionfold [67].

Falling prices and the growing number of metagenomic applications [4] leads to a rapidly growing amount of data. Large scale metagenomic studies can contain terabytes of raw sequencing data [57]. The storage required for sequencing data (including non-metagenomic) is expected to reach 2–40 exabytes per year in 2025, surpassing the requirements of fields like astronomy [58]. Having systems capable of processing this amount of data is therefore critical [57,63].

1.2 Machine Learning Trends

Another big trend in the last decade was the development of new and improved machine learning algorithms and techniques often summarized under the keyword "deep learning" [20,70].

The word "deep" refers to the fact that the machine learning models often use many processing layers and that the level of abstraction and the ability to learn complex relationships increases with every layer. As an example, a deep learning algorithm that is trained on images might detect simple edges in an image in the first layer. In the second layer it might combine several of these edges to detect simple shapes such as rectangles and in the final layer it could combine these shapes to detect complex objects. Adding yet another layer could enable the network to recognize the composition of objects to describe or classify a scene [70].

These algorithms are only possible by taking advantage of the increase in processing power and especially (GPGPU) as they can be computationally expensive and often require large amounts of data for processing [20, pp. 438–442].

Deep learning achieved record breaking results in many classification benchmarks as well as real life applications with a broad range of input data such as image, video, audio or text [70]. It has also been successfully applied to the field of genetics [76] including metagenomics [21].

2 Genetics and Metagenomics

2.1 Microorganisms

Microorganisms, like all living things, can be grouped into three "domains" called "bacteria", "archaea"and "eukaryotes" [69]. These domains differ in their evolutionary origin and in various properties such as the existence of a cell nucleus. Compared to organisms in general, microorganisms only include unicellular organisms.

Each of these unique cells contains molecular sequences in the form of deoxyribonucleic acid (DNA) and ribonucleic acid (RNA). Both DNA and RNA are built up using a sequence of nucleotides containing the bases adenine (A), cytosine (C), guanine (G) and thymine (T). In RNA uracil (U) is used in place of thymine (T) [1].

2.2 Differences Between DNA and RNA

There are several differences between DNA and RNA. Structurally DNA is made up of the famous double helix, consisting of two strands, where each of the nucleobases A, C, G and T on one strand is paired with a corresponding nucleobase on the complementary strand. A is paired with T and C is paired with G [1]. In comparison RNA usually has a single strand, so it does not form this double helix.

The complementary strands in DNA are biologically important for processes like cell division where the strands are separated and then rebuilt to replicate, but it has also important implications for sequencing since there are always two possible reads of a piece of DNA depending on which of the two strands is used for the translation.

From a functional perspective, DNA is responsible for storing and inheriting genetic information, while RNA has various functions within a cell such as the creation of proteins.

2.3 Genes and Proteins

Proteins are large molecules that execute many functions within cells and the body. The building blocks of proteins are organic molecules called amino acids. The order and type of amino acids determines the function of the protein. The instructions to form proteins are found within the DNA in sections called "genes". A part of the cell called the "ribosomes" is responsible for assembling the amino acids into proteins [52]. The ribosomes do not have direct access to the DNA though. For this reason, messenger RNA (mRNA) is used to create a copy of the gene from the DNA which is then transported to the ribosomes, where the protein synthesis is done [55]. The ribosomes are made up of proteins themselves along with another type of RNA called ribosomal RNA (rRNA) [52]. RRNA plays an important role in metagenomic studies as it can be used to identify the evolutionary ("phylogenetic") origin of an organism as will be discussed later.

2.4 Genomic vs Metagenomic Studies

The complete set of genetic material in an organism is called the "genome" [1]. The set of genomes from all microorganisms in a specific environment is called the "metagenome".

(Single) genome studies try to identify functional mechanisms within a single genome. For example, one use case of genomic studies is the identification of single-nucleotide polymorphisms (SNPs). SNPs, pronounced "Snips", are specific mutations of a single nucleotide within a genome [1]. SNPs can cause diseases like sickle-cell anemia [34], where the mutation causes irregularly shaped, sickled, red blood cells leading to blood disorders. SNPs are cataloged by the (NCBI) and assigned a unique reference number (the "rs" number) [56].

In comparison metagenomic studies usually do not care about individual mutations and instead work on a higher level by identifying whole genes or groups of organisms within a collection of many genomes that are analyzed at the same time [38]. Mutations can help though to identify the evolutionary relationship between organisms, which can be represented in a phylogenetic tree.

2.5 Phylogenetic Trees and Taxonomies

A phylogenetic tree displays the evolutionary relationships between species. Phylogenetic trees can be built by comparing the sequences of organisms. Since evolution happens by small mutations in the genetic sequences from one generation to the other, it can be assumed that big differences in the sequences correlate to distant relationships while small differences indicate a close relationship and a close common ancestor in the phylogenetic tree [48].

Different regions in the DNA and RNA are more affected by mutations than others. A challenge in creating phylogenetic trees is to find a region within these sequences which exists in all species and that has a mostly constant rate of mutation, so that the evolutionary distances can be accurately computed for all species [68]. Using only a specific region instead of the whole genome allows easier computation and lowers the cost of sequencing.

A popular choice for these regions lies within the rRNA which can be found in all living cells. The rRNA is structured into various subunits [52] which are named by their size in the Svedberg unit (S). T16S subunit in bacteria and archaea 18S subunit for eukaryotes contain both highly conserved regions (slow rate of evolution) as well as hypervariable regions (fast rate of evolution) [30,41]. While the former allows tracking of large evolutionary distances, the latter allows the differentiation between closely related species. The subunit can be further divided into smaller regions, which are used in metagenomic studies. The best region to use depends on the needs of the study. This is often a trade-off between the capabilities of the chosen sequencing platform, the total cost of sequencing as well as the desired phylogenetic "resolution" (ability to differentiate between closely related species) [8,52].

Using a phylogenetic tree a taxonomy can be created by labeling the different nodes and levels of a tree. The definitions and names of levels can change depending on the taxonomy used. Commonly they range from the "domain" as the highest level [69] (see also Sect. 2.1) to "species" at the lowest level. Commonly differentiated intermediate levels are "phylum", "class", "order", "family" and "genus" in order (from highest level to lowest level).

2.6 Structure of Metagenomic Studies

The goal of metagenomic studies is to sequence (read) and analyze the metagenome of one or more samples. Analyzing these samples is a process involving many steps.

Most studies can be distinguished into two categories: Those using "amplicon sequencing" and those using "shotgun sequencing" [41]. With amplicon sequencing a sample is prepared in a way that only specific parts of the DNA or RNA are sequenced. As was described in Sect. 2.5 these parts can be enough to identify an organism, assigning it a taxonomic classification using existing reference databases and placing it within a phylogenetic tree. For this reason, these parts are also called "barcode sequences".

The name "amplicon" stems from the fact, that these regions can be specifically selected within a sample and "amplified" (duplicated many times) using enzymes. Amplicon sequencing is a popular choice as it is relatively cheap while providing good results for taxonomic classification [6, pp. 56–59].

The other common approach is shotgun sequencing, where no special selection is done and sequences are sampled from the whole metagenome. Most sequencing platforms can only sequence fragments up to a specific length. This means that the sample has to be prepared in a way that cuts the genomes into small fragments. The fragments from all contained organisms in the sample will be mixed together which explains the name of "shotgun sequencing" as the exact fragments sampled from the complete metagenome is quite random.

Since shotgun sequencing has access to the whole metagenome it offers a wider range of possible studies. For example genes can be identified directly from the sequencing reads as part of a functional analysis to try to understand processes within a microbiome.

Even though shotgun sequencing seems more powerful than amplicon sequencing on first glance, there are good reasons to choose amplicon sequencing where sufficient. Since only a tiny part of the whole metagenome is sequenced in amplicon sequencing the cost is greatly reduced and less data needs to be analyzed and processed later [52, p. 112]. Also since all reads are focussed on regions that are well known with huge reference databases, the taxonomic composition of a sample can sometimes be better determined by this approach [6, pp. 56–59].

Regardless of whether amplicon sequencing or shotgun sequencing is used, the general workflow can be broken down into a series of individual steps that are taken from the initial sequencing up to the final result presentation. Figure 1 shows such a process for amplicon sequencing as well as shotgun sequencing. The figure also includes possible applications of machine learning, which will be discussed later.

It should be noted, that there is not a single template that can be applied to every study, some of the steps shown are optional and some studies might add additional steps. This is especially true for the analysis and visualization which highly depend on the study goal. The workflows should therefore only be considered examples that include the steps most commonly found.

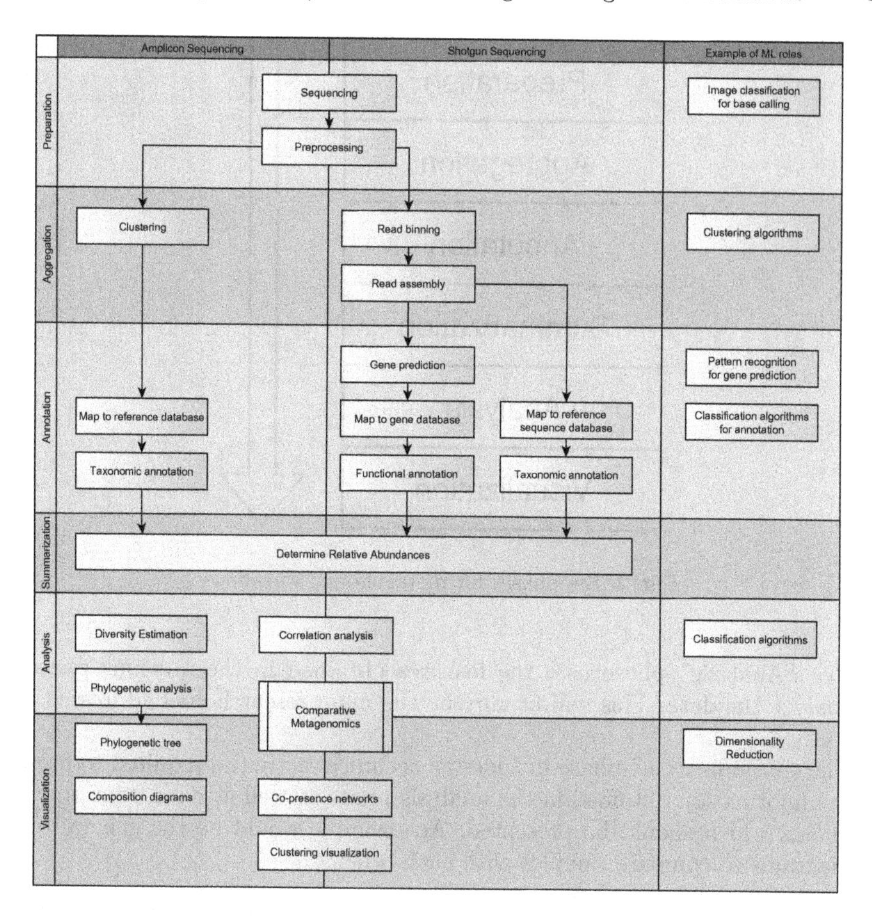

Fig. 1. Workflow for amplicon sequencing and shotgun sequencing with some applications for machine learning highlighted.

To simplify further discussion in this document, the actual tasks are sorted into six distinct phases shown in Fig. 1 and 2.

1. The "Preparation" phase encompasses the actual sequencing operation as well as quality control.
2. The "Aggregation" phase contains tasks that reduce, merge, cluster or otherwise aggregate sequences before further operations.
3. The "Annotation" phase is used to label or annotate individual sequences. The information used for annotation can come from external databases or from other methods such as pattern recognition.
4. The "Summarization" phase takes the information from individual sequences and transforms them into a comprehensive summary of the whole sample. This usually includes calculating the (relative) abundance of one or more features in the sample and preparing them for further analysis.

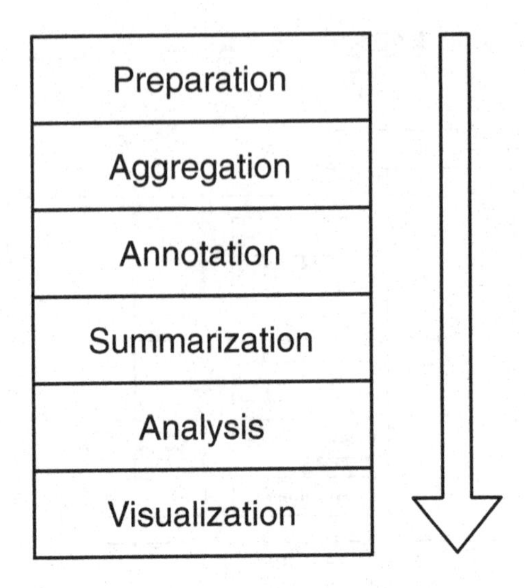

Fig. 2. Six phases for metagenomic workflows

5. The "Analysis" phase uses the features obtained in the previous phase to analyze the data. This will usually be the main research goal addressed in a study.
6. The "Visualization" phase includes all technical activities required to present the information obtained in the analysis phase as well as data from previous phases which should be presented. An example would be the generation of diagrams to compare samples with each other.

Having identified these phases, they will be used to describe the role of machine learning in the next section.

3 Roles of Machine Learning in Metagenomics

In metagenomic studies there are several parts which use machine learning algorithms or could potentially use them in the future. This section will go through the phases described earlier and identify machine learning applications in them. Unless otherwise mentioned the process will focus on sequencing results from high throughput sequencing (HTS) platforms like Illumina. Other emerging technologies like nanopore sequencing [43] will be mentioned at times where adequate.

3.1 Preparation

The preparation phase includes the actual sequencing of DNA molecules. The machinery of most sequencing platforms uses fluorescent nucleotides and different dyes to distinguish the four bases during sequencing. Photos are taken at different time steps and then analyzed to predict the bases present in the DNA molecules in order. This process is called "Base Calling". Base calling is complicated by multiple sources of errors during this reconstruction.

Machine learning can be applied to this problem. In one study two of the best performing algorithms (freeIbis and Ibis) were support vector machines (SVMs) [12]. The literature on using more modern deep learning techniques for base calling is however scarce. One possible reason for this could be that the results of simpler algorithms already have a very low error rate so that there is little room for improvement. This is supported by the fact that deep learning is successfully used for base calling in nanopore sequencing (an alternative emerging sequencing method), where the error rates are considerable higher [10,60].

The result of a sequencing operation is a collection of "reads" where each "read" contains the bases for one fragment along with quality metrics from the base calling step [41, p. 37]. The common data format for this is the FASTQ format, a simple text based format.

A preprocessing step will often be used after sequencing and before the execution of the rest of the pipeline to eliminate low quality reads or to trim bases that were not detected with a sufficiently high confidence based on the quality metrics present in the FASTQ file [41]. Since these are often simple threshold based techniques they will not be described in detail here. After preprocessing, the results are either saved again in the FASTQ format or converted to the FASTA format, which is similar to FASTQ, but discards the quality information.

3.2 Aggregation

Regardless of whether the individual reads are reassembled to a larger sequence or used directly, a common next step is to cluster reads together by similarity.

For amplicon sequencing, clustering is used to find reads for the same species. This is done by specifying an lower threshold for sequence similarity[1]. Sequences with a similarity above the threshold are clustered together into so called operational taxonomic units (OTUs), which are represented by the sequence of the corresponding cluster centroid.

Clustering is a typical machine learning application so there exists a wide range of algorithms used in this area. Since the distance metric used for clustering is often quite simple there is little practical usage of more advanced machine learning models [57].

The format for clustering is often FASTA for both the input and the output. While the input file contains all sequences, the output contains only the centroids of the detected clusters. Additional files may be produced that show which sequences have been assigned to which cluster.

In shotgun sequencing clustering algorithms can be useful to try to find reads belonging to the same organism or group of related organisms. As explained previously, HTS platforms require DNA molecules to be split up into fragments

[1] Frequently the threshold is 97% [74], although there is some debate whether this number is outdated [17].

with a few hundred bases at most for technical reasons [11]. The origin and order of these fragments is lost in the process [38]. "Binning" uses clustering algorithms to sort reads with similar properties into "bins". Within these bins, other algorithms can then be used to try to find overlaps between sequences ("sequence reassembly") and merging them together where possible [41, p. 39] [6, p. 60].

There are some promising results for genome reassembly using both classical machine learning (ML) algorithms as well as deep learning techniques, but most of them are still relatively new and their performance on real world samples is yet to be determined [47, p. 2123].

It should be noted that reassembly is not required for many studies, even in shotgun sequencing. For example if only the presence and abundance of certain genes in the sample needs to be known, then it can be sufficient to compare the fragments directly to adequate databases for the research topic [6, pp. 59–61].

The output of an assembler is often a FASTA file that contains all sequences that have been reassembled from the input reads. There are however alternative file formats that preserve the information how individual sequences have been constructed from the reads which are supported by a number of assemblers [27, 35].

3.3 Annotation

Annotation in metagenomics is the task of assigning one or more labels to the sequences or clusters previously identified. These labels can be of taxonomic nature (i.e. identifying the branch in a phylogenetic tree) or of functional nature (i.e. identifying genes in a sample). While taxonomic annotation tries to answer the question of "what is a sample composed of?", functional annotation tries to answer the question of "what do the components do?". In any case reference databases with sample sequences for the various labels are used.

For amplicon sequencing, taxonomic annotation is usually the only possibility, as the sequencing only contains the code for the amplicon itself and not for the whole genome as would be required to identify and label genes. One of the more popular tools for taxonomic annotation in amplicon sequencing is RDP classifier [66], a machine learning based approach using a Naïve Bayes classifier.

Although shotgun sequencing is often done for functional annotation, it is possible to do taxonomic annotation as well by matching the reads to suitable reference databases. In this group non machine learning based approaches like Kraken [15] which rely on exact substring matches are more popular. More generally, this also applies to functional annotation [57, p. 16]. One possible explanation is the large number of possible species and similarities between substrings in even distant species which will be further looked at as a challenge in Sect. 6.5.

Machine learning is also used in "gene prediction". Gene prediction tries to find genes within samples before matching them to existing databases or even to detect previously unknown genes. This can be a first step when exploring a new genome. In metagenomics the task is more difficult as complete genomes can usually not be assembled and the analysis has to be based on partial assemblies or individual reads alone. Most of these algorithms are based on Hidden Markov Models [57, p. 16]. Other popular tools for metagenomic gene prediction use neural networks [29] and there have also been successful attempts to apply deep learning to the task [73].

The output format for annotation tools are often text files containing a table of sequences and the assigned label. Additional columns are sometimes added for additional information like confidence. Many tools also support modern formats such as the JSON based BIOM format [40].

The result data for gene prediction depends on the specific needs of the study. It could be a text file containing the coordinates of genes within the input sequences or a protein translation of the predicted genes to do further functional annotation using protein databases [41, p. 47].

3.4 Analysis

As the analysis of samples is usually the main goal of a study with the other phases supporting this goal, it is also the most diverse one. Describing these tasks and the role of machine learning can therefore only be a sample of the whole range of possible methods.

A common theme across different studies and methods is the comparison of various samples with each other, which is sometimes summarized under the term "Comparative Metagenomics" [57, p. 14].

Comparative metagenomics tries to compare various metagenomic samples, often with the help of visualizations (see next section). This helps us to answer questions like "Is there a fundamental difference in the rumen microbiome between cattle with high methane emissions and cattle with low emissions?" [54], "Can fecal microbiomes be used as a proxy for rumen microbiomes?" [3] or "How can sick and healthy individuals be distinguished by their blood microbiome" [64] to name just a few.

There is a broad spectrum of possible methods to do these comparisons and to gain more insight into the composition of a sample. Many of them involve distance measures and statistics to express differences in quantitative form, other methods enable better visualization and exploration of the data to aid human interpretation [6, p. 66].

One of the common tasks for machine learning algorithms in this category is to directly classify samples in several categories based on their metagenomic profile (e.g. relative abundances of species or genes) [26,57, p. 14].

3.5 Visualization

Visualizations are an important tool to understand the data generated at the various steps. One example is the visualization of sample composition using taxonomic or functional annotation data. Figure 3a and 3b both show the taxonomic composition of a sample at various levels of the phylogenetic tree using two very distinct styles of visualization. Figure 5 demonstrates another example using a stacked bar chart to compare the composition of two distinct samples, which will be explained in detail in Sect. 5.2.

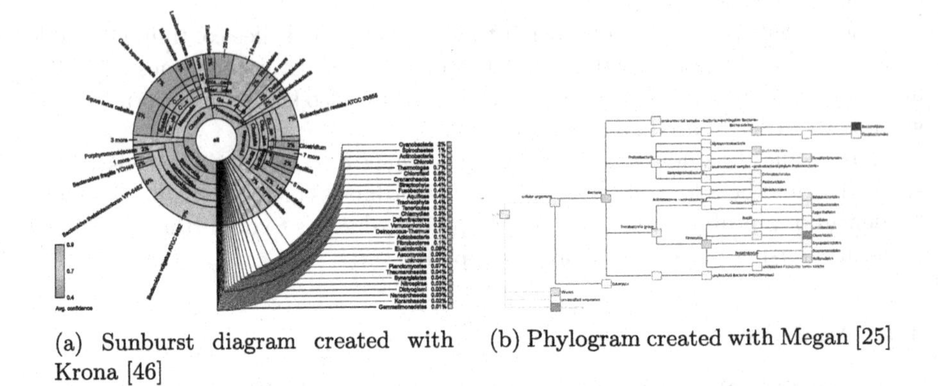

(a) Sunburst diagram created with Krona [46]

(b) Phylogram created with Megan [25]

Fig. 3. Taxonomic visualizations for microbiomes (using datasets from [37] and [49])

Another use case for visualizations is showing correlations between genes or organisms using networks. An example of this (see Fig. 4) will be further discussed in Sect. 5.1.

Machine learning often supports the creation of visualizations, especially if complex networks or graphs are used. An example is the visualization of clustering or binning (see Sect. 3.2).

The data to be clustered, in this case sequences, is highly dimensional, since we are comparing many features to determine the similarity between them (e.g. the individual characters or certain substrings, see also Sect. 6.7).

In order to display the results of clustering in a two dimensional graph that puts similar sequences close together and dissimilar sequences far from each other the number of dimensions of the input data has to be reduced to only two while still maintaining as much information about the distances between sequences as possible.

There are various machine learning algorithms that can perform this task of dimensionality reduction. A practical application for metagenomic binning is used in [13].

4 Metagenomic Processing Pipelines

There are numerous projects aiming to facilitate metagenomic analysis or biomedical analyses in general by providing step-by-step processing pipelines. The idea is to have individual components for each step in an analysis where the output of one step is the input of the next step. This provides great flexibility as the required steps can be configured individually depending on the requirements of the study while at the same time reuse is promoted by the possibility of reusing the same pipeline for several studies. It also allows easy evaluation of the underlying tools and algorithms as each step can easily be replaced with another approach as long as the input and output formats stay the same.

This section will provide some examples of these projects.

4.1 Galaxy

The Galaxy project [2] is a web based analysis platform for biomedical analyses including tools for metagenomic research [7,32]. It integrates several thousand tools in its "ToolShed" ready to be integrated into custom workflows that can be defined in a visual interface.

The tools cover all phases described—from the processing of raw sequence data down to the visualizations.

The project is enabled to support many concurrent users using an infrastructure scalable across multiple computing nodes. It can be used on free public servers, pay-as-you-go cloud services or installed locally.

4.2 MG-RAST

MG-RAST [18] is an analysis tool specifically tailored for metagenomics. It has a web based interface and provides automatic phylogenetic and functional annotation of sequence data which is uploaded in the portal. Since the focus is on ease of use and the analysis is limited to metagenomic data, the pipeline is fixed and customization is limited to setting several parameters before starting an analysis.

Besides offering analytics, MG-RAST also strives to be an extensive repository for metagenomic data with over 400 000 metagenomes containing more than 1 600 billion sequences (as of April 2020[2]).

4.3 MGnify (EBI Metagenomics)

The European Bioinformatics Institute (EBI) offers storage and analysis of metagenomic data under the name "MGnify'. The product was formerly called "EBI metagenomics" [42].

It uses a limited number of fixed pipelines depending on the type of study performed (e.g. shotgun or amplicon based analysis). The pipeline provides all usual processing steps including functional and taxonomic annotation and a range of visualization and comparison options.

4.4 Qiime

In contrast to the other tools in this section, Qiime [9] does not aim to be a fully fledged platform with ready-made workflows accessible through an easy to use interface. Rather than that it's a collection of python scripts that can be

[2] www.mg-rast.org.

used together to do metagenomic analyses locally. Using the command line as the primary interface provides a lot of possibility for customization and makes it easy to integrate other command line based tools into the workflow. Documentation of the steps in a metagenomic study is also easy by providing the executed command lines within the paper or in a shell script in a accompanying source repository.

Qiime provides a GUI as well as an API as alternatives mean to access its functionality.

The commands are designed to be run locally by default, although it is possible to run some of the jobs in parallel or on a cluster.

4.5 MetaPlat

The idea of MetaPlat is not only to provide comprehensive analysis tools for metagenomic data, but to support the complete life cycle of metagenomic studies, including archiving, taxonomy management and visualization of results. To achieve this it is integrated with the Knowledge Management Ecosystem Portal (KM-EP).

All components of MetaPlat are designed to be interchangeable to allow faster evolution of individual components and to help with academic research in individual areas. The architecture was designed based on best practices of Big Data systems, to ensure scalability from the beginning. Another goal is to use new and innovative machine learning models and visualizations to help researchers in understanding the collected data [31].

The bioinformatic workflow engine used by default in MetaPlat is called Simplicity [65], developed by the company NSilico.

MetaPlat is a EU funded Horizon 2020 project developed by several universities and other organizations, including some of the organizations represented by the authors of this paper.

5 Example: Rumen Microbiome Analysis with MetaPlat

In this section we will try to outline the process described previously on the specific example of rumen microbiome. This will be based on previous studies done on this subject [3,22,54]. We will assume the use of MetaPlat to implement the tasks described in the various phases although most principles apply to other bioinformatic pipelines as well.

5.1 Visualization of Gene Dependencies Using Shotgun Sequencing

In this example a study is performed to visualize gene dependencies and to understand their effect on methane production. The example is adapted from a study done by Zheng et al. [22] and prior work from Roehe et al. [54].

After sample preparation and shotgun sequencing on a HTS platform, the resulting FASTQ files are imported into MetaPlat along with relevant metadata for the study. A preconfigured metagenomic pipeline within MetaPlat will execute the steps described in these phases:

1. **Preparation**: Within this phase, duplicates, low quality reads and artifacts from the sequencing process itself are removed.
2. **Aggregation**: Overlapping reads are assembled where possible to obtain longer sequences (Read Assembly).
3. **Annotation**: The assembled sequences are mapped to the KEGG database [28] to check for known genes and their association with methane production (Functional Annotation).
4. **Summarization**: In this phase the relative abundances are computed for each recognized gene and saved alongside the information about methane production.
5. **Analysis**: The analysis consists of statistical computation of correlations between pairs of genes found in the samples based on the relative abundances. This allows determination on whether high occurrence of one gene leads to a decrease or increase in abundance of another gene. Mathematically, the degree of correlation or independence can be calculated using correlation measures. Applying correct correlation measures in the context of relative abundances in metagenomic studies is a complex task. This is because the relative abundance numbers are not independent of each other, even if the underlying absolute counts are.
   As an example, if the absolute count of gene A in a sample is increased without affecting the count of gene B, then there is no correlation between the count of the two genes. Looking at the relative abundances in the sample however, the increase of gene A, will decrease the percentage of gene B. Classical statistical measures of correlation would determine a (negative) correlation between these two genes, even if that does not reflect the true biological situation.
   In [22] this problem is solved by using an ensemble of various metrics, some of which are intrinsically robust against this compositional effects.
6. **Visualizations** are generated to make the results more easily understandable. In this case, a network-based approach was utilized to visualize the association between microbial genes as illustrated in Fig. 4, in which genes (identified from the KEGG database) are represented as nodes and links represent the co-presence association between genes. In addition the nodes have been colored to indicate genes associated with methane emissions (red) and genes associated with feed conversion efficiency (blue). The size of the nodes is proportional to the number of edges it has.

All intermediate and final results are saved within MetaPlat to allow easy access to the data and visualizations produced.

Interpretation. In the referenced study, modular structures were identified (as highlighted in Fig. 4). Module A contains many genes related to methane production. Further analysis showed that nineteen out of 20 methane emission specific genes identified by Roehe et al. [54] are contained in this module.

To confirm the biological relevance of this finding, the hypergeometric distribution probability (p value) was used to quantify the level of the enrichment of trait-specific genes contained in modules. For example, it has been found

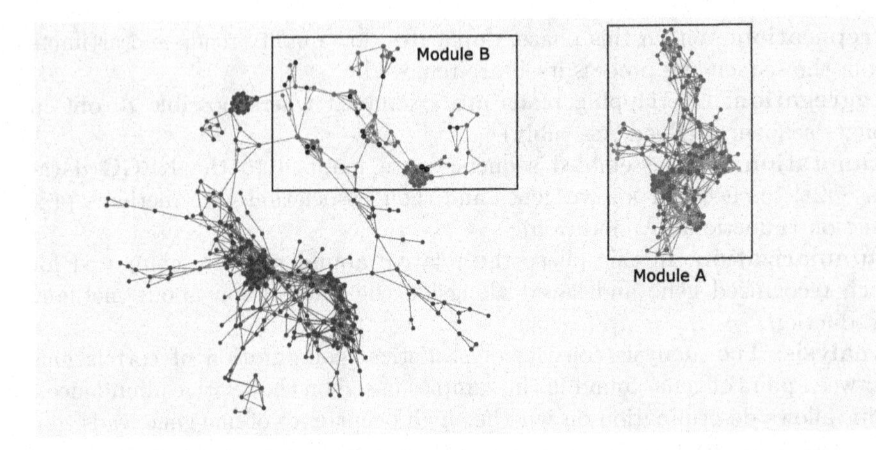

Fig. 4. Significant co-presence relationships among KEGG microbial genes in the rumen microbiome derived using a compendium of five similarity/dissimilarity metrics. Red nodes represent methane emission specific genes. Blue nodes are microbial genes associated with feed conversion efficiency. The size of nodes is proportional to node degree. (Color figure online)

that Module A is significantly enriched with methane emission specific genes ($p < 0.0001$), suggesting the co-presence network observed within this module is likely linked to methane production.

Understanding these dependencies is the first step in developing effective measures to reduce methane emissions and to increase feed conversion efficiency in rumen livestock.

5.2 Comparison of Rumen and Feces Microbiomes Using Amplicon Sequencing

In this example the focus is on comparing the composition of distinct metagenomic samples. Some of them collected from cattle rumen and some collected from feces. Since collecting fecal samples is a lot easier and less stressful to animals, the goal is to determine if the microbiome in feces can be used to infer information about the rumen microbiome. This example is adapted from the study done by Andrade et al. [3].

Like in the shotgun sequencing example, the samples are prepared and sequenced using a HTS platform. The sample preparation includes a step though that only selects and amplifies sequences from 16S 18S rRNA (amplicons). The sequences are imported and processed as following:

1. **Preparation**: As with the shotgun sequencing example, low quality reads from the input are removed.
2. **Aggregation**: In this phase clustering is used to group similar sequences together to create OTUs, which represent groups of similar organisms in the sample.

3. **Annotation**: The OTUs are mapped to a database of known microorganisms (Taxonomic Annotation). In this case the SILVA database [50] is used.
4. **Summarization**: Relative abundances are calculated for the encountered OTUs. Depending on the amount of data available and the possible resolution achieved in the taxonomic annotation this is done on different levels of the phylogenetic tree, such as order, family, genus or species.
5. **Analysis** is performed to determine metrics like the diversity of species found in the samples and the relationships between them such as co-presence or mutual exclusion similar to the analysis of gene dependencies in the shotgun example.
   As in the shotgun sequencing example care must be taken in determining the correlation between relative abundances. For taxonomic abundance counts the SparCC algorithm [19] can be used to try to determine the true correlations. Comparative metagenomics is used to interpret the calculated metrics and to compare the abundances obtained from the feces samples with those of the rumen samples to determine key differences.
6. **Visualizations** are generated to show the differences in the compared samples. A stacked bar graph is used to visualize the different abundances (Fig. 5). In addition a co-presence network is constructed to reveal relationships between microbiota in the rumen and feces.

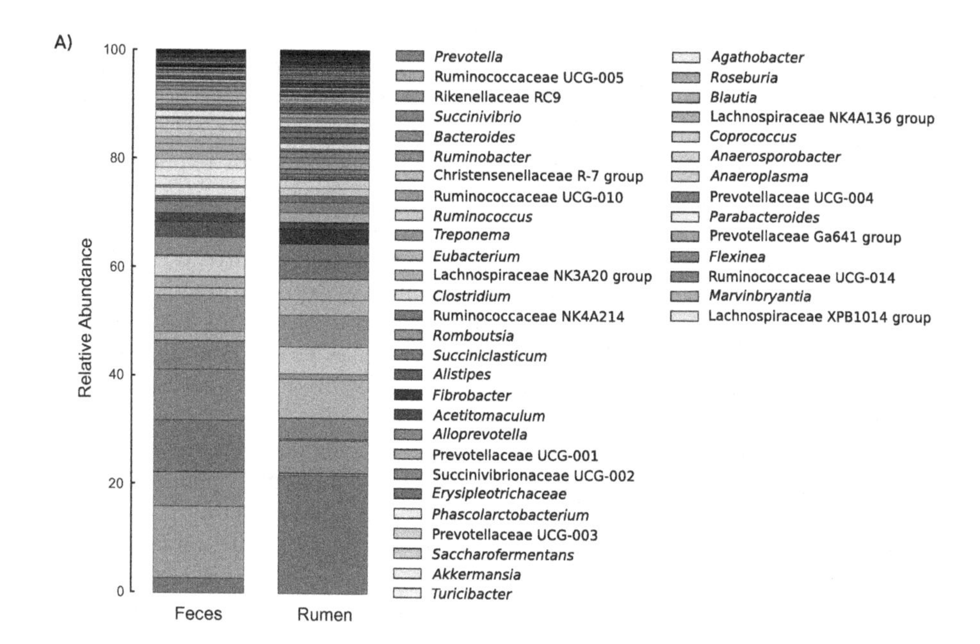

Fig. 5. Difference in microbial composition between feces and rumen. Taken from [3].

Interpretation. In the referenced study, it was found that the communities between the feces and rumen samples are quite distinct. This can also be seen in the stacked bar graph produced in the visualization step (Fig. 5).

The co-presence networks however revealed a significant and close abundance pattern between methane-producing kinds of archaea and other bacteria and eukaryotes that may reflect their relationship in these environments. Moreover, the networks also revealed that the archaea population from feces are highly dependent on the rumen population, indicating that fecal archaea could be used as markers for methane emission. This could allow future studies about methane emissions in cattle to use fecal samples as a proxy for rumen samples in some cases.

6 Challenges for Machine Learning in Metagenomics

As described earlier, machine learning can be used successfully in many key areas of metagenomics. There are however several challenges when applying machine learning to metagenomics, some of which might also impede broader usage of more advanced techniques like deep learning. The following list is a subset of commonly encountered challenges and was derived from relevant literature on metagenomics and machine learning.

6.1 Choosing the Right Model

Machine Learning provides a huge variety of possible algorithms. Looking at deep learning neural networks alone, there are many different network types as well as possible configurations (number of layers, neurons, etc.) to choose from. It is therefore a big challenge to find the right model even for experts in the field. This process can also involve a lot of trial and error where it is unclear if the final model will perform better than simpler models [71].

In order to really gain an advantage with deep learning we often try to "feed" more data into these networks. One of the promises of deep learning is that it is capable of finding new representations and deep connections from a large amount of features in the input data without requiring the same level of domain expertise and careful engineering of feature vectors as was required by classical machine learning techniques [20,70].

For example after identifying genes in the sequencing data, they can be combined with protein databases that categorizes their function. Depending on the goal of the analysis, combination of many databases can be useful.

Including additional data sources or analysis phases in the same network increases its complexity even further though.

6.2 Accessibility

Directly related to the problem of choosing the right model is a general lack of accessibility in machine learning. It can be assumed that experts in Metagenomics are usually not experts in machine learning and vice versa. A system that should be applicable to a wide range of metagenomic applications should therefore aim to be usable even for non data scientists. This is even more important when considering that data scientists are in high demand and not always available [39].

Having good user interfaces both for configuration of the models as well as the interpretation of the results could help to reduce this problem.

6.3 Explainability

Recently there is a push for more explainability in machine learning algorithms. For example the European Commission has committed itself to more trustworthy and secure use of artificial intelligence which includes explainable AI [23].

Although these policies are largely meant to protect citizens and may not apply to many metagenomic applications like the analysis of cattle rumen, they could affect applications where human microbiome analysis is done to support medical decision making.

Explainability is not easy to achieve in most machine learning models due to the complexity of their decision processes. This is especially true for deep learning where decisions are often based on thousands of neurons connected by million of edges computing billions of mathematical operations for a single classification decision.

For a model to provide real explainability it would need a concept of causality [36], but the training process is based on finding probabilistic patterns in the data. This leads to a black box model which might have exceptional performance but is unable to "explain" how it takes its decision.

It is an interesting debate whether explainability should come at the expense of accuracy [36]. Is it preferable to have a black box model that is 99% correct in predicting certain diseases or to have an explainable AI that is only correct 90% of time?

6.4 Reproducibility

Closely related to explainability is the concept of reproducibility. In an metagenomic analysis where many steps are needed from the initial raw data to the final visualization or result data it is crucial to be able to reproduce these steps whenever necessary. While this can be done by vigorously documenting each processing step, it is not an easy task as results can depend on the exact parameters of the involved tooling or even a specific environment or version number [16, p. 219]. It is also easy to make mistakes if these steps have to be performed by hand. The use of machine learning and trainable classifiers such as neural networks can increase this problem as the classification results can change with every retraining of the model even if the input data remains the same.

Pipelines as described in Sect. 4 can help to achieve this if they provide mechanisms to archive and execute specific pipeline configurations repeatedly.

6.5 Biological Diversity

The rumen microbiome in cattle can contain thousand of species of microorganisms with millions of genes [59]. Other environmental samples are estimated to contain millions of species [57].

A large number of these species are often unknown, which can complicate both taxonomic and functional annotation of the data. There is also a bias in the existing computational methods and databases towards bacterial data which can make the analysis of the whole metagenome including for example archaea and fungi more difficult [57] [33, pp. 218–219].

Even distant species often share a lot of similarities, which could be a reason why simple algorithms relying on exact matches are often preferred to less strict ML algorithms in taxonomic annotation tasks based on shotgun sequencing (see Sect. 3.3) [62]. There are however some indications that less reliance on exact matches could also be a strength for ML algorithms when dealing with species not part of the training set [57,62]. This can be especially important when comprehensive reference databases for the chosen environment do not exist yet as is often the case [6, p. 56].

6.6 Big Data

The biological diversity also affects the volume of data that needs to be processed. To reach a high taxonomic resolution (being able to classify organisms down to the species level for example) a large number of reads need to be produced by the sequencing machines which can easily lead to many gigabytes or even terabytes for a study [6, p. 59] [57].

ML and especially deep learning generally require a lot more computing resources (e.g. graphics processing unit (GPU) support) than simpler methods. The combination of both big data and ML can therefore easily push the boundaries of normal desktop computers and require specialized hardware or even big computing clusters and cloud architectures [14,57]. As was demonstrated in Sect. 4 not all pipelines in this field easily support this. Free, web based pipelines might also be hesitant to offer resource intensive, deep analysis methods if the operation incurs a heavy cost.

6.7 High Dimensionality and Low Number of Samples

While having lots of data usually helps in training classifiers as discussed earlier, the nature of metagenomics often leads to relatively few samples (e.g. rumen samples from a dozen cattle) with very high dimensionality (thousand or millions of species in the sample).

Modern machine learning algorithms like deep learning neural networks often train many parameters. While deep learning can generalize surprisingly well even if the number of training samples is a lot less than the number of parameters [72], these algorithms can still perform best by increasing the number of samples [75] [20, p. 20]. Datasets with a large number of samples are however rare as they are difficult to collect. Each sample has to be collected, prepared and processed individually which is time consuming and costly at large scale. For animal hosts this collection process can also be very stressful.

High dimensionality can also be a problem when combined with generally few samples as the neural network might not be able to select the important features on its own. This can sometimes be helped by performing heavy dimensionality reduction beforehand (e.g. only looking at relative abundances of species or genes, excluding genomic data during the sequencing process already or using computational methods [57]). It should be noted however that preselecting features and reducing the dimensionality also reduces possibly the greatest strength of deep learning to be able to deduce suitable data representations on its own [20, 70].

7 Applying the AI2VIS4BigData Reference Model

The AI2VIS4BigData is a reference model for the combined use of big data, artificial intelligence and visualization [53]. It combines the AI System Lifecycle [45] described by the OECD Expert Group on AI (AIGO) with Bornschlegl's IVIS4BigData reference model for Big Data analysis and visualization. Figure 6 shows the reference model. The model encompasses various user stereotypes, phases like model development, deployment and monitoring as well as relevant data types. It addresses both machine learning and symbolic AI models and puts a special focus on the need for AI transparency and explainability.

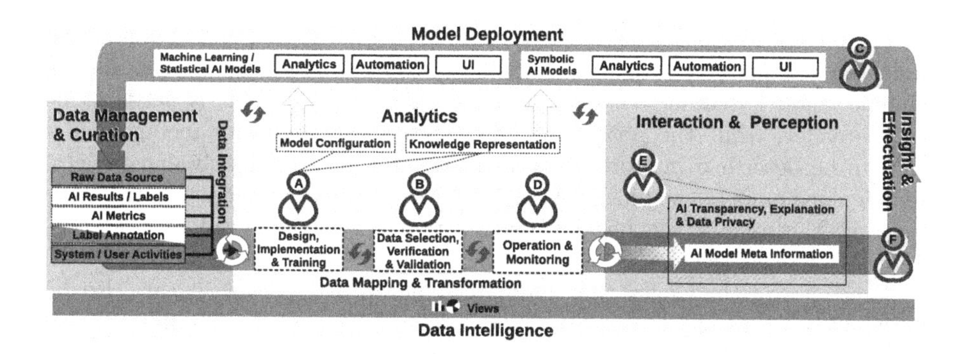

Fig. 6. The AI2VIS4BigData reference model [53]

As shown in the previous sections metagenomics is a big data application that uses machine learning and visualizations to derive new insights. A reference model combining all of these aspects has the potential to provide a common vocabulary and reference for discussion across different research teams in metagenomics and to improve collaboration and comprehension with other fields. We therefore consider the IVIS4BigData reference model highly relevant to our research.

The six phases of metagenomic studies described earlier can be mapped to the stages in the original IVIS4BigData reference model by Bornschlegl as well as the new AI2VIS4BigData reference model as shown in Fig. 7.

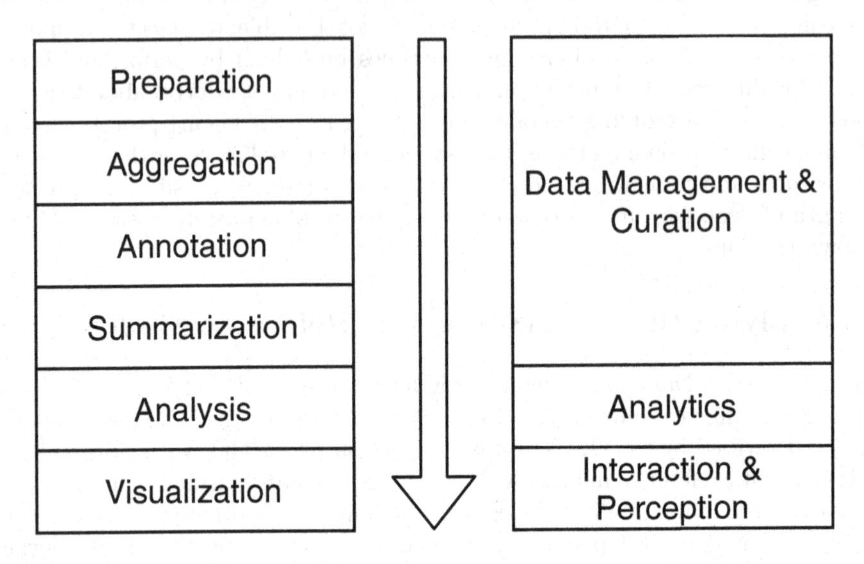

Fig. 7. The six phases of metagenomic studies and the matching stages in the reference model

The phases "Preparation", "Aggregation", "Annotation", and "Summarization" can be mapped to the "Data Management & Curation" stage. As the reference model is designed to apply to several research fields it needs to be more broader, while the phases described here are tailored for metagenomics and can be described in more detail using several phases for only one stage in the reference model. The phase "Analytics" can be directly mapped to the stage "Analysis". Similarly the phase "Visualization" is encompassed by the stage "Interaction & Perception".

Some of the challenges that have been described in Sect. 6 can also be described in terms of the reference model. The challenge of "accessibility" can be described as a lack of engineers fitting the roles of a "Model Designer". The challenge of "explainability" can be mapped to the element "AI Transparency & Explanation" in the reference model.

Lastly the reference model can also be useful to evaluate biomedical pipelines and platforms such as those described in Sect. 4. By mapping the stages of the reference model to a fixed or dynamic pipeline we can quickly identify missing elements as well as improve the comparability between systems. Using the user stereotypes we can check if they are represented in these systems appropriately.

8 Conclusion

This chapter described the role of machine learning in metagenomics. A common workflow consisting of six phases was identified and used to structure the remaining sections. Several challenges have been identified that might slow down further adaption of machine learning and specifically advanced methods like deep learning. A number of workflow systems have been analyzed to judge their suitability for combined use of machine learning and metagenomics. Lastly we took a look at the AI2VIS4BigData reference model and validated that it is highly relevant to the field. The reference model was checked both in general as well as in regards to the metagenomic workflow, the identified challenges and biomedical pipelines specifically.

References

1. Understanding genetics: A New York, Mid-Atlantic guide for patients and health professionals. Washington, DC (2009). ISBN 9780982162217
2. Afgan, E., et al.: The galaxy platform for accessible, reproducible and collaborative biomedical analyses: 2018 update. Nucleic Acids Res. **46**(W1), W537–W544 (2018). ISSN 0305-1048. https://doi.org/10.1093/nar/gky379. https://academic.oup.com/nar/article/46/W1/W537/5001157
3. Andrade, B.G.N., et al.: The structure of microbial populations in nelore git reveals inter-dependency of methanogens in feces and rumen. J. Anim. Sci. Biotechnol. **11**, 6 (2020). https://doi.org/10.1186/s40104-019-0422-x. ISSN 1674-9782
4. Nazir, A.: Review on metagenomics and its applications. Imperial J. Interdisc. Res. **2**(3), 277–286 (2016)
5. Belkaid, Y., Hand, T.W.: Role of the microbiota in immunity and inflammation. Cell **157**(1), 121–141 (2014). https://doi.org/10.1016/j.cell.2014.03.011. http://www.sciencedirect.com/science/article/pii/S0092867414003456
6. Bengtsson-Palme, J.: Strategies for taxonomic and functional annotation of metagenomes. In: Nagarajan, M. (ed.) Metagenomics, pp. 55–79, Academic Press, London (2018). https://doi.org/10.1016/B978-0-08-102268-9.00003-3. ISBN 9780081022689
7. Batut, B., et al.: ASaiM: a galaxy-based framework to analyze raw shotgun data from microbiota. bioRxiv, p. 183970 (2017). https://doi.org/10.1101/183970. https://www.biorxiv.org/content/10.1101/183970v1
8. Yang, B., Wang, Y., Qian, P.-Y.: Sensitivity and correlation of hypervariable regions in 16S rRNA genes in phylogenetic analysis. BMC Bioinform. **17**(1), 1–8 (2016). https://doi.org/10.1186/s12859-016-0992-y. https://bmcbioinformatics.biomedcentral.com/track/pdf/10.1186/s12859-016-0992-y. ISSN 1471-2105
9. Bolyen, E., et al.: Reproducible, interactive, scalable and extensible microbiome data science using QIIME 2. Nat. Biotechnol. **37**(8), 852–857 (2019). https://doi.org/10.1038/s41587-019-0209-9
10. Boža, V., Brejová, B., Vinař, T.: Deepnano: deep recurrent neural networks for base calling in minion nanopore reads. PLoS ONE **12**(6), e0178751 (2017). https://doi.org/10.1371/journal.pone.0178751

11. Buermans, H., den Dunnen, J.T.: Next generation sequencing technology: advances and applications. Biochimica et Biophysica Acta (BBA) Mol. Basis Dis. **1842**(10), 1932–1941 (2014). https://doi.org/10.1016/j.bbadis.2014.06.015. http://www.sciencedirect.com/science/article/pii/S092544391400180X. ISSN 0925-4439
12. Cacho, A., Smirnova, E., Huzurbazar, S., Cui, X.: A comparison of base-calling algorithms for illumina sequencing technology. Briefings Bioinform. **17**(5), 786–795 (2016). https://doi.org/10.1093/bib/bbv088. https://academic.oup.com/bib/article/17/5/786/2262186. ISSN 1467-5463
13. Laczny, C.C., et al.: Vizbin - an application for reference-independent visualization and human-augmented binning of metagenomic data. Microbiome **3**(1), 1–7 (2015). https://doi.org/10.1186/s40168-014-0066-1. ISSN 2049-2618
14. Chen, X.W., Lin, X.: Big data deep learning: challenges and perspectives. IEEE Access **2**, 514–525 (2014). https://doi.org/10.1109/ACCESS.2014.2325029
15. Wood, D.E., Salzberg, S.L.: Kraken: ultrafast metagenomic sequence classification using exact alignments. Genome Biol. **15**(3), 1–12 (2014). https://doi.org/10.1186/gb-2014-15-3-r46. https://genomebiology.biomedcentral.com/track/pdf/10.1186/gb-2014-15-3-r46. ISSN 1474-760X
16. Eck, S.H.: Challenges in data storage and data management in a clinical diagnostic setting. LaboratoriumsMedizin **42**(6), 219–224 (2018). https://doi.org/10.1515/labmed-2018-0054. ISSN 0342-3026
17. Edgar, R.C.: Updating the 97% identity threshold for 16S ribosomal RNA OTUs. Bioinformatics **34**(14), 2371–2375 (2018). https://doi.org/10.1093/bioinformatics/bty113
18. Meyer, F., et al.: The metagenomics RAST server - a public resource for the automatic phylogenetic and functional analysis of metagenomes. BMC Bioinform. **9**(1), 1–8 (2008). https://doi.org/10.1186/1471-2105-9-386. ISSN 1471-2105
19. Friedman, J., Alm, E.J.: Inferring correlation networks from genomic survey data. PLoS Comput. Biol. **8**(9), e1002687 (2012). https://doi.org/10.1371/journal.pcbi.1002687
20. Goodfellow, I., Bengio, Y., Courville, A.: Deep learning. MIT Press, Cambridge; London (2016). http://www.deeplearningbook.org/. ISBN 9780262035613
21. Arango-Argoty, G., Garner, E., Pruden, A., Heath, L.S., Vikesland, P., Zhang, L.: Deeparg: a deep learning approach for predicting antibiotic resistance genes from metagenomic data. Microbiome **6**(1), 1–15 (2018). https://doi.org/10.1186/s40168-018-0401-z. https://microbiomejournal.biomedcentral.com/track/pdf/10.1186/s40168-018-0401-z. ISSN 2049-2618
22. H. Zheng, H. Wang, R. Dewhurst, R. Roehe: Improving the inference of co-occurrence networks in the bovine rumen microbiome. IEEE/ACM Trans. Comput. Biol. Bioinform. 1 (2018). https://doi.org/10.1109/TCBB.2018.2879342. ISSN 1557-9964
23. Hamon, R., Junklewitz, H., Sanchez, I.: Robustness and explainability of Artificial Intelligence: From technical to policy solutions, EUR, vol. 30040. Publications Office of the European Union, Luxembourg (2020). ISBN 9276146601
24. Flint, H.J., Duncan, S.H., Scott, K.P., Louis, P.: Interactions and competition within the microbial community of the human colon: links between diet and health. Environ. Microbiol. **9**(5), 1101–1111 (2007). https://doi.org/10.1111/j.1462-2920.2007.01281.x. https://sfamjournals.onlinelibrary.wiley.com/doi/full/10.1111/j.1462-2920.2007.01281.x ISSN 1462-2920
25. Huson, D.H., Auch, A.F., Qi, J., Schuster, S.C.: Megan analysis of metagenomic data. Genome Res. **17**(3), 377–386 (2007). https://doi.org/10.1101/gr.5969107. ISSN 1088-9051

26. Wassan, J.T., Wang, H., Browne, F., Zheng, H.: A comprehensive study on predicting functional role of metagenomes using machine learning methods. IEEE/ACM Trans. Comput. Biol. Bioinform. **16**(3), 751–763 (2019). https://doi.org/10.1109/TCBB.2018.2858808. ISSN 1557-9964
27. Jaffe, D.B., MacCallum, I., Rokhsar, D.S., Schatz, M.C.: The FASTG format specification (v1. 00) (2012). http://fastg.sourceforge.net/FASTG_Spec_v1.00.pdf
28. Kanehisa, M., Goto, S.: KEGG: Kyoto encyclopedia of genes and genomes. Nucleic Acids Res. **28**(1), 27–30 (2000). https://doi.org/10.1093/nar/28.1.27. https://academic.oup.com/nar/article/28/1/27/2384332 ISSN 0305-1048
29. Hoff, K.J., Tech, M., Lingner, T., Daniel, R., Morgenstern, B., Meinicke, P.: Gene prediction in metagenomic fragments: a large scale machine learning approach. BMC Bioinform. **9**(1), 1–14 (2008). https://doi.org/10.1186/1471-2105-9-217. https://bmcbioinformatics.biomedcentral.com/track/pdf/10.1186/1471-2105-9-217 ISSN 1471-2105
30. Field, K.G., et al.: Molecular phylogeny of the animal kingdom. Science **239**(4841), 748–753 (1988). https://doi.org/10.1126/science.3277277. https://science.sciencemag.org/content/239/4841/748/tab-pdf. ISSN 1095-9203
31. Konstantinidou, N., et al.: Metaplat: a cloud based platform for analysis and visualisation of metagenomics data. In: Bleimann, U., Humm, B., Loew, R., Stengel, I., Walsh, P. (eds.) Proceedings of the Collaborative European Research Conference (CERC 2016) Cork (2016)
32. Pond, S.K., et al.: Windshield splatter analysis with the galaxy metagenomic pipeline. Genome Res. **19**(11), 2144–2153 (2009). https://doi.org/10.1101/gr.094508.109. ISSN 1088-9051
33. Kothari, R.K., et al.: Comprehensive exploration of the rumen microbial ecosystem with advancements in metagenomics. In: Nagarajan, M. (ed.) Metagenomics, pp. 215–229, Academic Press, London (2018). https://doi.org/10.1016/B978-0-08-102268-9.00011-2. ISBN 9780081022689
34. Kwiatkowski, D.P.: How malaria has affected the human genome and what human genetics can teach us about malaria. Am. J. Hum. Genet. **77**(2), 171–192 (2005)
35. Li, H.: GFA: graphical fragment assembly (GFA) format specification (2020). http://gfa-spec.github.io/GFA-spec/
36. London, A.J.: Artificial intelligence and black-box medical decisions: accuracy versus explainability. Hastings Cent. Rep. **49**(1), 15–21 (2019). https://doi.org/10.1002/hast.973
37. Louis, S., Tappu, R.M., Damms-Machado, A., Huson, D.H., Bischoff, S.C.: Characterization of the gut microbial community of obese patients following a weight-loss intervention using whole metagenome shotgun sequencing. PLoS ONE **11**(2), e0149564 (2016). https://doi.org/10.1371/journal.pone.0149564
38. Mardanov, A.V., Kadnikov, V.V., Ravin, N.V.: Metagenomics: a paradigm shift in microbiology. In: Nagarajan, M. (ed.) Metagenomics, pp. 1–13, Academic Press, London (2018). https://doi.org/10.1016/B978-0-08-102268-9.00001-X. ISBN 9780081022689
39. Markow, W., Braganza, S., Task, B.: The quant crunch: how the demand for data science skills is disrupting the job market (2017). https://www.ibm.com/downloads/cas/3RL3VXGA
40. McDonald, D., et al.: The biological observation matrix (BIOM) format or: how i learned to stop worrying and love the ome-ome. GigaScience **1**(1), 7 (2012). https://doi.org/10.1186/2047-217X-1-7

41. Méndez-García, C., Bargiela, R., Martínez-Martínez, M., Ferrer, M.: Metagenomic protocols and strategies. In: Nagarajan, M. (ed.) Metagenomics, pp. 15–54, Academic Press, London (2018). https://doi.org/10.1016/B978-0-08-102268-9.00002-1. ISBN 9780081022689
42. Mitchell, A.L., et al.: MGnify: the microbiome analysis resource in 2020. Nucleic Acids Res. **48**(D1), D570–D578 (2020). https://doi.org/10.1093/nar/gkz1035. https://academic.oup.com/nar/article/48/D1/D570/5614179. ISSN 0305-1048
43. Jain, M., Olsen, H.E., Paten, B., Akeson, M.: The oxford nanopore minion: delivery of nanopore sequencing to the genomics community. Genome Biol. **17**(1), 1–11 (2016). https://doi.org/10.1186/s13059-016-1103-0. https://genomebiology.biomedcentral.com/track/pdf/10.1186/s13059-016-1103-0. ISSN 1474-760X
44. Nagarajan, M. (ed.): Metagenomics: Perspectives, Methods, and Applications. Academic Press, London (2018). http://www.sciencedirect.com/science/book/9780081022689. ISBN 9780081022689
45. OECD: Artificial Intelligence in Society. OECD Publishing, Paris (2019). https://doi.org/10.1787/eedfee77-en. ISBN 9789264582545
46. Ondov, B.D., Bergman, N.H., Phillippy, A.M.: Interactive metagenomic visualization in a web browser. BMC Bioinform. **12**, 385 (2011). https://doi.org/10.1186/1471-2105-12-385. ISSN 1471-2105
47. Padovani de Souza, K., Setubal, J.C., Ponce de Leon F de Carvalho, A.C., Oliveira, G., Chateau, A., Alves, R.: Machine learning meets genome assembly. Briefings Bioinform. **20**(6), 2116–2129 (2019). https://doi.org/10.1093/bib/bby072
48. Penny, D., Hendy, M.D., Steel, M.A.: Progress with methods for constructing evolutionary trees. Trends Ecol. Evol. **7**(3), 73–79 (1992). https://doi.org/10.1016/0169-5347(92)90244-6. ISSN 01695347
49. Qin, J., et al.: A human gut microbial gene catalogue established by metagenomic sequencing. Nature **464**(7285), 59–65 (2010). https://doi.org/10.1038/nature08821. ISSN 0028-0836
50. Quast, C., et al.: The SILVA ribosomal RNA gene database project: improved data processing and web-based tools. Nucleic Acids Res. **41**(Database issue), D590–D596 (2013). https://doi.org/10.1093/nar/gks1219
51. Wallace, R.J., et al.: The rumen microbial metagenome associated with high methane production in cattle. BMC Genom. **16**(1), 1–14 (2015). https://doi.org/10.1186/s12864-015-2032-0. https://bmcgenomics.biomedcentral.com/track/pdf/10.1186/s12864-015-2032-0. ISSN 1471-2164
52. Ramazzotti, M., Bacci, G.: 16S rRNA-based taxonomy profiling in the metagenomics era. In: Nagarajan, M. (ed.) Metagenomics, chap. 5, pp. 103–119, Academic Press, London (2018). https://doi.org/10.1016/B978-0-08-102268-9.00005-7. http://www.sciencedirect.com/science/article/pii/B9780081022689000057. ISBN 9780081022689
53. Reis, T., Bornschlegl, M.X., Hemmje, M.L.: Towards a reference model for artificial intelligence supporting big data analysis. In: Proceedings of the 2020 International Conference on Data Science (ICDATA 2020) (2020)
54. Roehe, R., et al.: Bovine host genetic variation influences rumen microbial methane production with best selection criterion for low methane emitting and efficiently feed converting hosts based on metagenomic gene abundance. PLoS Genet. **12**(2), e1005846 (2016). https://doi.org/10.1371/journal.pgen.1005846
55. Eddy, S.R.: Non-coding RNA genes and the modern RNA world. Nat. Rev. Genet. **2**(12), 919–929 (2001). https://doi.org/10.1038/35103511. https://www-nature-com.ub-proxy.fernuni-hagen.de/articles/35103511. ISSN 1471-0064

56. Sherry, S.T., Ward, M., Sirotkin, K.: dbSNP-database for single nucleotide polymorphisms and other classes of minor genetic variation. Genome Res. **9**(8), 677–679 (1999). ISSN 1088-9051
57. Soueidan, H., Nikolski, M.: Machine learning for metagenomics: methods and tools (2015). https://arxiv.org/pdf/1510.06621
58. Stephens, Z.D., et al.: Big data: astronomical or genomical? PLoS Biol. **13**(7), e1002195 (2015). https://doi.org/10.1371/journal.pbio.1002195
59. Stewart, R.D., Auffret, M.D., Warr, A., Walker, A.W., Roehe, R., Watson, M.: Compendium of 4,941 rumen metagenome-assembled genomes for rumen microbiome biology and enzyme discovery. Nat. Biotechnol. **37**(8), 953–961 (2019). https://doi.org/10.1038/s41587-019-0202-3
60. Teng, H., Cao, M.D., Hall, M.B., Duarte, T., Wang, S., Coin, L.J.M.: Chiron: translating nanopore raw signal directly into nucleotide sequence using deep learning. GigaScience **7**(5) (2018). https://doi.org/10.1093/gigascience/giy037. https://academic.oup.com/gigascience/article/7/5/giy037/4966989
61. Vallianou, N.G., Stratigou, T., Tsagarakis, S.: Microbiome and diabetes: where are we now? Diabetes Res. Clin. Pract. **146**, 111–118 (2018). https://doi.org/10.1016/j.diabres.2018.10.008
62. Vervier, K., Mahé, P., Tournoud, M., Veyrieras, J.B., Vert, J.P.: Large-scale machine learning for metagenomics sequence classification. Bioinformatics **32**(7), 1023–1032 (2016). https://doi.org/10.1093/bioinformatics/btv683
63. Vu, B., et al.: A metagenomic content and knowledge management ecosystem platform. In: Yoo, I., Bi, J., Hu, X. (eds.) 2019 IEEE International Conference on Bioinformatics and Biomedicine, BIBM 2019, San Diego, CA, USA, 18–21 November 2019. IEEE (2019). ISBN 978-1-7281-1867-3
64. Walsh, P., et al.: Immunoadept - bringing blood microbiome profiling to the clinical practice. In: Zheng, H. (ed.) Proceedings, 2018 IEEE International Conference on Bioinformatics and Biomedicine, Piscataway, New Jersey, pp. 1577–1581. IEEE (2018). https://doi.org/10.1109/BIBM.2018.8621354. ISBN 978-1-5386-5488-0
65. Walsh, P., Carroll, J., Sleator, R.D.: Accelerating in silico research with workflows: a lesson in simplicity. Comput. Biol. Med. **43**(12), 2028–2035 (2013). https://doi.org/10.1016/j.compbiomed.2013.09.011. ISSN 0010-4825
66. Wang, Q., Garrity, G.M., Tiedje, J.M., Cole, J.R.: Naïve Bayesian classifier for rapid assignment of rRNA sequences into the new bacterial taxonomy. Appl. Environ. Microbiol. **73**(16), 5261–5267 (2007). https://doi.org/10.1128/AEM.00062-07. ISSN 0099-2240
67. Wetterstrand, K.A.: DNA sequencing costs: data from the NHGRI genome sequencing program (GSP) (2020). https://www.genome.gov/about-genomics/fact-sheets/DNA-Sequencing-Costs-Data
68. Woese, C.R., Fox, G.E.: Phylogenetic structure of the prokaryotic domain: the primary kingdoms. Proc. Natl. Acad. Sci. U.S.A. **74**(11), 5088–5090 (1977). https://doi.org/10.1073/pnas.74.11.5088. ISSN 0027-8424
69. Woese, C.R., Kandler, O., Wheelis, M.L.: Towards a natural system of organisms: proposal for the domains archaea, bacteria, and eucarya. Proc. Natl. Acad. Sci. **87**(12), 4576–4579 (1990). https://doi.org/10.1073/pnas.87.12.4576. https://www.pnas.org/content/87/12/4576. ISSN 1091-6490
70. LeCun, Y., Bengio, Y., Hinton, G.: Deep learning. Nature **521**(7553), 436–444 (2015). https://doi.org/10.1038/nature14539. https://www.nature.com/articles/nature14539.pdf. ISSN 1476-4687

71. Zela, A., Klein, A., Falkner, S., Hutter, F.: Towards automated deep learning: efficient joint neural architecture and hyperparameter search (2018). http://arxiv.org/pdf/1807.06906v1
72. Zhang, C., Bengio, S., Hardt, M., Recht, B., Vinyals, O.: Understanding deep learning requires rethinking generalization (2016). http://arxiv.org/pdf/1611.03530v2
73. Zhang, S.W., Jin, X.Y., Zhang, T.: Gene prediction in metagenomic fragments with deep learning. BioMed Res. Int. **2017**, 4740354 (2017). https://doi.org/10.1155/2017/4740354
74. Zhbannikov, I.Y., Foster, J.A.: Analyzing high-throughput microbial amplicon sequence data using multiple markers. In: Nagarajan, M. (ed.) Metagenomics, chap. 6, pp. 121–138. Academic Press, London (2018). https://doi.org/10.1016/B978-0-08-102268-9.00006-9. http://www.sciencedirect.com/science/article/pii/B9780081022689000069. ISBN 9780081022689
75. Zhu, X., Vondrick, C., Fowlkes, C., Ramanan, D.: Do we need more training data? Int. J. Comput. Vis. **119**(1), 76–92 (2016). https://doi.org/10.1007/s11263-015-0812-2. http://arxiv.org/pdf/1503.01508v1. ISSN 0920-5691
76. Zou, J., Huss, M., Abid, A., Mohammadi, P., Torkamani, A., Telenti, A.: A primer on deep learning in genomics. Nat. Genet. **51**(1), 12–18 (2019). https://doi.org/10.1038/s41588-018-0295-5

Intelligent Advanced User Interfaces for Monitoring Mental Health Wellbeing

Anna Esposito[1](✉), Zoraida Callejas[2], Matthias L. Hemmje[3], Michael Fuchs[4], Mauro N. Maldonato[5], and Gennaro Cordasco[1]

[1] Department of Psychology and IIASS, Università della Campania "Luigi Vanvitelli", Caserta, Italy
iiass.annaesp@tin.it, gennaro.cordasco@unicampania.it
[2] Department Software Engineering, University of Granada, Granada, Spain
zoraida@ugr.es
[3] Research Institute for Telecommunication and Cooperation (FTK), Dortmund, Germany
mhemmje@ftk.de
[4] Wilhelm Büchner University of Applied Science Hessen, Darmstadt, Germany
m.fuchs@globit.com
[5] Dipartimento di Neuroscience, Naples University "Federico", Naples, Italy
m.maldonato@gmail.com

Abstract. It has become pressing to develop objective and automatic measurements integrated in intelligent diagnostic tools for detecting and monitoring depressive states and enabling an increased precision of diagnoses and clinical decision-makings. The challenge is to exploit behavioral and physiological biomarkers and develop Artificial Intelligent (AI) models able to extract information from a complex combination of signals considered key symptoms. The proposed AI models should be able to help clinicians to rapidly formulate accurate diagnoses and suggest personalized intervention plans ranging from coaching activities (exploiting for example serious games), support networks (via chats, or social networks), and alerts to caregivers, doctors, and care control centers, reducing the considerable burden on national health care institutions in terms of medical, and social costs associated to depression cares.

Keywords: Artificial intelligence · Customer care · Biometric data · Social signal processing · Social behavior · Intelligent human-computer interfaces

1 Introduction

Depression is the most pervasive world population mental disorder, leading to significant social, occupational, and cognitive impairments in individuals' life. Depression is a source of social disabilities, and a main risk factor for suicide in older and young people (Dehaye et al. 2018; Groholt and Ekeberg 2009). Depression rarely occurs alone and is often accompanied by anxiety and stress (Horowitz 2010), or is in comorbidity with other mental disorders such as schizophrenia and dementia (Watson et al. 2019; Grover et al. 2017). The most obvious manifestations of depressive disorders are loss

T. Reis et al. (Eds.): AVI-BDA 2020/ITAVIS 2020, LNCS 12585, pp. 83–95, 2021.
https://doi.org/10.1007/978-3-030-68007-7_5

of interest, anhedonia, feelings of shame and guilt, low self-esteem, loss of sleep, and appetite, pervasive sadness not related to specific motivations (mood disorders), feelings of tiredness, poor concentration, reduced social contacts and emotional feelings, apathy (Yates et al. 2007; Freeman et al. 2017).

According to the World Health Organization (WHO) at the least 25% of people visiting family doctors live with depression (http://www.euro.who.int/en/health-topics/noncommunicable-diseases/mental-health/news/news/2012/10/depression-in-europe), and this number, projected to increase, is placing considerable burdens on national health care institutions in terms of medical, and social costs associated to depression cares.

Prevention, accurate diagnosis, appropriate treatments and constantly monitoring are crucial to reduce and limit the negative consequences of the disorder on patients' quality of life and the encumbrance of costs for public healthcare institutions (Olesen et al. 2012).

2 Questionnaires Assessing Depressive States

Research in depression is driven by the need of identifying indicators of the disease able to accurately predict its development. However, depression is difficult to detect, difficult to measure, and it is nontrivial to quantify the effectiveness of the suggested cares during the disorder's monitoring. Routinely screenings of depression are performed by means of semi-structured interviews (SCID, Structured Clinical Interview, https://www.appi.org/products/structured-clinical-interview-for-dsm-5-scid-5) recommended by the Diagnostic and Statistical Manual of Mental Disorders (recently updated to version 5, DSM-5). These interviews are extremely time consuming, may deliver heterogeneous measures (accounting of different mental disorders that may co-exist in comorbidity with depressive disorders), do not provide a clinically cut off in the outcome rates, require training to ensure reliable and valid interpretations of the results, and can be affected by biases resulting either from clinicians' theoretical orientations and training or clinicians overestimation of patient's progresses (that may occur when treatments' success is encouraged), or both. To avoid these pitfalls in the implementation of structured interviews for depression diagnoses, clinicians and researchers increasingly use self-report screening questionnaires, which do not require cumbersome time and special training for being administered, and whose ratings are highly correlated with those offered by professionals (Zimmerman et al. 2018).

Among the many clinically endorsed self report questionnaires, it is worth to mention the Beck Depression Inventory (BDI-II) (Beck et al. 1996), the Depression, Stress, and Anxiety Scales (DASS) (Lovibond and Lovibond 1995), the Patient Health Questionnaire for depression (PHQ) (Kroenke et al. 2001), the Geriatric Depression Scale (GDS) (Yeasavage et al. 1983), the Hamilton Depression Rating Scale (HDRS) (Hamilton 1960, 1967), the Major Depression Inventory (MDI) (Bech et al. 2015), the Center for Epidemiologic Studies Depression Scale (CES-D) (Lewinsohn et al. 1997), the Zung Self-Rating Depression Scale (SDS) (Zung 1965), the Montgomery-Äsberg Depression Rating Scale (MADRS) (Montgomery and Äsberg 1979), the Quick Inventory of Depressive Symptomatology (QIDS) (Rush et al 2003; Rush et al 2006), the Wechsler Depression Rating Scale (WDRS) (Wechsler et al. 1963); the Clinically Useful Depression Outcome Scale (CUDOS) (Zimmerman et al. 2008). In addition, since depression may co-occur with other mental disorders such as schizophrenia and dementia, specific self reports have been proposed for its assessment such as the Calgary Depression Scale for Schizophrenia (CDSS) (Addington et al. 1990) and the Cornell Scale for Depression in Dementia (CSDD) (Alexopoulos et al. 1988). These questionnaires are available in long, short, and even shorter forms both as clinician-rated and self report scales.

The validity of these clinician-rated and self report scales has been assessed by several authors (Torbey et al. 2015; Rabinowitz et al. 2019; da Silva et al. 2019; Rohan et al. 2016; Cunningham et al. 2011, among others) and criticisms have emerged. Some self reports have shown poor accord with clinicians' ratings (Möller 2000). Clinicians' expertise and restrictive inclusion criterions applied to assess the efficacy of treatments may affect clinicians' ratings (Landin et al. 2000). Patients' self reports may be biased by their interpretation of symptoms and disagreements with clinicians may reflect differences caused by language interpretation, importance assigned to the different scale's items, degree of severity assigned to symptoms, illiteracy or poor reading and comprehension abilities of patients, physical debility, compromised cognitive functioning and symptoms overlapping with other mental disorders (Hershenberg et al. 2020; Tolton et al. 2019; Ahmed et al. 2018; Grover et al. 2017; Shirazian et al. 2016; Dunlop et al. 2014, among others).

To overcome these drawbacks, it has become pressing to develop objective and automatic measurements with the intention of favoring fast, non-invasive, economical, and automated on-demand assistance. These decision tools should integrate available and/or emerging diagnostic means enabling an increased precision of diagnoses and clinical decision-makings.

The automatic detection of depressive states requires the identification of behavioral and physiological biomarkers which undergo to subtle changes (e.g., retardation in speech production) because of the disease and develop Artificial Intelligent (AI) models able to extract information from a complex combination of signals considered key symptoms. This will help medical professionals to rapidly formulate accurate diagnoses. An accurate detection is also important for implementing therapeutic interventions at an early stage of the disease, i.e., when treatments may be more effective. The proposed AI models should be able to recognize the detected depressive patterns and suggest personalized pre-modelled intervention plans ranging from coaching activities (exploiting for example serious games), support networks (via chats, or social networks), and alerts to caregivers, doctors, and care control centers.

3 Behavioral and Physiological Parameters Indicating Depressive States

Research in depression is driven by the need of identifying indicators of the disease able to accurately predict its development.

Among behavioral indicators of depression are:

- Scores of depressed patients to emotional facial expressions' decoding tests (Esposito et al. 2016a; Scibelli et al. 2016; Troncone et al. 2014).

- Speech analytics: For this purpose, different characteristics of verbal (such as acoustic variation of F0) and paralinguistic information (such as empty and filled pauses) can be used (Ringeval et al. 2017; Mendiratta et al. 2017; Esposito et al. 2016b; Alghowinem et al. 2013a, b; Cummins et al. 2015; Mundt et al. 2012).
- On-line handwriting and drawing features (Cordasco et al. 2019; Likforman-Sulem et al. 2017).
- Sentiment analysis, or psychological content analysis based on linguistic text-based algorithms, such as topic modeling (Gong and Poellabauer 2017), natural language processing (Dang et al. 2017) to identify links between produced words and psychological states.
- Faces, head, and gestural analysis (Almeida et al. 2014).

Among physiological indicators of depression are:

- Gaze points, eye movements, pupil dilation, and fixations' times, which provide measures of where someone is looking, how visually she/he scan the environment, the interest and the like for what is seen (eye tracking measurements). It has been shown that eye tracking measurements change significantly between depressed and control subjects (Sanchez-Lopez et al. 2019; Ypsilanti et al. 2020; Moirand et al. 2019)
- EEG signals describe the electrical activity of the brain over a period of time, as recorded from multiple electrodes placed on the scalp. Frontal EEG asymmetries refer to differences in the brain activity of the two frontal hemispheres and have been associated with individual's motivational and affective states. Relatively greater right (left) brain frontal activation is linked to negatively (positively) valenced emotions, and therefore frontal EEG asymmetries have been associated both with trait-like (such as personality traits) and state-dependent processes such as moods (Cai et al. 2020; Tolgay et al. 2020; Thibodeau et al. 2006). In addition, it has been shown that absolute EEG power in theta, alpha, beta, and gamma bands in depressed patients is significantly lower than healthy controls.
- Biofeedback markers such as skin conductance, and heart rates, have been investigated in relation to depressive states. Previous studies have found for example that depressed patients have lower or flat levels of skin conductance response than healthy controls (Vahey and Becerra 2015). Hearth rate variability (HRV) is a beat-to-beat variation in heart rate and is measured through electrocardiograms (ECGs). HRV is described both in time (using the standard deviation of normal heartbeats) and frequency domains distinguishing between high (HF - 0.15–0.4 Hz) and low frequencies (LF - 0.04–0.15 Hz) HRV. It was found that HF-HRV and not LF-HRV is reduced in depressed children and young depressed adults relative to healthy controls (Kemp et al. 2010) while LF-HRV is reduced in older depressed adults (Brown et al. 2018). These discordances in HRV were unified by which proved that both HF and LF-HRV measures were lower in depressed than in healthy subjects.

4 The MENHIR (Mental Health Monitoring Through Interactive Conversations) Project

Depression and anxiety are common disorders. Establishing how to treat them and when specific interventions may be necessary is quite difficult. A virtual assistant can help to monitor the symptoms and facilitate the definition of appropriate interventions. The MENHIR project (https://menhir-project.eu/) aims to develop conversational technologies to promote and assist people with mental health problems (depression and anxiety) and help them to manage their condition. The project partners (Spain, Germany, Italy and United Kingdom) intend to create a network to exchange and share their expertise for developing conversational assistants to support depressed individuals.

Such assistants should offer personalized social support through mental health education and continuous symptoms' monitoring providing valuable feedback and promoting physical and intellectual activities to improve patients' abilities to manage their conditions and prevent recurrence and relapse of depressive patterns. By providing automatic on-demand assistance, MENHIR aims to reduce social inequalities due to the cost of treating such disorders. In the proposed context, artificial intelligence is the theoretical structure from which to derive algorithms for information processing able to produce new representations of depressive disorders and offer generalized solutions for the nonstationary and non-linear input-output relations describing the disease.

Limitations due to the fact that algorithms of this type may not converge towards adequate solutions and produce meaningless results are surpassed by biologically inspired machine learning models that exploit behavioral analyses performed on communication signals (in the case of MENHIR essentially expressed by voice) instantiated in different scenarios and automated through audio/video processing, synthesis, detection and recognition algorithms. To realize an artificial intelligence aimed at humans it is necessary to understand the nature with which humans interact with each other through the multimodal exchange of signals that include voice, facial expressions, gestures, gaze, and body movements into a single perception. MENHIR aims to use speech behavioral analyses and mathematically structure symbolic and functional speech concepts to define computational models able to understand and synthesize the human capacity to communicate through voice individual choices, perceptions and actions. In addition, MENHIR establishes the need of data visualization for users and developers in order to guarantee that the proposed AI models will preserve human rights, human well-being, and privacy and security of their personal data. At the same time it will ensure that the proposed conversational systems are effective, competent, explainable, interpretable, and aware of their limitations, accounting of all relevant legal and compliance aspects as identified by the EU directives and the white paper (https://eur-lex.europa.eu/legal-content/EN/TXT/?uri=CELEX%3A32016L2102, 2016, https://ec.europa.eu/info/publications/white-paper-artificial-intelligence-european-approach-excellence-and-trust_en, February 2020) on artificial intelligence. A data visualization model, called AI2VIS4BigData Reference Model, is under study by MENHIR's partners (Reis et al. 2020; Bornschlegl et al. 2016) and is going through modifications and re-assessment in order to satisfy the specific MENHIR context.

5 Automatic Detection of Depressive States Exploiting Speech

Speech is, among the behavioral data, the most exploited to detect depressive states, since depression causes psychomotor retardation, i.e. depressed speech exhibits a "slow" auditory dimension (Marazziti et al. 2010; Bennabi et al. 2013) and is perceived as sluggish. This sluggishness is due to changes in prosodic and acoustic features of the produced speech. Automatic detection of depression through speech analysis aims to accomplish: a) the discrimination between depressed and healthy subjects and b) the discrimination among different degree of depression (e.g. typical, mild, moderate, severe). A typical automatic classifier consists of two parts: the speech processing module that extract prosodic, and spectral features from speech, and the application of a computational method to predict the belonging of the data to one of the two classes (e.g. depressed and non-depressed subjects) or to multiple severity categories (e.g. mild, moderate, and severe depression).

Generally, when learning algorithms are involved, the computational method requires a training phase to learn an association between the available data and categories to be learned, and a testing phase where an unseen speech sample is assigned to one of the learned categories. Support Vector Machine (SVM), Gaussian Mixture Models (GMM), K-Nearest Neighbors (K-NN), Artificial Neural Network (ANN) are among the most utilized classifiers to detect depression, and exploit several spectral and prosodic speech features (Jiang et al. 2017; Cummins et al. 2015). The performance of these classifiers is reported in terms of accuracy (percentage of subjects attributed to a class that actually belong to such a class) and/or recall (percentage of samples belonging to a given class that have actually been attributed to that class). Most of these studies reported an accuracy of more than 70% demonstrating that this automatic approach can be a useful tool for helping clinicians in the diagnosis of depression, in addition to traditional diagnostic instruments.

Experiments reported in literature on this line of investigation show noticeable achievements. Scherer et al. (2013), extracted glottal features from speech signals collected from a sample of 39 subjects (14 depressed) whose depression degree was assessed through the Patient Health Questionnaire (PHQ-9, Kroenke et al. 2001) and on these features trained a SVM classifier, obtaining an accuracy of 75%. Alghowinem et al. (2013a, b) tested spontaneous and read speech of 30 depressed patients - diagnosed with severe depression through the HDRS questionnaire - and matched them with 30 healthy subjects. Speech was processed extracting several spectral features such as pitch, MFCCs, energy, intensity, loudness, formants, jitter shimmer, voice quality, Harmonic Noise Ratio. A SVM classifier trained on these features produced a recall of 68–69% on spontaneous and 61–64% on read speech respectively. On the same speech recordings, the performances of SVM, Hierarchical Fuzzy Signature (HFS), MLP, GMM and fusion methods were assessed (Alghowinem et al. 2013b). The fusion of GMM and SVM classifiers produced a recall of 81%, followed by a recall of 76% obtained with SVM.

Kiss et al. (2016) recruited a sample of 53 Hungarian and 11 Italian depressed patients (diagnosed by psychiatrists and assessed with BDI-II with respect to the depression degree) matched with 53 Hungarian and 11 Italian controls. From reading speech they extracted spectral (formants, Jitter and Shimmer) and prosodic (variance of intensity, range of fundamental frequency, total length of pauses, articulation and speech rate) features which were given as input to a SVM and ANN classifiers. Performance reached an accuracy of 75% for both classifiers when Hungarian speech were used on training and testing data, and 77% when Hungarian speech was used for training and Italian speech for testing. Jiang et al. (2017) extracted different low descriptors from recordings obtained in readings, interviews, and picture descriptions tasks obtained from 85 depressed subjects (diagnosed through PHQ-9 scores) matched with 85 controls. The performance of SVM, GMM and K-NN classifiers were compared on this data. Findings showed a slightly higher accuracy of SVM (65%) with respect to GMM and K-NN (60–62%) classifiers. When classifiers' performances were compared on tasks, speech from pictures' description provided better accuracy 68% than interview (63%) and reading (60%) tasks. Mendiratta et al. (2017) extracted F0 and MFCC features from the spontaneous speech of 12 depressed subjects (diagnosed by psychiatrists), and 12 matched controls and clustered the two groups through a self-organizing map (SOM) neural network, obtaining an accuracy of 80%. Scibelli et al. (2018) exploited recordings of spontaneous and read speech from 62 depressed patients (diagnosed by psychiatrists) and 54 healthy controls. Speech sample were transformed in input vectors having as components 384 low level descriptors (among those Root Mean Square (RMS) of the energy, MFCC coefficients (MFCC), Zero Crossing Rate (ZCR)). A SVM classifier was trained on these vectors obtaining a 75% discrimination accuracy, which was independent from gender, depression-related pathology, and length of the pharmacological treatment (if any).

Currently, new audio analyses have been proposed that rely on linguistic text-based methods, such as topic modeling (Gong and Poellabauer 2017), natural language processing (Dang et al. 2017), articulatory features associated to vowel production (such as front and back vowels and phonetical markedness, Stasak et al. 2017a, b), as well as, linguistic stress associated to vowel duration, loudness (Stasak et al. 2019) and affect based measures, all of them along with spectral selection measures (Williamson et al. 2016). These new approaches were presented, starting from 2013, at the Audio/Visual Emotion Challenges (AVEC), either as primary challenges AVEC 2013, AVEC 2014, AVEC 2015, or as sub-challenges AVEC 2016, AVEC 2017, AVEC 2018 (Valstar et al. 2016, 2014, 2013; Ringeval et al. 2018, 2017, and 2015). The AVEC 2019 edition, https://sites.google.com/view/avec2019/, is a challenge on states of mind where depression plays a fundamental role, and where signal processing and machine learning methodologies are called to compete as tools offering the most effective performances to accurately detect mental health and behavioral disorders from audio and video, and text data.

6 Conclusions

There is a huge demand to develop complex autonomous systems capable of assisting people with depression. One solution is to develop complex autonomous systems, in the form of socially and emotionally believable ICT interfaces capable of detecting the onset of such disorders, providing, where possible, initial on-demand support to patients, offering doctors' sustenance for diagnoses and treatments, suggesting strategies for favoring social inclusion and wellbeing and "meeting" users' expectations and demands. These interfaces should exploit data by sensors, and data analysis by artificial intelligent and user-friendly conversational interfaces which naturally integrated behavioral and psychological features derived for depressed people's daily life observations providing emotional and psychological support to them, their doctors and caregivers, enabling advance in diagnostics and healthcare support through non-obtrusive technologies that favor the physical, cognitive, social and mental wellbeing of depressed individuals. However, this task is intrinsically complex requiring the need of a holistic approach that accounts for the multiple factors affecting depression, including personality traits, social and contextual information, and cultural diversities (Esposito and Jain 2016). "The goal is to provide experimental and theoretical models of behaviors for developing a computational paradigm that should produce [ICT interfaces] equipped with a human level [of] automaton intelligence" (Esposito et al. 2015, p. 48). Such ICT interfaces can be exploited as automatic diagnostic tools for the diagnosis of different degrees of depressive states and in general for detecting from interactional exchanges reliable behavioral and contextual information. The challenge is how to make available the data collected from multiple sources and differently processed to intelligent computational devices for a cross-multimodal analysis and how endorse them of an effective ability to intelligently process behavioral and contextual information.

Acknowledgements. The research leading to these results has received funding from the EU H2020 under grant agreement N. 769872 (EMPATHIC) and 823907 (MENHIR), and from the Italian projects SIROBOTICS, MIUR, PNR 2015-2020, DD1735, 13/07/2017, and ANDROIDS, V:ALERE, UniCampania, D.R. 906 del 4/10/2019, prot. 157264, 17/10/2019. 7.

References

Addington, D., Addington, J., Schissel, B.: A depression rating scale for schizophrenics. Schizophr. Res. **3**(4), 247–251 (1990)

Ahmed, A.T., et al.: Mapping depression rating scale phenotypes onto Research Domain Criteria (RDoC) to inform biological research in mood disorders. J. Affect. Disord. **238**, 1–7 (2018)

Alghowinem, S., Goecke, R., Wagner, M., Epps, J., Breakspear, M., Parker, G.: Detecting depression: a comparison between spontaneous and read speech. In: 2013 IEEE International Conference on Acoustics, Speech and Signal Processing, pp. 7547–7551 (2013a)

Alghowinem, S., et al.: A comparative study of different classifiers for detecting depression from spontaneous speech. In: 2013 IEEE International Conference on Acoustics, Speech and Signal Processing (ICASSP), pp. 8022–8026 (2013b)

Bornschlegl, M.X., et al.: *IVIS4BigData:* a reference model for advanced visual interfaces supporting big data analysis in virtual research environments. In: Bornschlegl, Marco X., Engel, F.C., Bond, R., Hemmje, M.L. (eds.) AVI-BDA 2016. LNCS, vol. 10084, pp. 1–18. Springer, Cham (2016). https://doi.org/10.1007/978-3-319-50070-6_1

Almeida, E., Ferruzca, M., del Pilar Morales Tlapanco, M.: Design of a system for early detection and treatment of depression in elderly case study. In: Cipresso, P., Matic, A., Lopez, G. (eds.) MindCare 2014. LNICST, vol. 100, pp. 115–124. Springer, Cham (2014). https://doi.org/10.1007/978-3-319-11564-1_12

Alexopoulos, G.S., Abrams, R.C., Young, R.C., Shamoian, C.A.: Cornell scale for depression in dementia. Biol. Psychiatry **23**, 27184 (1988)

Bech, P., Timmerby, N., Martiny, K., Lunde, M., Soendergaard, S.: Psychometric evaluation of the Major Depression Inventory (MDI) as depression severity scale using the LEAD (Longitudinal Expert Assessment of All Data) as index of validity. Psychiatry **15**, 190 (2015)

Beck, A.T., Steer, R.A., Brown, G.K.: Manual for the Beck Depression Inventory-II. Psychological Corporation, San Antonio (1996)

Bennabi, D., Vandel, P., Papaxanthis, C., Pozzo, T., Haffen, E.: Psychomotor retardation in depression: a systematic review of diagnostic, pathophysiologic, and therapeutic implications. BioMed Res. Int. (2013), Article ID 158746, 18 pages (2013). http://dx.doi.org/10.1155/2013/158746

Brown, L., Karmakar, C., Gray, R., Jindal, R., Lim, T., Bryant, C.: Heart rate variability alterations in late life depression: a meta-analysis. J. Affect. Disord. **235**, 456–466 (2018)

Cai, H., Qu, Z., Li, Z., Zhang, Y., Hu, X., Hu, B.: Feature-level fusion approaches based on multimodal EEG data for depression recognition. Inf. Fusion **59**, 127–138 (2020)

Cordasco, G., Scibelli, F., Faundez-Zanuy, M., Likforman-Sulem, L., Esposito, A.: Handwriting and drawing features for detecting negative moods. In: Esposito, A., Faundez-Zanuy, M., Morabito, F.C., Pasero, E. (eds.) WIRN 2017 2017. SIST, vol. 103, pp. 73–86. Springer, Cham (2019). https://doi.org/10.1007/978-3-319-95095-2_7

Cummins, N., Scherer, S., Krajewski, J., Schnieder, S., Epps, J., Quatieri, T.F.: A review of Depression and suicide risk assessment using speech analysis. Speech Commun. **71**, 10–49 (2015)

Cunningham, J.L., Wernroth, L., von Knorring, L., Berglund, L., Ekselius, L.: Agreement between physicians' and patients' ratings on the Montgomery-Äsberg Depression Rating Scale. J. Affect. Disord. **135**, 148–153 (2011)

Dang, T., et al.: Investigating word affect features and fusion of probabilistic predictions incorporating uncertainty in AVEC 2017. In: Proceedings of the Seventh Annual Workshop on Audio/Visual Emotion Challenge, Mountain View, CA, pp. 27–35 (2017)

da Silva, A.K., Reche, M., da Silva Lima, A.F., de Almeida Fleck, M.P., Edison Capp, E., Milman Shansis, F.: Assessment of the psychometric properties of the 17- and 6-item Hamilton Depression Rating Scales in major depressive disorder, bipolar depression and bipolar depression with mixed features. J. Psychiatr. Res. **108**, 84–89 (2019)

Dehaye, M., Leemans, C., Loas, G.: Elderly's suicide attempt. Rev. Med. Brux. **39**, 15–21 (2018)

Dunlop, B.W., McCabe, B., Eudicone, J.M., Sheehan, J.J., Baker, R.A.: How well do clinicians and patients agree on depression treatment outcomes? Implications for personalized medicine. Hum. Psychopharmacol. **29**, 528–536 (2014)

Esposito, A., Esposito, A.M., Likforman-Sulem, L., Maldonato, M.N., Vinciarelli, A.: On the significance of speech pauses in depressive disorders: results on read and spontaneous narratives. In: Esposito, A., et al. (eds.) Recent Advances in Nonlinear Speech Processing. SIST, vol. 48, pp. 73–82. Springer, Cham (2016a). https://doi.org/10.1007/978-3-319-28109-4_8

Esposito, A., Esposito, A.M., Vogel, C.: Needs and challenges in human computer interaction for processing social emotional information. Pattern Recogn. Lett. **66**, 41–51 (2015)

Esposito, A., Jain, L.C.: Modeling social signals and contexts in robotic socially believable behaving systems. In: Esposito, A., Jain, L.C. (eds.) Toward Robotic Socially Believable Behaving Systems - Volume II. ISRL, vol. 106, pp. 5–11. Springer, Cham (2016). https://doi.org/10.1007/978-3-319-31053-4_2

Esposito, A., Scibelli, F., Vinciarelli, A.: A pilot study on the decoding of dynamic emotional expressions in major depressive disorder. In: Bassis, S., Esposito, A., Morabito, F.C., Pasero, E. (eds.) Advances in Neural Networks. SIST, vol. 54, pp. 189–200. Springer, Cham (2016b). https://doi.org/10.1007/978-3-319-33747-0_19

Freeman, D., Sheaves, B., Goodwin, G.M., Yu, L.M., Nickless, A., Harrison, P.J., Hinds, C.: The effects of improving sleep on mental health (OASIS): a randomized controlled trial with mediation analysis. Lancet Psychiatry **4**(10), 749–758 (2017)

Gong, Y., Poellabauer, C.: Topic modeling based on multi-modal depression detection. In: Proceeding of the Seventh Annual Workshop on Audio/Visual Emotion Challenge, Mountain View, CA, pp. 69–76 (2017)

Groholt, B., Ekeberg, Ø.: Prognosis after adolescent suicide attempt: mental health, psychiatric treatment, and suicide attempts in a nine-year follow-up study. Suicide and Life-Threat. Behav. **39**(2), 125–136 (2009)

Grover, S., Sahoo, S., Dua, D., Chakrabarti, S., Avasthi, A.: Scales for assessment of depression in schizophrenia: factor analysis of Calgary depression rating scale and Hamilton depression rating scale. Psychiatry Res. **252**(2017), 333–339 (2017)

Hamilton, M.: A rating scale for depression. J. Neurol. Neurosurg. Psychiatry **23**, 56–62 (1960)

Hamilton, M.: Development of a rating scale for primary depressive illness. Br. J. Soc. Clin. Psychol. **6**, 278–296 (1967)

Hershenberg, R., et al.: Concordance between clinician-rated and patient reported outcome measures of depressive symptoms in treatment resistant depression. J. Affect. Disord. **266**, 22–29 (2020)

Horwitz, A.V.: How an age of anxiety became an age of depression. Milbank Q. **88**(1), 112–138 (2010)

Jiang, H., et al.: Investigation of different speech types and emotions for detecting Depression using different classifiers. Speech Commun. **90**, 39–46 (2017)

Kemp, A.H., Quintana, D.S., Gray, M.A., Felmingham, K.L., Brown, K., Gatt, J.M.: Impact of depression and antidepressant treatment on heart rate variability: a review and meta-analysis. Biol. Psychiat. **67**(11), 1067–1074 (2010)

Kiss, G., Tulics, M.G., Sztahó, D., Esposito, A., Vicsi, K.: Language independent detection possibilities of depression by speech. In: Esposito, A., et al. (eds.) Recent Advances in Nonlinear Speech Processing. SIST, vol. 48, pp. 103–114. Springer, Cham (2016). https://doi.org/10.1007/978-3-319-28109-4_11

Kroenke, K., Spitzer, R., Williams, J.: The PHQ-9. Validity of a brief depression severity measure. J. Gen. Intern. Med. **16**, 606–613 (2001)

Landin, R., DeBrota, D.J., DeVries, T.A., Potter, W.Z., Demitrack, M.A.: The impact of restrictive entry criterion during the placebo lead-in period. Biometrics **56**(1), 271–278 (2000)

Lewinsohn, P.M., Seeley, J.R., Roberts, R.E., Allen, N.B.: Center for Epidemiologic Studies Depression Scale (CES-D) as a screening instrument for depression among community-residing older adults. Psychol. Aging **12**(2), 277–287 (1997)

Likforman-Sulem, L., Esposito, A., Faundez-Zanuy, M., Clémençon, S., Cordasco, G.: EMOTHAW: a novel database for emotional state recognition from handwriting and drawing. IEEE Trans. Hum.-Mach. Syst. **47**(2), 273–284 (2017). http://ieeexplore.ieee.org/document/7807324/

Lovibond, P.F., Lovibond, S.H.: The structure of negative emotional states: comparison of the depression anxiety stress scales (DASS) with the Beck Depression and Anxiety Inventories. Behav. Res. Therapy **33**(3), 335–343 (1995)

Marazziti, D., Consoli, G., Picchetti, M., Carlini, M., Faravelli, L.: Cognitive impairment in major depression. Eur. J. Pharmacol. **626**, 83–86 (2010)

Mendiratta, A., et al.: Automatic detection of depressive states from speech. In: Esposito, A., Faudez-Zanuy, M., Morabito, F.C., Pasero, E. (eds.) Multidisciplinary Approaches to Neural Computing. SIST, vol. 69, pp. 301–314. Springer, Cham (2018). https://doi.org/10.1007/978-3-319-56904-8_29

Moirand, R., Galvao, F., Brunelin, J.: Early shifts of emotional attention as a possible predictor of remission in patients with depression receiving ECT: preliminary results of an eye-tracker study. L'Encéphale **45**(2), 73 (2019)

Möller, H.J.: Rating depressed patients: observer- vs self-assessment. Eur. Psychiatry **15**, 160–172 (2000)

Montgomery, S.A., Äsberg, M.: A new depression scale designed to be sensitive to change. Br. J. Psychiatry **134**, 382–389 (1979)

Mundt, J.C., Vogel, A.P., Feltner, D.E., Lenderking, W.R.: Vocal acoustic biomarkers of depression severity and treatment response. Biol. Psychiatry **72**, 580–587 (2012)

Olesen, J., Gustavsson, A., Svensson, M., Wittchen, H.U., Jonsson, B.: The economic cost of brain disorders in Europe. Eur. J. Neurol. **19**(1), 155–162 (2012)

Rabinowitz, J., et al.: Consistency checks to improve measurement with the Montgomery-Äsberg Depression Rating Scale (MADRS). J. Affect. Disord. **256**, 143–147 (2019)

Reis, T., Bornschlegl, M.X., Hemmje, M.L.: Towards a reference model for artificial intelligence supporting big data analysis. In: Proceedings of the 2020 International Conference on Data Science (ICDATA 2020) (2020)

Ringeval, F., et al.: AVEC 2017 – Real-life depression, and affect recognition workshop and challenge. In: Proceedings of the 7th International Workshop on Audio/Visual Emotion Challenge (AVEC), co-located with the 25th ACM International Conference on Multimedia (ACM MM), pp. 3–9. ACM, Mountain View (2017)

Ringeval, F., et al.: AV+EC 2015 – The first affect recognition challenge bridging across audio, video, and physiological data. In: Proceedings of the 5th International Workshop on Audio/Visual Emotion Challenge (AVEC), co-located with the ACM International Conference on Multimedia (ACM MM), pp. 3–8. ACM, Brisbane (2015)

Ringeval, F., et al.: 2018 AVEC 2018 workshop and challenge: bipolar disorder and cross-cultural affect recognition. In: Proceedings of the 8th International Workshop on Audio/Visual Emotion Challenge (AVEC), co-located with the 26th ACM International Conference on Multimedia (ACM MM), Seoul, Republic of Korea, 22 October 2018

Rohan, K.J., et al.: A protocol for the Hamilton Rating Scale for Depression: Item scoring rules, Rater training, and outcome accuracy with data on its application in a clinical trial. J. Affect. Disord. **200**, 111–118 (2016)

Rush, A.J., et al.: The 16-Item Quick Inventory of Depressive Symptomatology (QIDS), clinician rating (QIDS-C), and self-report (QIDS-SR): a psychometric evaluation in patients with chronic major depression. Biol. Psychiatry **54**, 573–583 (2003)

Rush, A.J., et al.: An evaluation of the quick inventory of depressive symptomatology and the Hamilton Rating Scale for Depression: a sequenced treatment alternative to relieve depression trial report. Biol. Psychiatry **59**, 493–501 (2006)

Sanchez-Lopez, A., Koster, E.H.W., Put, J.V., De Raedt, R.: Attentional disengagement from emotional information predicts future depression via changes in ruminative brooding: a five-month longitudinal eye-tracking study. Behav. Res. Ther. **118**, 30–42 (2019)

Scibelli, F., Troncone, A., Likforman-Sulem, L., Vinciarelli, A., Esposito, A.: How major depressive disorder affects the ability to decode multimodal dynamic emotional stimuli. Frontiers (2016). https://doi.org/10.3389/fict.2016.00016. IN ICT, vol. 3, ISSN 2297-198X

Scibelli, F., et al.: Depression speaks: automatic discrimination between depressed and non-depressed speakers based on nonverbal speech features. In: Proceedings of IEEE International Conference on Acoustics, Speech and Signal Processing (ICASSP), pp. 6842–6846, Calgary, AB, Canada, 15–20 April 2018 (2018)

Scherer, S., Stratou, G., Gratch, J., Morency, L.: Investigating voice quality as a speaker-independent indicator of depression and PTSD. In: Proceedings of Interspeech. ISCA, Lyon, France, pp. 847–851 (2013b)

Shirazian, S., Grant, C.D., Aina, O., Mattana, J., Khorassani, F., Ricardo, A.C.: Depression in chronic kidney disease and end-stage renal disease: similarities and differences in diagnosis, epidemiology, and management. Kidney Int. Rep. **2**(1), 94–107 (2016). https://doi.org/10.1016/j.ekir.2016.09.005. Published 20 Sept 2016

Stasak, B., Epps, J., Goecke, R.: Elicitation design for acoustic depression classification: an investigation of articulation effort, linguistic complexity, and word affect. In: Proceedings of INTERSPEECH Conference, Stockholm, Sweden, pp. 834–838 (2017a)

Stasak, B., Epps, J., Lawson, A.: Analysis of phonetic markedness and gestural effort measures for acoustic speech-based depression classification. In: Proceedings of the ACII Conference, Parramatta, Australia, pp. 1–6 (2017b)

Stasak, B., Epps, J., Goecke, R.: An investigation of linguistic stress and articulatory vowel characteristics for automatic depression classification. Comput. Speech Lang. **53**, 140–155 (2019)

Thibodeau, R., Jorgensen, S.R., Kim, S.: Depression, anxiety, and resting frontal EEG asymmetry: a meta-analytic review. J. Abnorm. Psychol. **115**, 4 (2006)

Tolgay, B., Dell'Orco, S., Maldonato, M.N., Vogel Carl Trojano L., Esposito, A.: EEGs as potential predictors of virtual agent's' acceptance. In Proceedings of 10th IEEE International Conference in Cognitive Infocommunication, Naples, 23–25 October 2019 (2020)

Tolton, D., Steffens, D., Chan, G.: Patient versus clinician rated depression scores: a comparison of participant scores on the Carroll Depression Scale and the Hamilton Depression Rating Scale. Am. J. Geriatric Psychiatry **27**(3)S 124–125 (2019)

Torbey, E., Pachana, N.A., Dissanayaka, N.N.W.: Depression rating scales in Parkinson's disease: a critical review updating recent literature. J. Affect. Disord. **184**, 216–224 (2015)

Troncone, A., Palumbo, D., Esposito, A.: Mood effects on the decoding of emotional voices. In: Bassis, S., Esposito, A., Morabito, F.C. (eds.) Recent Advances of Neural Network Models and Applications. SIST, vol. 26, pp. 325–332. Springer, Cham (2014). https://doi.org/10.1007/978-3-319-04129-2_32

Vahey, R., Becerra, R.: Galvanic skin response in mood disorders: a critical review. Int. J. Psychol. Psychol. Ther. **15**(2), 275–304 (2015)

Valstar, M., Schuller, B., Krajewski, J., Cowie, R., Pantic, M.: AVEC 2013, Workshop summary for the 3rd International Audio/Visual Emotion Challenge and Workshop (AVEC 2013). In: Proceedings of the MM, Barcelona, Spain, October 2013, pp. 1085–1086. ACM (2013)

Valstar, M., Schuller, B., Krajewski, J., Cowie, R., Pantic, M.: AVEC 2014: The 4th International Audio/Visual Emotion Challenge and Workshop. In: Proceedings of the MM, Orlando (FL), USA, November 2014, pp. 1243–1244. ACM (2014)

Valstar, M., Gratch, J., Schuller, B., Ringeval, F., Cowie, R., Pantic, M.: AVEC 2016. Summary for AVEC 2016: depression, mood, and emotion recognition workshop and challenge. In: Proceedings of the 24th ACM International Conference on Multimedia (ACM MM), pp. 1483–1484. ACM, Amsterdam (2016)

Yates, W.R.: Clinical features of depression in outpatients with and without co-occurring general medical conditions in STAR* D: Confirmatory analysis. Primary Care Companion J. Clin. Psychiatry **9**(1), 7–15 (2007)

Ypsilanti, A., Robson, A., Lazuras, L., Powell, P.A., Overton, P.G.: Self-disgust, loneliness and mental health outcomes in older adults: an eye-tracking study. J. Affect. Disord. **2661**, 646–665 (2020)

Yeasavage, J.A., et al.: Development and validation of a geriatric depression screening scale: a preliminary report. J. Psychiatr. Res. **17**, 3749 (1983)

Watson, B., Tatangelo, G., McCabe, M.: Depression and anxiety among partner and offspring carers of people with dementia: a systematic review. The Gerontologist **59**(5), e597–e610 (2019)

Wechsler, H., Grosser, G.H., Busfield, B.L.: The depression rating scale. Arch. Gen. Psychiatry **9**, 334–343 (1963)

Williamson, J.R., et al.: Detecting depression using vocal, facial, and semantic communication cues. In: Proceedings of the Sixth International Workshop on Audio/Visual Emotion Challenge (AVEC), Amsterdam, The Netherlands, pp. 11–18 (2016)

Zimmerman, M., Chelminski, I., McGlinchey, J.B., Posternak, M.A.: A clinically useful depression outcome scale. Compr. Psychiatry **49**, 131–140 (2008)

Zimmerman, M., Walsh, E., Friedman, M., Boerescu, D.A., Attiullah, A.: Are self-report scales as effective as clinician rating scales in measuring treatment response in routine clinical practice? J. Affect. Disord. **225**, 449–452 (2018)
Zung, W.W.K.: Self-rating depression scale. Arch. Gen. Psychiatry **12**, 63–70 (1965)

Towards Explainable Artificial Intelligence and Explanation User Interfaces to Open the 'Black Box' of Automated ECG Interpretation

Khaled Rjoob[1(✉)], Raymond Bond[1], Dewar Finlay[1], Victoria McGilligan[2], Stephen J. Leslie[3], Ali Rababah[1], Aleeha Iftikhar[1], Daniel Guldenring[4], Charles Knoery[3], Anne McShane[5], and Aaron Peace[6]

[1] Faculty of Computing Engineering and Built Environment, Ulster University, Jordanstown, Northern Ireland, UK
rjoob-k@ulster.ac.uk
[2] Faculty of Life and Health Sciences, Centre for Personalised Medicine, Ulster University, Londonderry, Northern Ireland, UK
[3] Department of Diabetes and Cardiovascular Science, University of the Highlands and Islands, Centre for Health Science, Inverness, Scotland, UK
[4] HTW Berlin, Wilhelminenhofstr. 75A, 12459 Berlin, Germany
[5] Emergency Department, Letterkenny University Hospital, Donegal, Ireland
[6] Western Health and Social Care Trust, C-TRIC, Ulster University, Londonderry, Northern Ireland, UK

Abstract. This an exploratory paper that discusses the use of artificial intelligence (AI) in ECG interpretation and opportunities for improving the explainability of the AI (XAI) when reading 12-lead ECGs. To develop AI systems, many principles (human rights, well-being, data agency, effectiveness, transparency, accountability, awareness of misuse and competence) must be considered to ensure that the AI is trustworthy and applicable. The current computerised ECG interpretation algorithms can detect different types of heart diseases. However, there are some challenges and shortcomings that need to be addressed, such as the explainability issue and the interaction between the human and the AI for clinical decision making. These challenges create opportunities to develop a trustworthy XAI for automated ECG interpretation with a high performance and a high confidence level. This study reports a proposed XAI interface design in automatic ECG interpretation based on suggestions from previous studies and based on standard guidelines that were developed by the human computer interaction (HCI) community. New XAI interfaces should be developed in the future that facilitate more transparency of the decision logic of the algorithm which may allow users to calibrate their trust and use of the AI system.

Keywords: Artificial intelligence (AI) · ECG interpretation · Explainable AI (XAI)

T. Reis et al. (Eds.): AVI-BDA 2020/ITAVIS 2020, LNCS 12585, pp. 96–108, 2021.
https://doi.org/10.1007/978-3-030-68007-7_6

1 Artificial Intelligence

Artificial intelligence (AI) is defined as the ability of computers to perform tasks that humans usually perform to make decision based on prior knowledge and experiences. AI is an umbrella term for many intelligent technologies, but AI encompasses machine learning (ML) and deep learning (DL) (which is considered a branch of ML). One of the distinctions between traditional ML and DL is the process of feature engineering. In DL, there is no hand-crafted feature engineering (feature extraction and selection), while traditional ML normal requires feature engineering. Hence, traditional ML systems are often more explainable than DL because the feature engineering process shows the contribution of each feature in making the decision. ML is divided into three branches: 1) supervised ML, 2) semi-supervised ML and 3) unsupervised ML. In supervised ML, a dataset is labelled, and it is used to solve a classification or regression problem, while semi-supervised ML uses semi-labelled/partially labelled dataset which includes small number of labelled cases and large amount of unlabelled cases. In unsupervised ML, the dataset is unlabelled, and it's used for example to solve clustering problems which can be a method used to discover labels. AI has several technologies including: 1) machine learning; 2) expert systems, 3) natural language processing (NLP), 4) computer vision, 5) speech recognition, 6) planning and 7) robotics. In the last two decades, AI has shown promise in medicine, however, AI has shortcomings including: 1) machine learning often requires a large amount of data to learn and 2) a lack of transparency. However, AI systems are likely to be more explainable and transparent in the coming few years according to published works that demonstrate new methods to solve the AI transparency problem. Developing AI systems must follow general principles: 1) preserve human rights, 2) preserve well-being, 3) data agency, 4) effectiveness, 5) transparency, 6) accountability, 7) awareness of misuse, 8) competence [1]. Table 1 shows the explanation of each principle and Fig. 1 shows the dependency between these principles [1–3] .

Table 1. General principles of developing AI system.

Principle	Explanation
Human rights	AI shall be operated to respect and protect internationally recognised human rights and must be fully taken into account by AI companies, research institutions, government and individuals
Well-being	Increasing an prioritising human well-being should be considered by AI system creators because it is a primary success criteria of AI systems and avoiding negative unintended consequences such as decreasing economic growth for society, which means high quality AI systems without considering well-being can still have negative consequences on society's mental health, sense of themselves, ability to achieve goals, and other dimensions of well-being
Data agency	AI developers shall provide people with the ability to securely share and access their data, to maintain people's ability to have a control over their identity

(*continued*)

Table 1. (*continued*)

Principle	Explanation
Effectiveness	AI developers and operators should define a metric or benchmark for their AI system to measure the effectiveness of the developed system. Because AI will not be trusted unless it shows effective performance in use and it does not cause harm which can delay or prevent its adoption. So, industry associations such as IEEE and ISO should work on developing standard metrics for measuring on the effectiveness of AI systems
Transparency	A key concern over AI systems is that they must be transparent with different levels for each range of stakeholders to know why and how a system made this decision particularly, especially in systems that have real consequences to human safety such as medical diagnosis which requires "rationale" and "logic" explanations. In terms of AI, "transparency" also addresses the interpretability and explainability of the system. Both interpretability and explainability augment AI transparency. However, there is a difference between interpretability and explainability regarding to user experience (UX) level (developer, an accident investigator, user in the legal process, data scientist or public user). Interpretability enables AI systems to be understood by users of all experience levels (from public user to data scientist). While explainability enables data scientists to understand "why a model behaves that way?", and then they can explain "why" to users of all experience levels (public users or developer). Lack of explainability and interpretability (which results less transparency) increase the difficulty of accountability and for calibrating how must trust a human should put on a machine decision
Accountability	People need clarity about the manufacture and deployment of AI systems to establish responsibility and accountability to avoid any potential harm. Hence, accountability is not possible without transparency, so they are intricately linked to transparency. AI system manufacturers are perhaps accountable in order to address legal issues culpability. It should be possible to put equal culpability among responsible developers which include designers, manufacturers and operators to avoid fear within people
Awareness of misuse	New AI systems might have a risk coming from misuse of AI which could be deliberate or accidental such as misuse of personal data, hacking or system manipulation. Unfortunately, cases of AI hacking or unintended consequences have happened before such as the "Microsoft Tay" AI chatbot which was hacked. Hence, a new kind of education is required for people to be informed of the risks of AI misuse. GDPR provide procedures to deal with the misuse of recorded personal data

(*continued*)

Table 1. (*continued*)

Principle	Explanation
Competence	Operators of AI systems should be able to understand how and why an AI system made its decision and the effects of those decisions. Additionally, they should know when they need to check AI decisions and when they have to overrule them. Hence, Creators of AI systems should ensure that operators of their systems have experience, the knowledge and skill of how to use them safely and appropriately

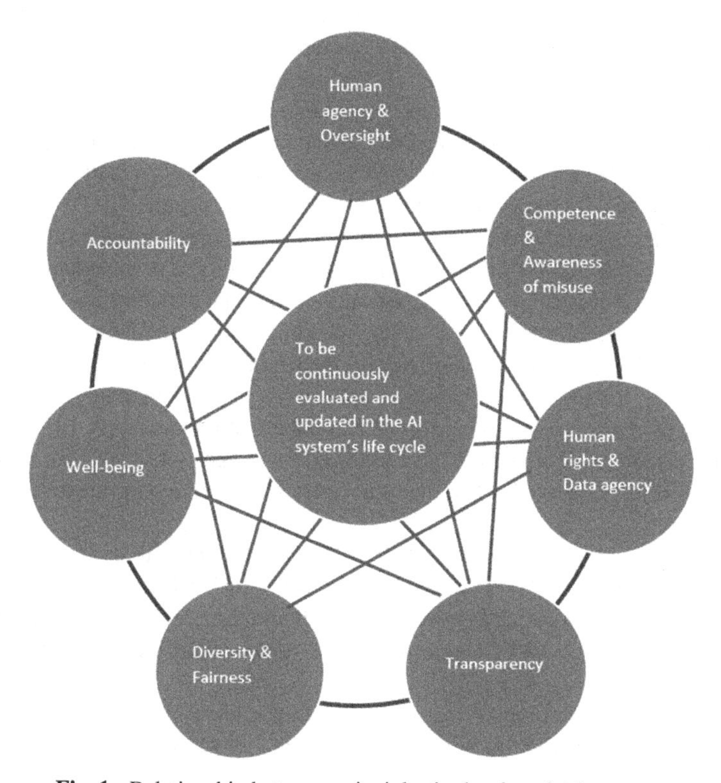

Fig. 1. Relationship between principles in developed AI systems.

The aim of this work is to show the current work of AI in electrocardiology (ECG), especially in ECG interpretation and how to improve it using transparent AI by discussing opportunities and challenges. Also, the paper suggests a new explainable AI (XAI) interface design to develop a trustworthy ECG interpreter by combining AI interpretation and human interpretation.

2 Automated ECG Interpretation-Challenges and Opportunities

AI is a rapidly evolving area in medicine, especially cardiology. Hence, it's used to perform different tasks such as heart rate monitoring, ECG interpretation and diagnosis. Automatic ECG interpretation (AEI) started from 1950s and it was expected that computers would have promising results in ECG interpretation [4]. Computers were used for ECG interpretation to improve the ECG interpretation accuracy of physicians and to support an expedited and accurate decision that would improve patient outcomes and reduce costs. However, inexperienced physicians might not be able to avoid automation bias when using an AI decision to assist them in their interpretation, because incorrect automated diagnosis (AD) can reduce ECG interpreter's diagnostic accuracy and confidence which indicates there is an automation bias, especially with non-cardiology fellows which means automation bias effects more on less expert physicians. Influences of automatic ECG interpretation was investigated on ECG interpreters. Hence, it showed ECG certainty index can improve interpreter's diagnostic accuracy and confidence [5–8]. The occurrence of lead misplacement in ECG acquisition is also challenging to detect and can mislead the algorithm to a false positive or false negative [9, 10] (challenge). Also, most of the algorithms to date are rule-based and use symbolic reasoning even though the algorithm outputs do not present any decision logic or metadata (challenge). Europe and United States have developed an international standard for AEI to reduce the variation in ECG interpretation by using the similar measurements [4, 11].

Additionally, in order to standardise the interpretation of the ECG, a glossary of diagnostic terms for ECG interpretation was created to be shared by readers of electrocardiography. However, an international standard is still missing [4, 12] (challenge). Hence, the current status of using AEI is reviewed for suggestions and close cooperation between expert physicians and AEI manufacturers is required to optimise performance [4, 11].

The Food and Drug Administration (FDA) approved algorithms to be used in the clinical environment such as "Azure Machine Learning", which was developed successfully through collaboration between Microsoft and the Cleveland Clinic to integrate computational techniques in ECG interpretation to detect abnormal arrhythmia event by focusing on the ICU [13, 14].

Another success example of translating machine learning to the clinic to detect silent atrial fibrillation (AF) is AliveCor. It received clearance from the FDA and it is now widely used in clinical practice. Hence, Mayo Clinic plans to collaborate with AliveCor developers to develop a technology to discover hidden morphological features from ECG data. Additionally, a portable device was developed using support vector machine to diagnose heart diseases in real-time using ECG such as atrial fibrillation and myocardial ischaemia with a high sensitivity and specificity [13, 14].

In addition, 3D computer simulations were developed to help in ECG interpretation findings from using ML. However, traditional ML algorithms such as decision tree and logistic regression are more transparent and explainable than other ML such as support vector machines. While DL is less transparent and not explainable because it automates feature extraction while traditional ML requires handcrafted feature before classification. Hence, DL does not show which feature was responsible for making the decision [13, 14].

Modern ECG devices have a digital output such as XML file however, most of recorded ECGs are still paper based. Hence, converting paper to digital could be helpful to remove noise in background and to exchange data between healthcare providers easily (opportunity). Digitizing paper ECGs and open these ECGs using interactive devices such as tablets could afford interactive design with meta information and explanation which allow the user to use and interrogate AI logic without the need to access raw samples from proprietary storage formats [15–17] (opportunity).

3 Artificial Intelligence Transparency

Previous studies that were carried out in different disciplines such as philosophy, cognitive science and psychology to interpret "how people define, evaluate and present explanations?", found that people employ social expectations and certain cognitive biases in the explanation process [18]. People tend to select a few causes out of infinite number of causes to explain their decisions. Also, human do not usually ask why event "A" happened, but rather ask why "A" happened instead of event "B".

In addition, likelihood is considered important in explanations. Hence, explainable AI could be developed based on these types of findings from research in other disciplines. Miller et al. [18] shows that research which do not use social science to build frameworks for AI explanation could lead to failure in AI explainability. Because the AI explainability issue is not just related to AI itself, it is also related to a human–agent interaction which is defined as the intersection of human–computer interaction, social science, and artificial intelligence as shown in Fig. 2 according to HCI community [18, 19].

Explanations that tell what, how and why are major importance. Four major mechanisms (backward propagation, perturbation, activation optimization, and proxy) were therefore developed for making AI explainable. The backward propagation method is used to explain deep neural network models by generating importance scores for the inputs/features. Backward propagation starts from the last layer (predicted outputs/labels) and computes the contribution from each neuron in the previous layer to the target and this is repeated down to the first layer. This mechanism uses different methods to compute contribution from each neuron such as DeepLIFT, layer-wise relevance propagation (LRP), smoothGrad, guided backprop (GB) and integrated gradients (IG). The main difference between these methods is the way that they compute the contribution [20]. The perturbation mechanism generates noise on the desired input features separately and observes the impact on the performance and summarising the impact in importance scores. Local interpretable model-agnostic explanations (LIME) is a method that uses a perturbation mechanism to compute importance scores using a linear model [21]. The activation optimization mechanism is used to generate explanations of hidden layers working in deep neural networks. It searches for input pattern that minimise or maximise hidden layers response according to the target. Hence, it can be formulated or considered as an optimisation problem but by optimising input features rather than hyper parameters [22]. While, proxy mechanism is often used to replace DNN with more explainable AI models such as decision trees (DT) by constructing DT that mimics DNN structure. So, the main concept proxy mechanism is mapping the complex AI models to more explainable AI model to solve the explainability problem. However, this mechanism was only applicable with shallow neural networks [23].

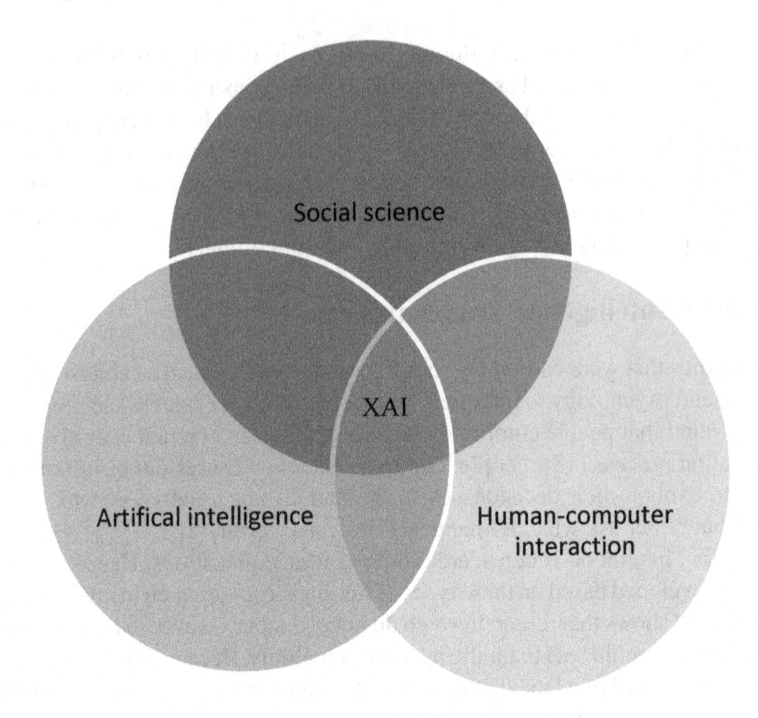

Fig. 2. Explainable artificial intelligence scope.

There are common dimensions to categorise explanation mechanisms: 1) explanation scope (global or local understanding), 2) model complexity to be explained, 3) is the explanation method applicable to all ML model or only for one model and 4) in which stage of model creation should the explanation be applied. To reduce the gap between explainable AI (XAI) algorithms and use, the HCI society encourages work on user-centered approaches and call for interdisciplinary collaboration to build sufficient frameworks on XAI. Hence, design practitioners from different backgrounds and jobs were recruited to build a question bank on how to build a comprehensive XAI model. Table 2 shows the question bank according to the recruited designers main feedback and questions [24].

Building high quality user interface design should follow these guidelines: 1) make elements perform intuitive and maintain it discoverable, 2) keep interface design simple, 3) consider the user's attention regarding to your interface layout and avoid including buttons excessively, 4) minimise the number of actions for each task, 5) put controls near element user wants to control, 6) consider default settings such as pre-filled forms to reduce user burden and 7) try to use reusable designs that were used before to be a good practice [25, 26].

4 Explainable Artificial Intelligence in ECG Interpretation

Automated ECG interpretation algorithms that are used in clinical practice today present simple diagnostic statements (such as 'Acute anterior MI') to the end-user on the header

Table 2. Question bank from previous research to build a clear user interface.

Question bank
What is the type of dataset? (input)
What is the out type? (output)
How accurate are the predictions? (performance)
What the overall logic in the built system? (global)
Why and how this instance gives this specific prediction?
Why and how are the other labels not predicted?
What the AI system will predicted if it is given another instance?
How the given instance should be changed to give the other prediction?
What is the range of change permitted to get the same prediction?
How to improve the system?

of the paper along with basic measurements/features that the system computed (e.g. width of the QRS, cardiac axis, heart rate etc.) Hence, the ECG algorithms today do not inform the end user of the features used in making the diagnostic decision or the decision logic. In addition, the algorithms do not inform the end-user about how certain the AI is nor does it inform the user about the expected accuracy of the algorithm for suggested diagnoses. Researchers at Ulster University have developed more explainable computerised decision support systems such as the interactive progressive based interpretation (IPI) system that was developed using a differential diagnoses algorithm (DDA) to suggest multiple diagnoses (and their decision logic) to improve ECG interpretation accuracy [27]. IPI + DDA approach showed promising results by improving diagnostic accuracy. Nevertheless, computerised ECG interpretation does augment physician's decision making.

Attention/heat maps are another solution to solve explainability issues, especially for the case of deep learning (DL). For example, attention/heat maps were generated for ECG interpreters to detect whether there is a lead misplacement or not. So, generating attention/heat maps from the last layer (which represents high level features) in DL can show which feature was responsible for making the decision and contributed more in the final prediction. Also, generated attention/heat maps could suggest to decision makers (ECG interpreters) the features that should be considered more in the clinical decision-making process and may help clinicians notice new features [28]. Fumeng Yang et al. [29] found that the combination of a human, a visual explanation and an ML algorithm perform better than the human and ML algorithm separately, because visual explanation leads to a higher level of trust and self-confidence. Including transparency in AI increases user understandability of the AI and allows the AI to be interrogatable at the point of need. Hence, visualizations and model performance are the most important information when establishing trust with AI [30]. Based on HCI community suggestions, AI principles, explanation mechanism, question bank and user interface guidelines, a suggested XAI model was developed to show how XAI interface design could look like as shown in Fig. 3.

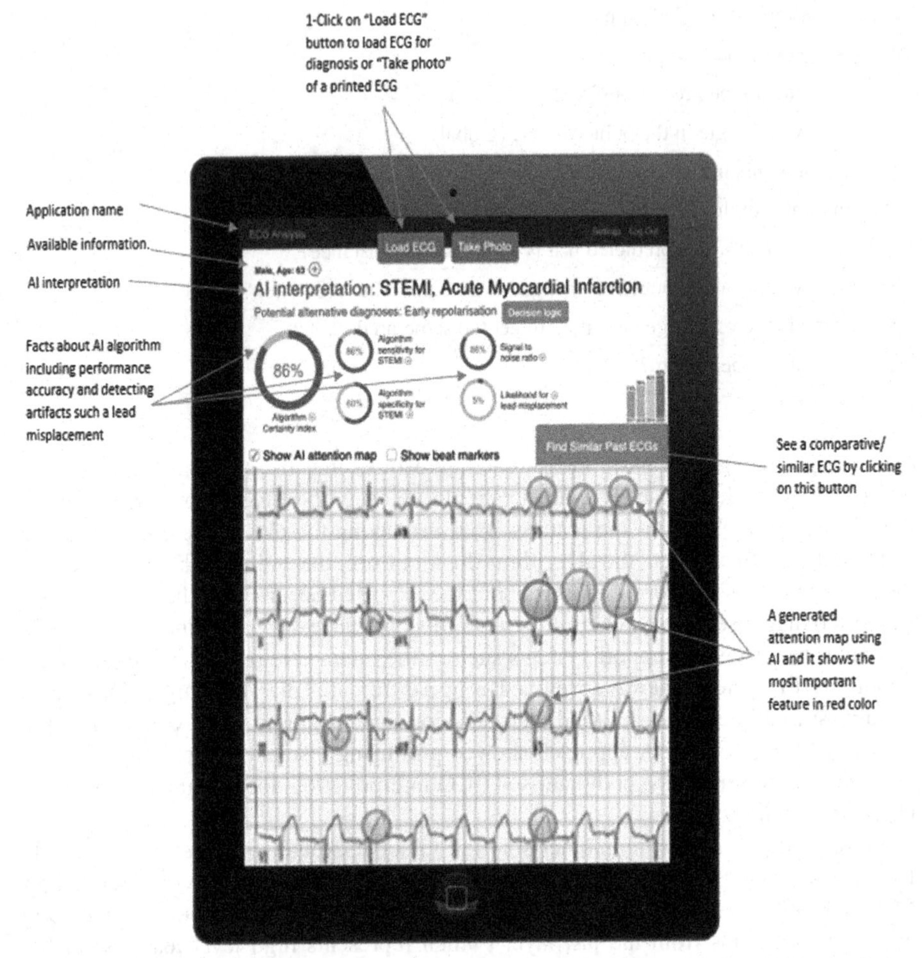

Fig. 3. Suggested XAI interface according to aforementioned recommendations. This user interface involves clicking one of two buttons ("Upload ECG" or "Take a photo" of an ECG). The user can input general metadata about the ECG such as patient age and gender. The physician can view prior similar ECGs with their diagnoses from a large database of ECGs by clicking on the "Show prior similar ECGs" button. AI algorithms interpret the same ECG. An attention map shows the most important features that were considered by the AI for making its classification. Moreover, facts about algorithm are presented, including signal to noise ratio, confounding decisions, rules, potential artifacts and an algorithm certainty index for calibrating human-machine trust.

5 Model Validation

The proposed work in this paper was projected onto the AI2VIS4BigData model (a reference model for AI, Big Data analysis and visualisation) as shown in Fig. 4.a, which was developed by Thoralf Reis et al. [32]. The AI2VIS4BigData model is an attempt to close the gap between AI, Big Data and visualisation. Figure 4.b shows how the infrastructure of the proposed model in this paper will integrate with the AI2VIS4BigData model. In terms of AI user stereotypes, the proposed model could have a model designer, a domain expert (who has knowledge in ECG interpretation), a model deployment engineer who is responsible for integrating the proposed model into the production environment, a model operator to manage and monitor the model in the production environment, a model governance officer who controls the whole process of the proposed model development and is responsible for ensuring that the proposed model is accountable by embedding transparency and explainability into the system. Finally, a model end user would be the clinician who is using the AI enabled ECG interpretation system.

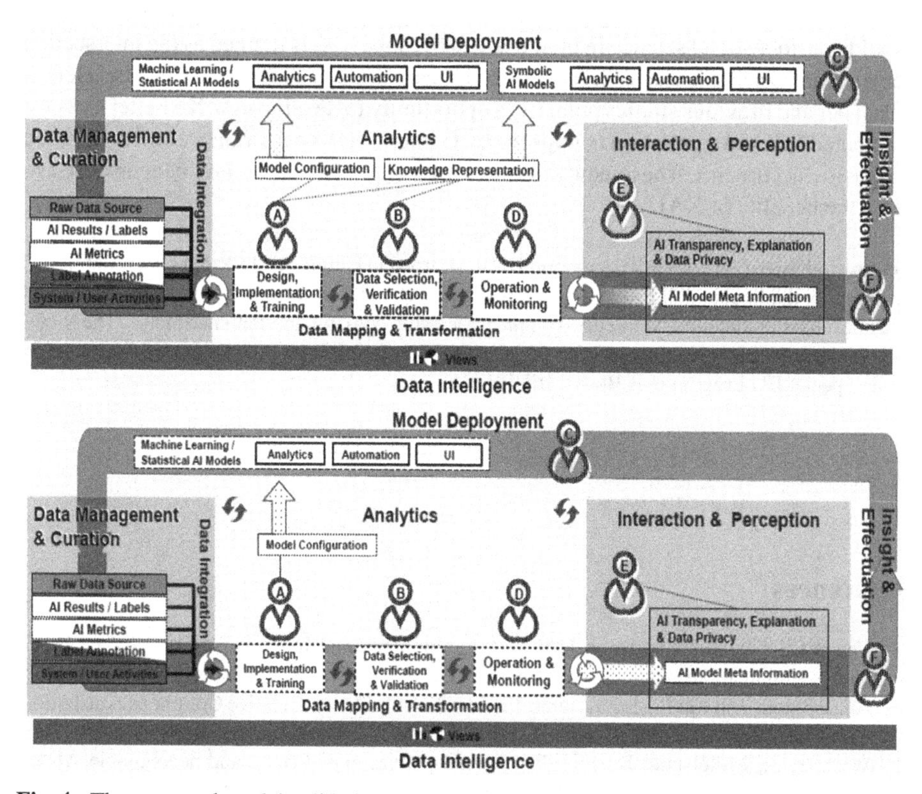

Fig. 4. The proposed model validation. a: represents the AI2VIS4BigData reference model. b: represents how the infrastructure of the proposed model will look like after integrating it with the AI2VIS4BigData model.

6 Conclusion and Discussion

Computerised ECG interpretation can include ML to enable automated ECG interpretation. However, there were some challenges such as algorithm transparency which mean the prediction is unexplainable. Researchers have shown that ECG algorithms that simply present a decision without any explainability can yield automation bias in the reader. Automation bias is when a reader simply accepts the machine's without critical review [6]. Hence, there are clear opportunities to improve automated ECG interpretation by providing a XAI user interface during ECG interpretation. Applying XAI could enhance ECG interpretation and as a consequence improve decision making in cardiology. There are different methods to develop an XAI interface such as showing attention/heat map for DL approaches or the rules for symbolic approaches. It is important to highlight which features were important and considered for making the prediction which as a result could calibrate the interpreter's trust and decrease automation bias in ECG interpretation. Furthermore, XAI could solve non-technology challenges such as the physicians adoption of AI, because AI is often considered a "black-box" and only −50% of physicians are familiar with AI technologies [31]. According to HCI guidelines, XAI developers should consider social science in their designs because XAI is defined as the intersection between human–computer interaction, social science, and artificial intelligence. Hence, this paper and previous studies point to an opportunity to develop new XAI interfaces for automated ECG interpretation to improve ECG interpreter's performance and to improve diagnostic accuracies. These new interfaces should be developed and benchmarked to show the benefits of XAI.

Acknowledgment. This work is supported by the European Union's INTERREG VA programme, managed by the Special EU Programmes Body (SEUPB). The work is associated with the project – 'Centre for Personalised Medicine – Clinical Decision Making and Patient Safety'. The views and opinions expressed in this study do not necessarily reflect those of the European Commission or the Special EU Programmes Body (SEUPB).

References

1. The IEEE Global Initiative on Ethics of Autonomous and Intelligent Systems (The IEEE Global Initiative). Ethically Aligned Design: A Vision for Prioritizing Human Well-being with Autonomous and Intelligent Systems, First Edition (EAD1e), Creative Commons Attribution Non-Commercial 4.0 United States License. https://ethicsinaction.ieee.org/#read
2. Wachter, S., Mittelstadt, B., Floridi, L.: Transparent, explainable, and accountable AI for robotics. Sci. Robot. (2017) https://doi.org/10.1126/scirobotics.aan6080
3. European Commission. Ethics guidelines for trustworthy AI. Retrieved from https://ec.europa.eu/futurium/en/ai-allianceconsultation/guidelines/1
4. Schläpfer, J., Wellens, H.J.: Computer-interpreted electrocardiograms: benefits and limitations. J. Am. Coll. Cardiol. **70**, 1183–1192 (2017). https://doi.org/10.1016/j.jacc.2017.07.723

5. Bond, R., et al.: Automation bias in medicine: the influence of automated diagnoses on interpreter accuracy and uncertainty when reading electrocardiograms. J. Electrocardiol. **51**, S6–S11 (2018). https://doi.org/10.1016/j.jelectrocard.2018.08.007
6. Knoery, C.R., Bond, R., et al.: SPICED-ACS: study of the potential impact of a computer-generated ECG diagnostic algorithmic certainty index in STEMI diagnosis: towards transparent AI. J. Electrocardiol. **57**, S86–S91 (2019). https://doi.org/10.1016/j.jelectrocard.2019.08.006
7. Finlay, D., et al.: Effects of electrode placement errors in the EASI-derived 12-lead electrocardiogram. J. Electrocardiol. **43**, 606–611 (2010). https://doi.org/10.1016/j.jelectrocard.2010.07.004
8. Bond, R., Dewar, D., et al.: Human factors analysis of the CardioQuick Patch®: a novel engineering solution to the problem of electrode misplacement during 12-lead electrocardiogram acquisition. J. Electrocardiol. **49**, 911–918 (2016). https://doi.org/10.1016/j.jelectrocard.2016.08.009
9. Rjoob, K., Bond, R., et al.: Data driven feature selection and machine learning to detect misplaced V1 and V2 chest electrodes when recording the 12-lead electrocardiogram. J. Electrocardiol. **57**, 39–43 (2019). https://doi.org/10.1016/j.jelectrocard.2019.08.017
10. Rjoob, K., Bond, R.: Machine learning improves the detection of misplaced v1 and v2 electrodes during 12-lead electrocardiogram acquisition. In: Computing in Cardiology (CinC), pp. 1–4. IEEE (2019). https://doi.org/10.22489/CinC.2019.035
11. Smulyan, H.: The computerized ECG: friend and foe. Am. J. Med. **132**, 153–160 (2018). https://doi.org/10.1016/j.amjmed.2018.08.025
12. Mason, J.W., et al.: Recommendations for the standardization and interpretation of the electrocardiogram: part II: electrocardiography diagnostic statement list a scientific statement from the American Heart Association Electrocardiography and Arrhythmias Committee, Council on Clinical Cardiology; the American College of Cardiology Foundation; and the Heart Rhythm Society Endorsed by the International Society for Computerized Electrocardiology. J. Am. Coll. Cardiol. **49**, 1128–1135 (2017). https://doi.org/10.1016/j.jacc.2007.01.025
13. Lyon, A., et al.: Computational techniques for ECG analysis and interpretation in light of their contribution to medical advances. J. R. Soc. Interface **15**, 20170821 (2018). https://doi.org/10.1098/rsif.2017.0821
14. Mark Estes, N.A.: Computerized interpretation of ECGs supplement not a substitute. Circulation: Arrhythmia and Electrophysiology. Vol. 6, pp. 2–4 (2013) https://doi.org/10.1161/CIRCEP.111.000097
15. Ravichandran, L., et al.: Novel tool for complete digitization of paper electrocardiography data. IEEE J. Transl. Eng. Health Med. **1**, 1800107–1800107 (2013). https://doi.org/10.1109/JTEHM.2013.2262024
16. Baydoun, M., et al.: High precision digitization of paper-based ECG records: a step toward machine learning. IEEE J. Transl. Eng. Health Med. **7**, 1–8 (2019). https://doi.org/10.1109/JTEHM.2019.2949784
17. Brisk, R., Bond, R., et al.: Deep learning to automatically interpret images of the electrocardiogram: Do we need the raw samples? J. Electrocardiol. **57**, S65–S69 (2019). https://doi.org/10.1016/j.jelectrocard.2019.09.018
18. Miller, T., et al.: Explainable AI: beware of inmates running the asylum or: how I learnt to stop worrying and love the social and behavioural sciences. arXiv preprint arXiv:1712.00547 (2017)
19. Miller, T., et al.: Explanation in artificial intelligence: insights from the social sciences. Artif. Intell. **267**, 1–38 (2019). https://doi.org/10.1016/j.artint.2018.07.007
20. Lundberg, S., et al.: A unified approach to interpreting model predictions. arXiv:1705.07874 (2017)

21. Ribeiro, M.T., et al.: "Why should i trust you?": explaining the predictions of any classifie. In: Proceedings of the 22nd ACM SIGKDD International Conference on Knowledge Discovery and Data Mining, pp. 1135–1144 (2016). https://doi.org/10.1145/2939672.2939778
22. Montavon, G., et al.: Methods for interpreting and understanding deep neural networks. Digit. Sig. Proc. **73**, 1–15 (2018). https://doi.org/10.1016/j.dsp.2017.10.011
23. Zilke, J.R., Loza Mencía, E., Janssen, F.: DeepRED–Rule Extraction from Deep Neural Networks. In: Calders, T., Ceci, M., Malerba, D. (eds.) DS 2016. LNCS (LNAI), vol. 9956, pp. 457–473. Springer, Cham (2016). https://doi.org/10.1007/978-3-319-46307-0_29
24. Liao, Q.V., et al.: Questioning the AI: informing design practices for explainable AI user experiences. In: Proceedings of the ACM CHI Conference on Human Factors in Computing Systems (CHI 2020), pp. 1–15 (2020). https://doi.org/10.1145/3313831.3376590
25. Badashian, A.S., Mahdavi, M., Pourshirmohammadi, A.: Fundamental usability guidelines for user interface design. In: International Conference on Computational Sciences and Its Applications, pp. 106–113 (2008). https://doi.org/10.1109/ICCSA.2008.45
26. Low, S., et al.: Enhancing user experience through customisation of UI design. Procedia Manuf. **3**, 1932–1937 (2015). https://doi.org/10.1016/j.promfg.2015.07.237
27. Cairns, A.W., Bond, R.R., et al.: A decision support system and rule-based algorithm to augment the human interpretation of the 12-lead electrocardiogram. J. Electrocardiol. **50**, 781–786 (2017). https://doi.org/10.1016/j.jelectrocard.2017.08.007
28. Alqaraawi, A., et al.: Evaluating saliency map explanations for convolutional neural networks: a user study. In: Proceedings of the 25th International Conference on Intelligent User Interfaces, pp. 275–285 (2020). https://doi.org/10.1145/3377325.3377519
29. Yang, F., et al. How do visual explanations foster end users' appropriate trust in machine learning?. Proceedings of the 25th International Conference on Intelligent User Interfaces March 2020, pp. 189–201, https://doi.org/10.1145/3377325.3377480
30. Drozdal, J., et al.: Trust in AutoML: exploring information needs for establishing trust in automated machine learning systems. In: Proceedings of the 25th International Conference on Intelligent User Interfaces, pp. 297–307 (2020). https://doi.org/10.1145/3377325.3377501
31. DAIC (AUGUST 08, 2019). Retrieved from https://www.dicardiology.com/content/half-hospital-decision-makers-plan-invest-ai-2021
32. Reis, T., Bornschlegl, M.X., Hemmje, M.L.: Towards a reference model for artificial intelligence supporting big data analysis. In: Proceedings of the 2020 International Conference on Data Science (ICDATA2020) (2020)

Recognition and Visualization of Facial Expression and Emotion in Healthcare

Hayette Hadjar[1(✉)], Thoralf Reis[1], Marco X. Bornschlegl[1], Felix C. Engel[2], Paul Mc Kevitt[3], and Matthias L. Hemmje[2]

[1] University of Hagen, Faculty of Mathematics and Computer Science, 58097 Hagen, Germany
{hayette.hadjar,thoralf.reis, marco-xaver.bornschlegl}@fernuni-hagen.de

[2] Research Institute for Telecommunication and Cooperation, FTK, Dortmund, Germany
{fengel,mhemmje}@ftk.de

[3] Ulster University, Derry/Londonderry, Northern Ireland
p.mckevitt@ulster.ac.uk

Abstract. To make the SenseCare KM-EP system more useful and smart, we integrated emotion recognition from facial expression. People with dementia have capricious feelings; the target of this paper is measuring and predicting these facial expressions. Analysis of data from emotional monitoring of dementia patients at home or during medical treatment will help healthcare professionals to judge the behavior of people with dementia in an improved and more informed way. In relation to the research project, SenseCare, this paper describes methods of video analysis focusing on facial expression and visualization of emotions, in order to implement an "Emotional Monitoring" web tool, which facilitates recognition and visualization of facial expression, in order to raise the quality of therapy. In this study, we detail the conceptual design of each process of the proposed system, and we describe our methods chosen for the implementation of the prototype using *face-api.js* and *tensorflow.js* for detection and recognition of facial expression and the *PAD space* model for 3D visualization of emotions.

Keywords: Emotion recognition · Facial expression analysis · Emotion visualization · Emotion monitoring · Convolutional Neural Networks (CNNs) · Affective computing

1 Introduction

Emotion analysis is important, because emotions penetrate many aspects of our lives, by informing the decisions we make and how we choose to communicate our thoughts to others and to ourselves. The data obtained can facilitate the diagnosis of emotional needs related to anxiety, depression or other kinds of mental illnesses. Healthcare for people with dementia living in their homes has become essential and health professionals need more information on patient behavior to prevent deterioration of their health. It is very important to intervene and predict this deterioration before it happens, avoiding the worst outcomes. In this context, the work reported here monitors the emotional state of the

T. Reis et al. (Eds.): AVI-BDA 2020/ITAVIS 2020, LNCS 12585, pp. 109–124, 2021.
https://doi.org/10.1007/978-3-030-68007-7_7

patient at home by recording videos, and analyzing video frames for facial recognition content and providing temporal trends and visualizations. The therapist or healthcare professional can intervene in the case of anxiety or depression for a dementia patient evident in the results before their mental state deteriorates further. Hence, primary care professionals will have an improved overview of the emotional wellbeing of patients through SenseCare [1]. SenseCare integrates data streams from multiple sensors and fuses data from these streams to provide a global assessment that includes objective levels of emotional insight, well-being, and cognitive state. There is potential to integrate this holistic assessment data into multiple applications across connected healthcare and various other inter-related and independent domains. SenseCare is thematically aligned with the current EU Horizon 2020 themes of "Internet of Things", "Connected Health", "Robotics" (including emotional robotics) and the "Human Brain Project". SenseCare has identified three application scenarios: (i) Assisted Living Scenario, (ii) Emotional Monitoring Scenario, (iii) Shared care giving Scenario. This work is focused on the second application scenario, *Emotional Monitoring* which deals with the emotional monitoring of people with dementia during medical treatment. Healthcare professionals will be better informed about the behavior of patient, by using SenseCare in order to raise the quality of therapy. Processing of voluminous data streams from video recordings, on the basis of the recently introduced Information Visualization for Big Data (IVIS4BigData) model [2] elaborates data stream types addressed by our visualization approach.

The visualization of emotions can be applied to Psychiatry and Neurology and relates to the diagnosis of people suffering from mental health problems such as e.g., dementia and depression. Human emotions are hypothetical constructs based on physiological and psychological data. The aim of the work reported here proposes to find solutions for the following points:

- The representation of emotions.
- The detection and recognition of emotion.
- The visualization of people's emotional states from video recordings, real-time and offline video analysis processing, and how users will comprehend the results.
- The visualization and exploration of emotion dynamically over time.

The remainder of this paper is organized as follows. Section 1 presents the state of the art of Convolutional Neural Networks (CNNs), facial Expression Emotion detection from video recordings, and visualization of dynamic emotion (over time). In Sect. 2 we detail conceptual designs of modeling of solutions for recognition and visualization of emotion. Section 3 describes our chosen methods for implementation of the prototype for recognition and visualization of facial expression and emotion, and finally we conclude in Sect. 4 also discussing future work.

2 State of the Art

Emotional Intelligence (EI) is a term designating a specific intelligence concept originally introduced by Daniel Goleman in 1995 [3]. Goleman defined emotional intelligence as the ability to identify, assess, and control the emotions of oneself, of others, and of groups. First, we focus here on, *Emotion representation.*

SenseCare comprises the implementation of a web-based software platform for the *Emotional Monitoring Scenario* (see Fig. 1).

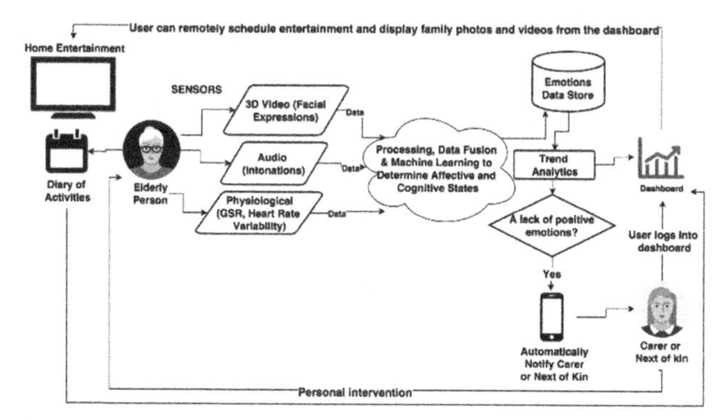

Fig. 1. SenseCare: framework for monitoring and caring for the emotional wellbeing of older people [4].

The SenseCare platform:

- Manages data streams from multiple sensors (e.g.: video frames for facial recognition of emotional states, sensory wearables for physiological emotion analytics).
- Fuses these data streams to provide a global assessment that includes objective levels of wellbeing and emotional state.
- Visualization of the global assessment.

The SenseCare platform layered software architecture is detailed in Fig. 2 below:

Convolutional Neural Networks (CNNs) are the most popular neural network model employed in image classification [5], CNNs comprise several layers, such as the Convolutional Layer, Non-Linearity Layer, Rectification Layer, Rectified Linear Units (ReLU), Pooling Layer, Fully Connected Layer, Dropout Layer. We have chosen five CNN models:

1- **AlexNet** [6]: is designed to effectively classify video shots into different views (i.e., long, medium, close-up, crowd/out-of-field) which is promising and novel in terms of its application to video shot classification. AlexNet employs five CONV layers including RELU and response normalization layers to extract the maximum feature maps form input frames for training the dataset with maximum accuracy.

2- **VGGNet** [7]: the runner-up at ILSVRC-2014, was developed by Simonyan and Zisserman. Similar to AlexNet, it employs only 3×3 convolutions, with one stride and zero-padding, but lots of filters. VGGNet consists of 138 million parameters, which can be partly challenging to handle. VGGFace [8] refers to a series of models developed for face recognition and demonstrated on benchmark computer vision datasets by members of the Visual Geometry Group (VGG) at the University of Oxford. There are two main VGG models for facial recognition, *VGGFace* and *VGGFace2*.

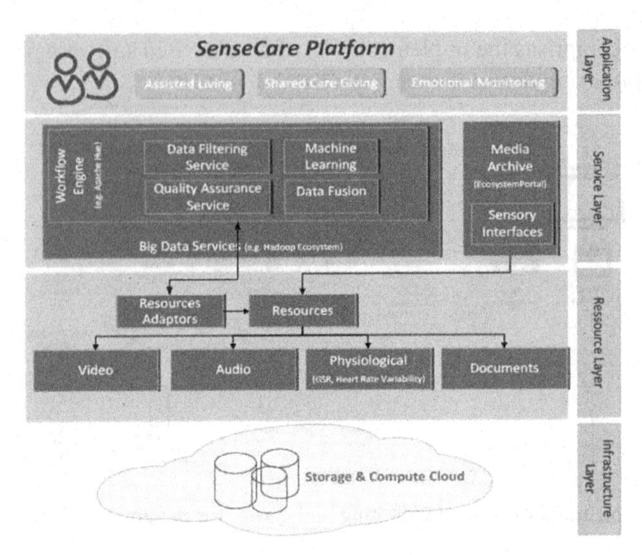

Fig. 2. SenseCare platform layered software architecture [1]

3- **ResNet** [10]: presented at the ILSVRC-2015, ResNet (Residual Neural Network) introduced a new architecture with "skip connections", and features large batch normalization. It realizes a top-5 error rate of 3.57% which beats human-level performance on this dataset. By adding identity "shortcut connections" x (input) in a residual network, the skip connections between layers add the outputs from previous layers to the outputs of stacked layers. The new layer is able to train much deeper networks than learn something different apart from outputs which have already been encoded in the previous layer. An implementation of Residual Nets in Keras can be found here [36]. Keras is a deep learning API written in Python, running on top of the machine learning platform TensorFlow. ResNet-152 has the least top-1 and top-5 error rates compared to other shallow ResNet models for classification on ImageNet validation.
4- **Convolutional 3D Neural Network (C3D) model** [11] generates short-term spatiotemporal features of video, LSTM (Long Short-Term Memory) accumulates those consecutive time-varying features to characterize long-term dynamic behaviors, and a multilayer perceptron (MLP) evaluates emotion in a video clip by regression on the emotion space (see Fig. 3).
5- **ZFNet [9]:** is the ILSVRC-2013 winner, possessing an architecture similar to AlexNet with a slight modification of hyperparameters in the middle convolutional layers of AlexNet. It realizes a top-5 error rate of 14.8% which is today already half of the prior mentioned non-neural error rate [17].

Existing solutions stream frames from a video stream over a network with OpenCV [18], for the following advantages: (i) firstly, building a security application that requires all frames to be sent to a central hub for additional processing and logging, (ii) secondly, the client machine may be highly resource-constrained (such as a Raspberry Pi) and lack the necessary computational horsepower required to run computationally expensive

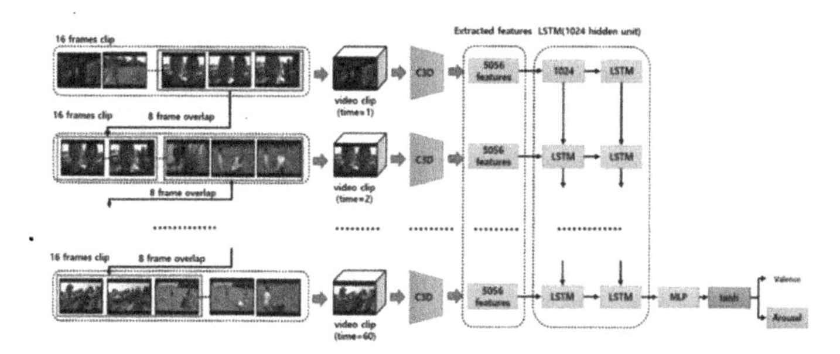

Fig. 3. C3D model [11]

algorithms (such as CNNs). An example is the client/server relationship for ImageZMQ [19] video streaming with OpenCV.

A real-time automatic facial expression system [12] was designed, implemented and tested with an FPGA implementation, and a Local Binary Pattern (LBP) algorithm was implemented for comparison in MATLAB and an FPGA, and FeelTrace of each frame for the extraction of activation and valence values for the database.

Software for emotion recognition from facial expressions employs the FURIA algorithm (Fuzzy Unordered Rule Induction Algorithm) [13] to offer timely and appropriate feedback based on learners' facial expressions, in order to validate the use of webcam data for real-time and accurate analysis of facial expressions in e-learning environments.

How should we measure the well-being of a population over time? Many ways approaches exist to measure variability in real-time. However, the variability in itself is inadequate without a mode of index of temporal dependencies from one moment to another. Results on unconstrained visual explorations of natural emotional faces (i.e., free eye movements) [14], confirm the significant gains obtained through EFRP (Eye Fixation Related Potential) analysis using the GLM (General Linear Model) method and open the way for effective analyzes of dynamic emotional ecological stimuli.

3 Methodology

Here we discuss methodology for operation of the SenseCare recognition and visualization of facial expression and emotion.

3.1 Video Recognition Process

Classifying video presents unique challenges for machine learning models. Video has the added property of temporal features in addition to the spatial features present in 2D images. An overview of the video recognition process using CNNs is shown in Fig. 4:

As shown in Fig. 4, the video frames are split into individual frames and on each frame, face detection is executed. Each individual frame is fed back into the system for face feature detection. For *feature extraction*, in the first learning stage *video input* is pre-trained with CNN models such as C3D, AlexNet, ResNet, VGGNet or ZFnet. In the second learning stage on *training linear classifiers*:

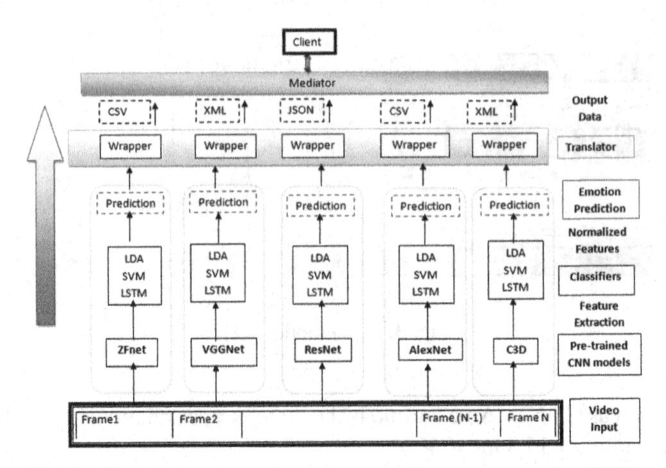

Fig. 4. Global overview of video recognition process using CNNs

Following feature extraction, there is a binary classification task for each frame employing:

- Long short-term memory (LSTM) is a particular type of Recurrent Neural Network (RNN) which performs better than the standard version [15]. The goal of LSTMs is to capture long-distance dependencies in a sequence, such as the context words.
- A Softmax classifier or a Support Vector Machine (SVM) classifier [20] employed to capture the emotion-specific information. The fusion of CNN and SVM classifiers provides better results compared to individual classifier performance.
- Linear discriminant analysis (LDA): a method employed recognition machine learning for face image to separate two or more classes of objects or events, for dimensionality reduction before later classification.

Emotion prediction: at the conclusion of processing, linear classifiers automatically predict emotional states by referring to training sets for *anger, disgust, fear, happiness, sadness*, and *surprise*. Results are stored in data files in .CSV or .XML format, and a mediator provides output to the client.

3.2 Emotion Visualization Process

An overview of the emotion visualization process is detailed in Fig. 5. The SenseCare user interface sends requests to the computer vision pipeline application. Results from video recognition are stored in data files in XML, CSV, or JSON format. The visualization prototype uses a wrapper to select data, and a web server in the mediator sends responding customized graphs of emotions as output results to the SenseCare user interface.

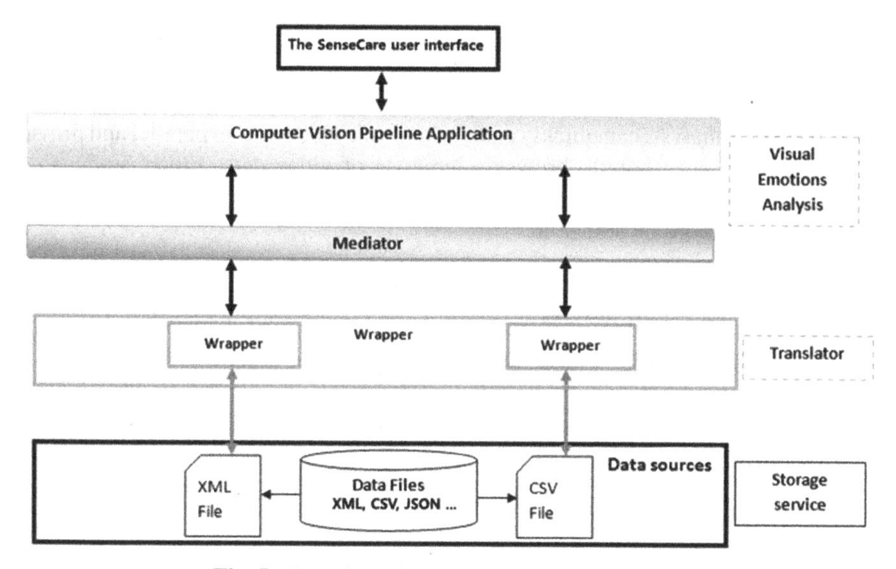

Fig. 5. Overview of emotion visualization process

4 Implementation Methods

For the implementation of the *SenseCare Emotional Monitoring* Scenario prototype, each operation requires specific hardware and software to succeed. Figure 6 illustrates the workflow of real-time and offline facial expression video analysis. Real-time video analysis uses video streamed from the webcam as data input. Offline video analysis uses

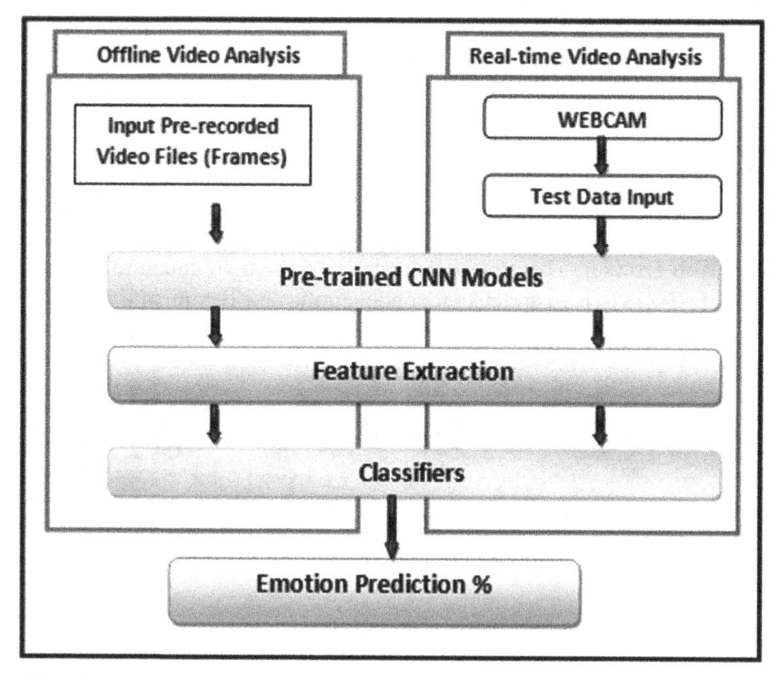

Fig. 6. The workflow of real-time and offline facial expression video analysis

us input pre-recorded video files. The same processing operations will be completed in both processes using pre-trained CNN models for feature extraction and classifiers for emotion prediction.

Offline video analysis can quickly analyze multiple video files in parallel and provide useful alerts with snapshots to browse a large set of video data. Video Streams can continuously capture video data from the webcam and store terabytes of data per hour from hundreds of thousands of sources.

4.1 Real-Time Video Streaming

In Fig. 7 the architecture for remote streams video recovery is shown.

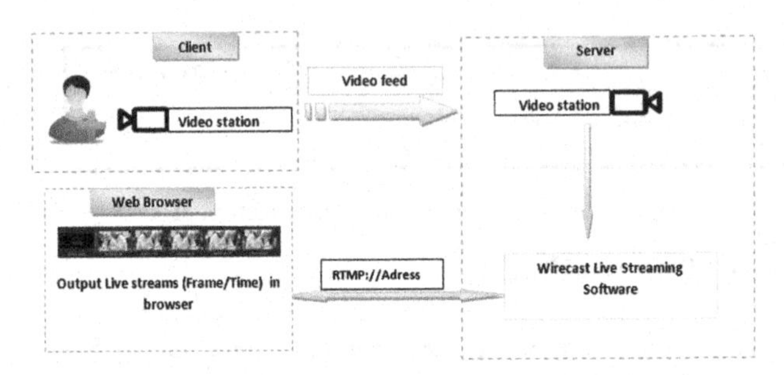

Fig. 7. SenseCare videoconferencing client/server relationship

The proposed solution employs two video stations (see Fig. 8), one in the client part (e.g., patient at home), and the second in the server part server part (e.g., at hospital). The Video stations consist of input and output ports to transmit video feeds. The external capture card plugs into the server using the appropriate Thunderbolt connection between Camera and Wirecast Live Streaming Software, to receive improved image quality. The RTMP (Real Time Messaging Protocol) address is added (e.g., public IP set) as a source for broadcast in the Wirecast Live Streaming software. The end-user must download and install the Flash browser plugin in order to playback audio and video streamed by RTMP in a Web browser. This videoconferencing system architecture is employed in the WebTV of CERIST (Research Centre on Scientific and Technical Information) [21].

Fig. 8. Remote streaming video station at CERIST [21]

4.2 Real-Time Video Analysis

The basic software components for real-time analysis of video frames taken from live video streams are as follows:

- Acquire frames from the video source
- Select the frames to be analyzed
- Submit these frames to the API
- Each result of the analysis returned is consumed by the API call

4.3 Detection and Recognition of Emotion

Essential steps in Face Recognition processing are summarized as follows:

1. *Face Detection*: Locate one or more faces in the image and mark with a bounding box.
2. *Face Alignment*: Normalize the face for consistency with the database, such as e.g., geometry and photometrics.
3. *Feature Extraction*: Extract features from the face that can be employed in the face recognition task (4.).
4. *Face Recognition*: Perform matching of the face against one or more known faces in a prepared database.

Face detection is an essential step in emotion recognition systems. It is the first step in our system to define a region of interest for feature extraction.

We have chosen *Face-api.js* [22] and *Tensorflow.js* [23] for video processing. *Face-api.js* is a JavaScript API for face recognition in the browser with *Tensorflow.js*. *TensorFlow.js* is a library for building and executing machine learning algorithms in JavaScript. *TensorFlow.js models* run in a web browser and in the *Node.js* environment. *TensorFlow.js* has empowered a new set of developers from the extensive JavaScript community to build and deploy machine learning models and enabled new classes of on-device computation [24]. For face recognition, a *ResNet-34* like architecture is applied to calculate a face descriptor, a feature vector with 128 values.

4.3.1 Face Detection, Landmark Detection and Alignment

Face-api.js solely implements an SSD (Single Shot Multibox Detector) MobileNets v1 based CNN for face detection. MobileNets relies on a streamlined structure that uses detachable deep convolution to create deep and light neural networks. This app also implements an optimized *Tiny Face Detector*, basically an even tinier version of *Tiny Yolo v2* [25] utilizing depthwise separable convolutions instead of regular convolutions, and finally also employed MTCNN (Multi-task Cascaded Convolutional Neural Network) [26]. The neural networks return the bounding boxes of each face, with their corresponding scores. The default model *face_landmark_68_model* and the tiny model *face_landmark_68_tiny_model* return the 68 point face landmarks of a given face image.

4.3.2 Face Expression Recognition

Face images can be extracted and aligned in the face recognition network, which is based on a *ResNet-34* type structure and basically matches the structure applied in dlib's face recognition model [27]. *Face-api.js* is prepared to evaluate faces detected and allocates a score (from 0 to 1) for each expression, *neutral, happy, sad, angry, fearful, disgusted, surprised,* in real-time with a webcam. The facial expression recognition model performs with reasonable accuracy. The model has a size of roughly 310 kb and implements several CNNs. It was trained on a variety of images from open access public data sets as well as images extracted from the web. The API employs a *Euclidean distance* classifier to find best matches in*/data/faces.json* [28].

The results are optimized for the web and for mobile devices. We have used videos from CERIST-WebTV for testing the API (see Fig. 9).

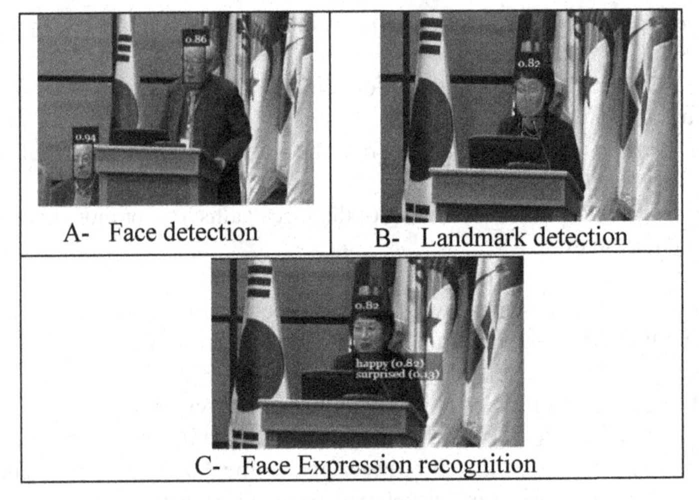

Fig. 9. Demonstration of face detection, landmark detection, face expression Recognition.

In the case of real-time video, SenseCare selects a frame from the video and analyses the images every 500 ms, so the following step is how to return the results for a particular image in JSON format.

4.3.3 Confusion Matrix

A confusion matrix is employed in evaluating the correctness of a classification model. In classification problems, 'accuracy' refers to the number of correct predictions made by the predictive model over the rest of the predictions. The four public face expression databases are CK+, Oulu-CASIA, TFD, and SFEW [30]. CK+ (Extended Cohn-Kanade dataset) consists of 529 videos from 123 subjects, 327 of them annotated with eight expression labels.

Experiential results of the confusion matrix for face expression recognition in videos are shown in Fig. 10.

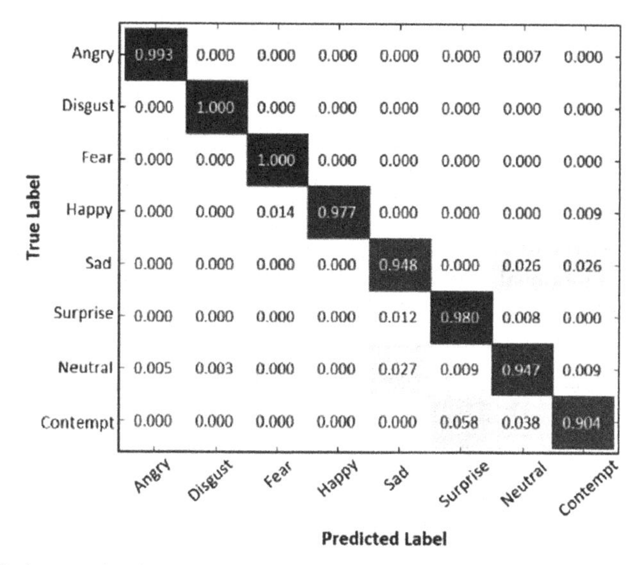

Fig. 10. Confusion matrix of CK + for the eight classes problem. (darker color = higher accuracy) [16].

'Accuracy' refers to the number of correct predictions made by the predictive model over the rest of the predictions. Accuracy is used when the target variable classes in the data are nearly balanced, but is not used if the target variables in the data are the majority of one class.

$$\text{Accuracy} = \frac{(\text{TP} + \text{TN})}{(\text{TP} + \text{TN} + \text{FP} + \text{FN})}$$

TR = True Positive, TN = True Negative, FP = False Positive, FN = False Negative.

4.4 Emotion Visualization

There are two ways of representing affective states in video content: (1) discrete affective categories, and (2) continuous affective dimensions.

4.4.1 Implementing the Affective Model

Dimensional models of emotion attempt to visualize human emotions by determining where they are located in 2 or 3 dimensions. Most dimensional models include *valence* and *arousal* or *intensity* dimensions. For example, The *Circumplex model* of affect [30] defines two dimensions, *pleasure* and *arousal*, whilst the PAD (Pleasure-Arousal-Dominance) [31] emotional state model uses 3. *PAD space*: Pleasure-Arousal-Dominance is a psychological model proposed by Albert Mehrabian. The PAD model is employed in describing and measuring emotional states. It's one of the 3D models that that has gained popularity in affective computing. The PAD model allows us to differentiate anger (positive dominance) from fear (negative dominance).

As shown in Fig. 11, dimensions (PAD-axes) are:

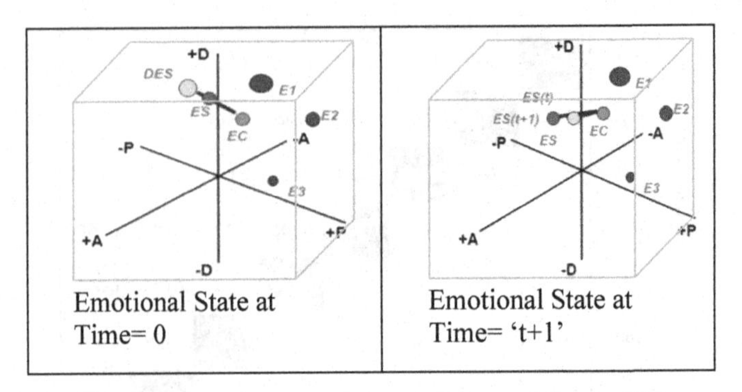

Fig. 11. Exploration of emotions in PAD model space [32]

- Pleasure/Valence (P)
- Arousal (A)
- Dominance (D)

DES denotes Default Emotional State, *Ei*, Emotions, and *ES(t)*, Emotional State.

The following labels describe the resulting octants of the PAD model:

(+ P+ A + D) *Exuberant*, (-P-A-D) *Bored*, (+ P-A + D) *Relaxed*, (-P + A-D) *Anxious*, (+ P + A-D) *Dependent*, (-P-A + D) *Disdainful*, (+ P-A-D) *Docile*, (-P + A + D) *Hostile*.

Intensity of Emotional State (ESi) is defined as follows:

ESi = ||ES||, if ESi ∈[0.0, 0.57], *Slightly*

ESi ∈ [0.57, 1.015], *Moderate*

ESi ∈ [1.015, 1.73], *Highly*

Emotional data is mapped in PAD space and takes the following form:

Visualization space = {PAD positions (XYZ-axes), Val, color of emotion}.

Val = % emotion prediction.

Building interactive visualizations using WebVR and NodeJS technologies [33] allows synchronous or real-time communication in the web application.

Figure 12 shows how the Websocket operates in SenseCare, including user do action change position or rotation, socket emit action (socket emit), the server NodeJS received data, and sends (socket on) to update information for all users connected in this space.

Figure 13 shows simulation of emotion dynamics in the PAD model space:

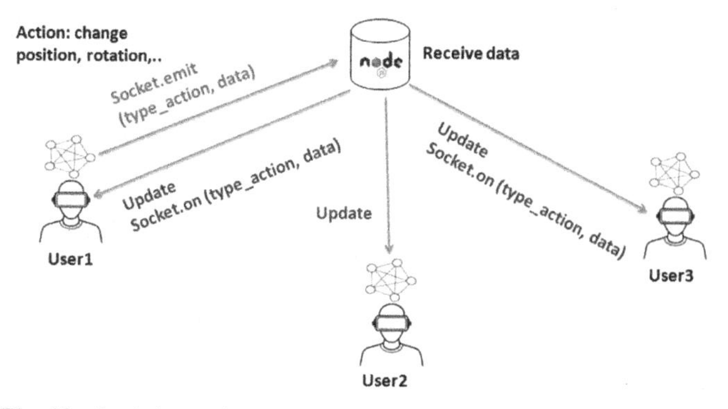

Fig. 12. Real-time collaborative data communication and visualization

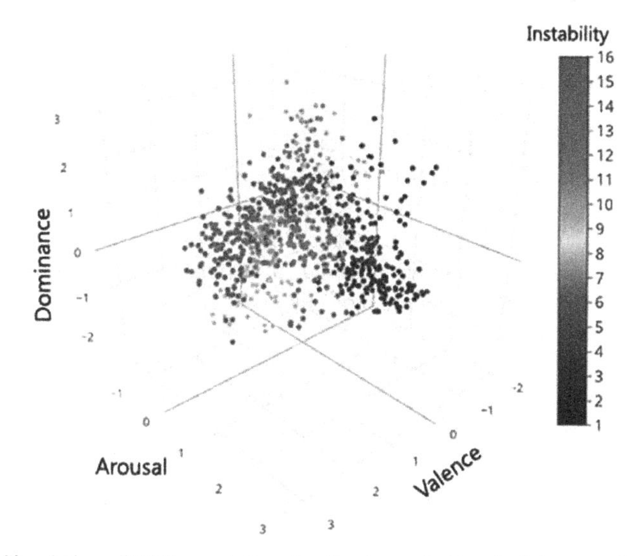

Fig. 13. Simulation of PAD annotation distributions of video facial expression analysis

4.5 AI2VIS4BigData Model

Processing large data streams from video recordings (in real-time and offline) to be visualized fits with the AI2VIS4BigData reference model (see Fig. 14). AI2VIS4BigData model [34] is based on AI transparency, explanation, and data privacy. It is also based on the life cycle of the AIGO AI system [35] and the reference model IVIS4BigData [2] of Bornschlegl for the analysis and visualization of Big Data.

A = Model Designer, B = Domain Expert, C = Model Deployment Engineer, D = Model Operator (MLOps), E = Model Governance Officer, F = Model End User.

All the elements of the AI2VIS4BigData model such as AI models, user stereotypes, and data management are relevant to our visualization approach.

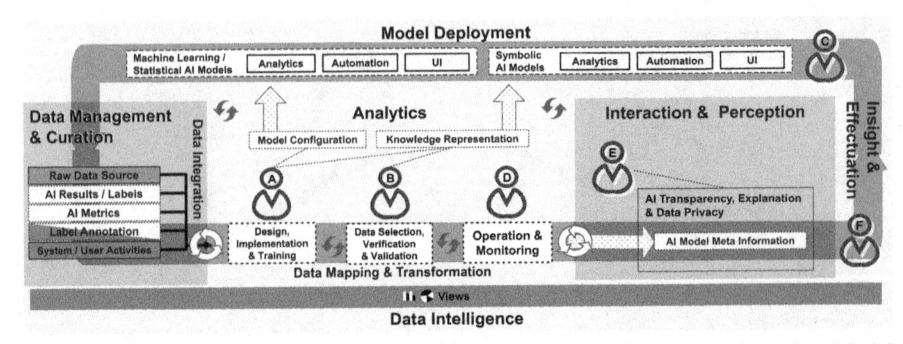

A = Model Designer, B = Domain Expert, C = Model Deployment Engineer, D = Model Operator (MLOps), E = Model Governance Officer, F = Model End User.

Fig. 14. AI2VIS4BigData: A reference model for AI supporting Big Data analysis [34].

5 Conclusion and Future Work

In order to develop major advances in emotion analysis, there must be adequate techniques for combining and analyzing complex signals. This research explores two architectures for the *Emotional Monitoring Scenario*, for processing video of a dementia patient recorded at home. Existing techniques for video face expression recognition employing CNNs and classifiers are detailed, including the exploration of emotional states using *PAD Space* model. Future work includes:

a- Finding solutions to manage and store (streaming & offline) video analysis results in the cloud (format JSON, CSV, XML, Databases).
b- Developing a web tool for visualization of emotional states and possibly including collaborative visualization.
c- Testing the SenseCare prototype in a live setting with live patients.

Future improvements will include new visual representations, views, and the collection of additional types of data such as eye-movement monitoring.

Our primary challenge is to develop a cloud-based affective computing system capable of processing and fusing multiple sensory data streams to provide cognitive and emotional intelligence for AI connected healthcare systems employing sensory and machine learning technologies, in order to augment patient well-being with more effective treatment across multiple medical domains.

Acknowledgements. This research has been developed in the context of the SenseCare project. SenseCare has received funding from the European Union's H2020 Programme under grant agreement No 690862. However, this paper reflects only the authors' views and the European Commission is not responsible for any use that may be made of the information it contains.

References

1. Engel, F., et al.: Sensecare: towards an experimental platform for home-based, visualisation of emotional states of people with dementia. In: Bornschlegl, M.X., Engel, F.C., Bond, R., Hemmje, M.L. (eds.) AVI-BDA 2016. LNCS, vol. 10084, pp. 63–74. Springer, Cham (2016). https://doi.org/10.1007/978-3-319-50070-6_5
2. Bornschlegl, M.X., et al.: IVIS4BigData: a reference model for advanced visual interfaces supporting big data analysis in virtual research environments. In: Bornschlegl, M.X., Engel, F.C., Bond, R., Hemmje, M.L. (eds.) AVI-BDA 2016. LNCS, vol. 10084, pp. 1–18. Springer, Cham (2016). https://doi.org/10.1007/978-3-319-50070-6_1
3. Goleman, D.: Emotional Intelligence. Bantam Books, Inc, New York (1995)
4. Bond, R.R., et al.: SenseCare: using affective computing to manage and care for the emotional wellbeing of older people. In: Giokas, K., Bokor, L., Hopfgartner, F. (eds.) eHealth 360°. LNICST, vol. 181, pp. 352–356. Springer, Cham (2017). https://doi.org/10.1007/978-3-319-49655-9_42
5. Machine Intelligence and Signal Processing, Ebook. In: Proceedings of International Conference, Springer, Singapore, MISP (2019). ISBN 978-981-13-0923-6
6. Minhas, R.A., Javed, A., Irtaza, A., Mahmood, M.T., Joo, Y.B.: Shot classification of field sports videos using alexnet convolutional neural network. Appl. Sci. **9**(3), 483 (2019)
7. Simonyan, K., Zisserman, A.: Very deep convolutional networks for large-scale image recognition. In: ICLR (2015)
8. Brownlee, J.: Deep Learning for Computer Vision: Image Classification, Object Detection, and Face Recognition in Python. Machine Learning Mastery, Vermont, Australia (2019)
9. Lim, Y.K., Liao, Z., Petridis, S., Pantic, M.: Transfer learning for action unit recognition. CoRR abs/1807.07556 (2018)
10. He., K., Zhang, X., Ren, S., Sun, J.: Deep residual learning for image recognition. In: Proceedings of the IEEE Conference on Computer Vision and Pattern Recognition, pp. 770–778 (2016)
11. Kim, Byoungjun, Lee, Joonwhoan: A deep-learning based model for emotional evaluation of video clips. Int. J. Fuzzy Logic Intell. Syst. **18**(4), 245–253 (2018)
12. Turabzadeh, S., Meng, H., Swash, R.M., Pleva, M., Juhar, J.: Facial expression emotion detection for real-time embedded systems. Technologies **6**, 17 (2018)
13. Bahreini, K., van der Vegt, W., Westera, W.: A fuzzy logic approach to reliable real-time recognition of facial emotions. Multi. Tools Appl. **78**, 18943–18966 (2019)
14. Guérin-Dugué, A., Roy, R.N., Kristensen, E., Rivet, B., Vercueil, L., Tcherkassof, A.: Temporal dynamics of natural static emotional facial expressions decoding: a study using event- and eye fixation-related. Potentials. Front. Psychol. **9**, 1190 (2018). https://doi.org/10.3389/fpsyg.2018.01190
15. Long short-term memory. Neural Comput. **9** (8), 1735–1780. https://doi.org/10.1162/neco.1997.9.8.1735. PMID 9377276
16. Ding, H., Zhou, S.K., Chellappa, R.: FaceNet2ExpNet: regularizing a deep face recognition net for expression recognition. In: 12th IEEE International Conference on Automatic Face and Gesture Recognition, pp. 118–126 (2017)
17. Vasudevan, C.: Concepts and Programming in PyTorch: A way to dive into the technicality, BPB Publications (2018). ISBN 9388176057, 9789388176057
18. OpenCV (Open Source Computer Vision Library), link: https://opencv.org/. Accessed 23 June 2020
19. Rosebrock, A.: Live video streaming over network with OpenCV and ImageZMQ. https://www.pyimagesearch.com/2019/04/15/live-video-streaming-over-network-with-opencv-and-imagezmq/. Accessed 23 June 2020

20. Rao, K.S., Koolagudi, G.: Emotion Recognition using Speech Features, Springer New York (2013). https://doi.org/10.1007/978-1-4614-5143-3
21. Research Centre on Scientific and Technical Information, link: http://www.cerist.dz. Accessed 23 June 2020)
22. Face-api.js, JavaScript API for face detection and face recognition in the browser and nodejs with tensorflow.js, link: https://github.com/justadudewhohacks/face-api.js/. Accessed 23 June 2020
23. TensorFlow.js, JavaScript library for machine learning, link: https://www.tensorflow.org/js. Accessed 23 June 2020
24. Smilkov, D., et al.: Tensorflow.js: Machine learning for the web and beyond. arXiv preprint arXiv:1901.05350 (2019)
25. Tiny YOLO v2 object detection with tensorflow.js, Link: https://github.com/justadudewhohacks/tfjs-tiny-yolov2. Accessed 23 June 2020
26. Zhang, K., Zhang, Z., Li, Z., Qiao, Y.: Joint face detection and alignment using multitask cascaded convolutional networks. IEEE Sig. Process. Lett. **23**(10), 1499–1503 (2016)
27. Dlib C ++ Library, link: http://dlib.net/. Accessed 23 June 2020
28. Realtime Face Recognition in the Browser, link: https://morioh.com/p/ddbc538212df. Accessed 23 June 2020
29. Ding, H.S., Zhou, K., Chellappa, R.: FaceNet2ExpNet: regularizing a deep face recognition net for expression recognition. In: 2017 12th IEEE International Conference on Automatic Face & Gesture Recognition (FG 2017), Washington, DC, pp. 118–126 (2017). https://doi.org/10.1109/fg.2017.23
30. Russell, J.: A circumplex model of affect. J. Pers. Soc. Psychol. **39**(6), 1161–1178 (1980). https://doi.org/10.1037/h0077714
31. Mehrabian, A.: Pleasure-arousal-dominance: a general framework for describing and measuring individual differences in temperament. Curr. Psychol. **14**, 261–292 (1996)
32. Tavara, D.D.L.A.: Visualization of Affect in Faces Based on Context Appraisal. Doctoral Thesis, University of Balearic Islands, Spain (2012)
33. Hadjar, H., Meziane, A., Gherbi, R., Setitra, I., Aouaa, N.: WebVR based interactive visualization of open healthdata. In: International conference on Web Studies (WS.2 2018), October 3–5, 2018, Paris, France. ACM, New York, NY, USA, p. 8 (2018)
34. Reis, T.M.X., Bornschlegl, M.L.H.: Towards a reference model for artificial intelligence supporting big data analysis. In: Proceedings of the 2020 International Conference on Data Science (ICDATA 2020) (2020)
35. OECD, Artificial Intelligence in Society (2019)
36. Keras implementation of residual networks, link: https://gist.github.com/mjdietzx/0cb95922aac14d446a6530f87b3a04ce. Accessed 23 June 2020

Machine Learning in Healthcare: Breast Cancer and Diabetes Cases

Abbas Cheddad(✉)

Department of Computer Science, Blekinge Institute of Technology, 371 79 Karlskrona, Sweden
abbas.cheddad@bth.se

Abstract. This paper provides insights into a workflow of different applications of machine learning coupled with image analysis in the healthcare sector which we have undertaken. As case studies, we use personalized breast cancer screenings and diabetes research (i.e., *Beta-cell* mass quantification in mice and diabetic retinopathy analysis). Our tools play a pivotal role in evidence-based process for personalized medicine and/or in monitoring the progression of diabetes as a chronic disease to help for better understanding of its development and the way to combat it. Although this multidisciplinary collaboration provides only succinct description of these research nodes, relevant references are furnished for further details.

Keywords: Medical image analysis · Applied machine learning · Breast cancer · Diabetes

1 Introduction

The computer science has a long history of serving other disciplines among which is the medical field. This interaction manifests itself in the form of secure transmission of medical data [1], bioinformatics (i.e., sequencing and genome analysis), biomedical imaging, etc. The latter is a field that involves creating a visual representation of the examined specimen/body that can be used for medical diagnoses and clinical analyses. Biomedical imaging involves the use of various technologies such as X-Rays, CT- scans, magnetism (MRI), ultrasound, mammography, light (endoscopy, OCT), optical projection tomography (OPT) or radioactive pharmaceuticals (nuclear medicine: SPECT, PET), etc.

All these medical technologies output digital visual representations in the form of images or a stack of images. In order to fathom the complex characteristics of these visualizations, deep/machine learning is usually adopted. Deep learning (DL) is a widely discussed topic in computer vision. It is a subset of machine learning (ML) that mimics the functionality of the human brain, by having different neurons being activated by certain events. The most common usage for this is image classification or image-based non-linear regression. These are useful within various fields, especially in the medical field, where it can for example assist doctors in identifying various diseases, or in predicting age of people lacking proper identification or, for some reasons, age was not disclosed and recorded in the registry.

T. Reis et al. (Eds.): AVI-BDA 2020/ITAVIS 2020, LNCS 12585, pp. 125–135, 2021.
https://doi.org/10.1007/978-3-030-68007-7_8

In this paper, we describe previous multidisciplinary projects which signify systematic use of algorithms and tools from the mathematical, statistical, data, and computer sciences towards solving/understanding particular healthcare issues. As shown in the abstract, the workflow shall be illustrated through two case studies. For breast cancer, on one hand, new biomarkers apart from breast mammographic density and molecular profiles are developed, and on the other hand, machine learning algorithms are deployed to mimic a common commercial tool of volumetric breast density estimation on full field digital mammograms (FFDM) which such a tool is unable to process. For diabetes, we show how shallow machine learning algorithms are capable of removing artefacts from the output data of the OPT scanner. Such enhancements enabled us to enormously increase the precision of quantification of Beta-cell mass in the pancreases of healthy and diabetes mice. The software we developed is provided for free and is used by several research centres around the globe. Additionally, diabetic retinopathy analysis using deep learning is also highlighted.

1.1 Image Processing

Imaging science plays a crucial role in a wide spectrum of science fields ranging from remote sensing and automated surveillance to medical and biological fields. X-rays, positron emission tomography (PET) [2] and magnetic resonance imaging (MRI) [3] are just few examples of how imaging technology has propelled medical science into the next level, see Fig. 1.

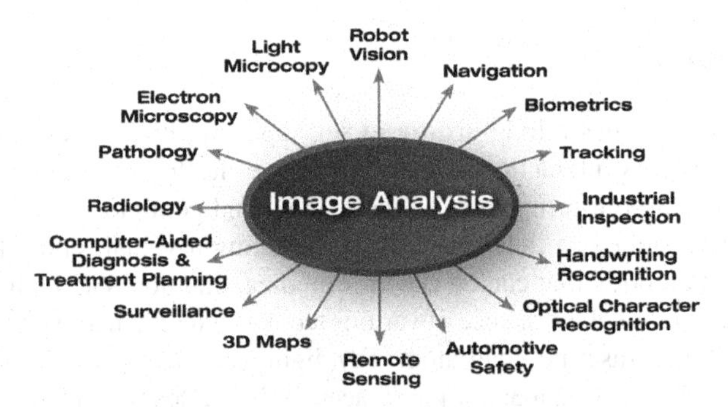

Fig. 1. Image analysis at a macro-scale.

1.2 Machine Learning (ML)

In simple words, a computer program that learns from previous experience/data to optimize its performance to achieve certain task describes the process of machine learning. It is seen as a subset of artificial intelligence (AI). From the training point of view, supervised and unsupervised learning can be viewed as two facets of the same machine learning field. From the algorithmic complexity, such field is divided into shallow learning and deep learning. An in-depth insight about the topic is warranted in [4].

2 Machine Learning Applications

2.1 ML in Breast Cancer Research

A digital mammogram is a normal mechanism to be examined to detect breast cancer, either during the screening time or as part of a clinical work up procedure. There has been intensive research into the features/information contained in a mammogram w.r.t its value in assisting the prediction of breast cancer risk. Breast tissue density is reflected in the amount of fibroglandular tissue which exists in the breast. It appears in mammograms as bright regions as compared to its surrounding regions (i.e., the fatty tissue). The proportion of the dense tissue to the total breast area is formally known as percent density (PD) and has been shown to be a strong determinant of breast cancer risk [5, 6], independently of other established risk factors.

Mimicking Volpara. The PD (area density) as a risk factor for breast cancer has been traditionally measured from mammograms (screened film or FFDM images) using a semi-automatic tool called Cumulus [7]. A decade ago, a software that stems from a PhD thesis, called *Volpara*™, was proposed [8] which models the breast as 3D structure from mammograms. It is an FDA cleared algorithm for measuring volumetric density on both 2D medio-lateral oblique (MLO) and 2D cranio-caudal (CC) raw FFDM digital mammograms. By design, Volpara is unable to work on processed FFDM or on digitised film mammogram images. That is, its algorithm assumes that pixel values are proportional to exposure, which is not the case for processed images since the pixel values are non-linearly transformed to enhance the contrast [9]. As it is the routine at hospitals to discard raw FFDM images and store only their processed version, we provided our approach in [10] for volumetric density measurement which is based on mimicking Volpara. The approach is termed CASAM-Vol[1], which is obtained as a weighted combination of statistical and morphological features (measured in processed images) and acquisition related tags, with weights obtained by training a random forests, an ensemble learning nonparametric statistical method for classification and regression developed by Breiman [11], to predict log Volpara measurements (from raw images). We are providing the software for free, see Fig. 2, though Fig. 2(b) option has currently certain limitations.

- The supported type is the processed FFDM images (a.k.a., For Presentation).
- The supported ViewPosition tags are MLO and CC views.
- The current supported machines and models are as depicted in Fig. 3.
- The following acquisition parameters must be encoded into the header file of the FFDM images in order for the function "Volumteric PD" to work:

KVP, ExposureTime, XrayTubeCurrent, Exposure, ExposureInuAs, BodyPartThickness, CompressionForce, AnodeTargetMaterial, RelativeXrayExposure, OrganDose, FilterMaterial.

Risk Prediction. As shown above, we developed two algorithms for processed images, an automated area-based approach (CASAM-Area) and a volumetric-based approach

[1] CASAM is an acronym for Computer Aided Statistical Assessment of Mammograms.

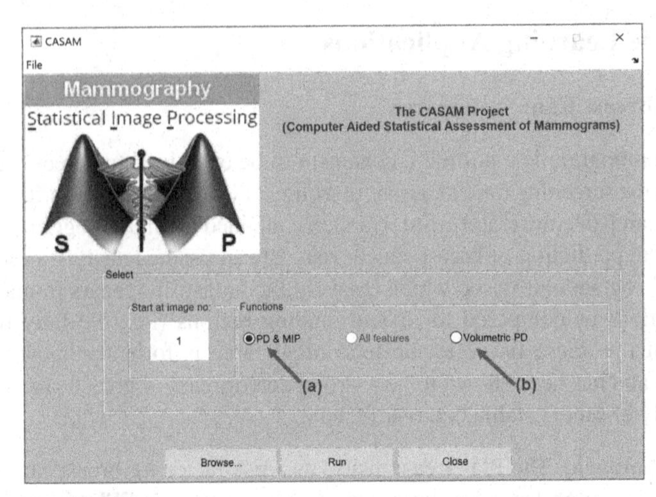

Fig. 2. Mammography Statistical Image Processing software's main window. (a) calculates area percent density (CASAM-Area) and mean intensity of the pectoral muscle, (b) calculates the volumetric density from FFDM MLO and CC processed views generated by specific manufacturers' models.

Machine code	Manufacturer	Manufacturer model name	Station name
0	GE MEDICAL SYSTEMS	Senographe Essential VERSION ADS_53.40	GEMAM-KLN1
1	GE MEDICAL SYSTEMS	Senographe Essential VERSION ADS_53.40	GEMAM-SCR2
2	GE MEDICAL SYSTEMS	Senographe Essential VERSION ADS_53.40	HBGMG03
3	GE MEDICAL SYSTEMS	Senographe Essential VERSION ADS_53.10.10	HBGMG03
4	GE MEDICAL SYSTEMS	Senographe Essential VERSION ADS_53.40	LKAMG01
5	GE MEDICAL SYSTEMS	Senograph DS VERSION ADS_53.40	SCR1
6	Sectra Imtec AB	L30	BDCHK1
7	Sectra Imtec AB	L30	SECTRA_MDM_1
8	Sectra Imtec AB	MDM 1.5	BDCHK2
9	Sectra Imtec AB	MDM 1.5	BDCHK3
10	Philips Digital Mammography Sweden AB	L30	BDCHK1
11	Philips Digital Mammography Sweden AB	L30	BDCHK2
12	Philips Digital Mammography Sweden AB	L30	BDCHK3
13	Philips Digital Mammography Sweden AB	L30	BDCHK4
14	Philips Digital Mammography Sweden AB	L30	SECTRA_MDM_1

Fig. 3. CASAM-vol current supported models.

(CASAM-Vol). Subsequently, we contrast the three methods, CASAM-Area, CASAM-Vol and Volpara directly and in terms of association with breast cancer risk by fitting logistic regression models and a known genetic variant for mammographic density and breast cancer, *rs10995190* in the gene *ZNF365* (coded 0/1/2, treated as continuous variable) by fitting linear regression models. Associations with breast cancer risk were evaluated using images from 47 breast cancer cases and 1011 control subjects. The genetic association analysis was based on 1011 control subjects.

All three measures of mammographic density were associated with breast cancer risk and *rs10995190*, more into this study can be found in [10]. In a related work, unlike common practice of discarding the pectoral muscle when computationally examining mammograms, we rather opt to explore it to test its association with breast cancer. Surprisingly, we found that such association does exist even after adjusting the model for common covariant (e.g., age, BMI) and percent density; to explore more, we refer the reader to our publication in [12, 13]. We also explored additional image-based features, namely, tissue stiffness, in conjunction with interval and screen-detected breast cancer [14]. The general workflow of our framework w.r.t mammography for risk assessment of breast cancer is illustrated in Fig. 4.

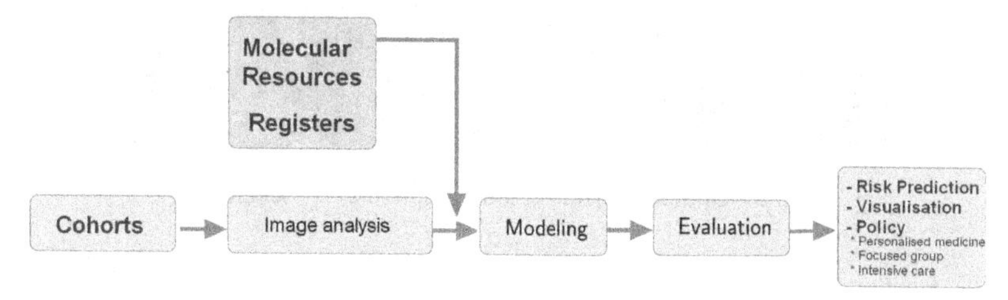

Fig. 4. A workflow to illustrate the process from data and modelling to evaluation.

2.2 ML in Diabetes Research

As we speak, there is no available total remedy for the chronic disease; diabetes. Research into this area has intensified over the last decade to find solutions to combat the disease.

OPT Scan Optimization. It is in this context that an EU's 7th Framework Programme named VIBRANT (In Vivo Imaging of Beta-cell Receptors by Applied Nano Technology) was conceived. The project aims to develop new non-invasive methods for biomedical imaging of the pancreas and involves a number of laboratories across Europe, see VIBRANT's Project Final Report [15]. Our part of the project involved exploiting new bioimaging technology, in combination with classical molecular genetics, in the hope to better understand the underlying mechanisms of pancreatic formation and development of diabetes. In this case, we used OPT technology to image the insulin producing cells of the pancreas (the B-cells) and their distribution to examine how this is affected during the development of diabetes in pancreases extracted from diabetes-prone mice. The OPT scanner is shown in Fig. 5.

Specimen Automatic Centring. Ideally, specimen must be mounted so that they land on what is called the optical axis of rotation (OAR) to ensure that reconstruction of images is done properly as images are captured through the 360° rotation. The blurring effect that results from manual mounting increases as the amount of OAR misalignment increases. An approach to improving OPT is therefore to introduce an efficient and automatic way to position specimens at the OAR (see Fig. 6). To this end, we developed a method called Centre of Mass based Axis Rotation (COM-AR), which captures and adjusts alignment

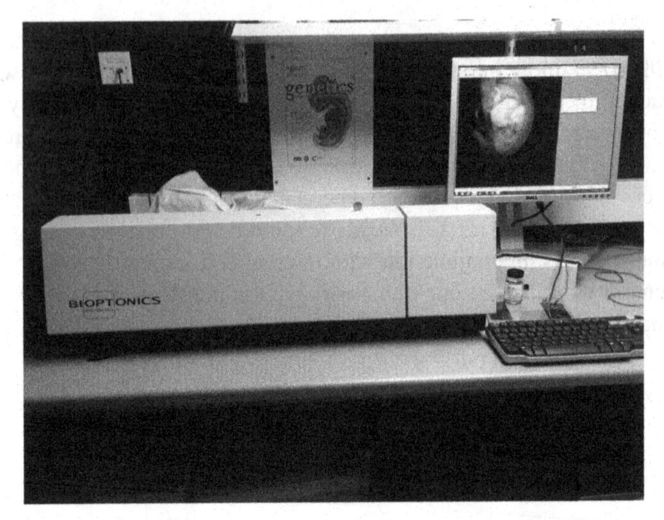

Fig. 5. Optical projection tomography (OPT) scanner.

errors and calculates the required displacements in the reconstructed 3D images using specialised algorithms. The algorithm benefits from the expectation–maximization (EM) algorithm.

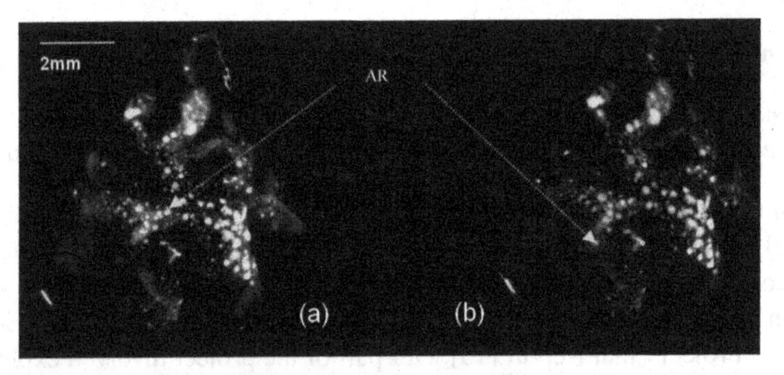

Fig. 6. Centring a specimen at the OAR, shown is a tomographic slice after reconstruction. (a) using COM-AR and (b) manually centred.

Artefacts Removal. We have also addressed a number of other related issues to enhance the overall performance of OPT [16]. For instance, if well calibrated, COM-AR automatically corrects for the (X, Z) alignment offset with respect to the 3D world coordinates. However, this does not address shifts along the Y coordinate, best known as the post-alignment in the reconstruction process. We have therefore developed an algorithmic approach based on Fourier transforms and linear regression to fix this issue, the effect of which can be seen in Fig. 7.

The software package is also provided for free and is used in several research centre worldwide, the algorithms underlying it are described in [16]. An example window of the software is shown in Fig. 8.

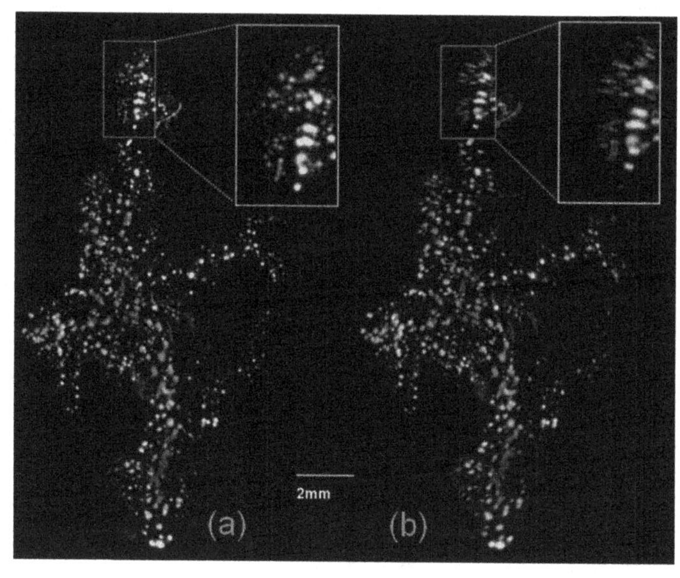

Fig. 7. Volume rendering of a specimen (pancreas labelled for islet *B-cell* insulin) using the proposed approach (a) and the variance-based approach -the OPT commercial software package- (b).

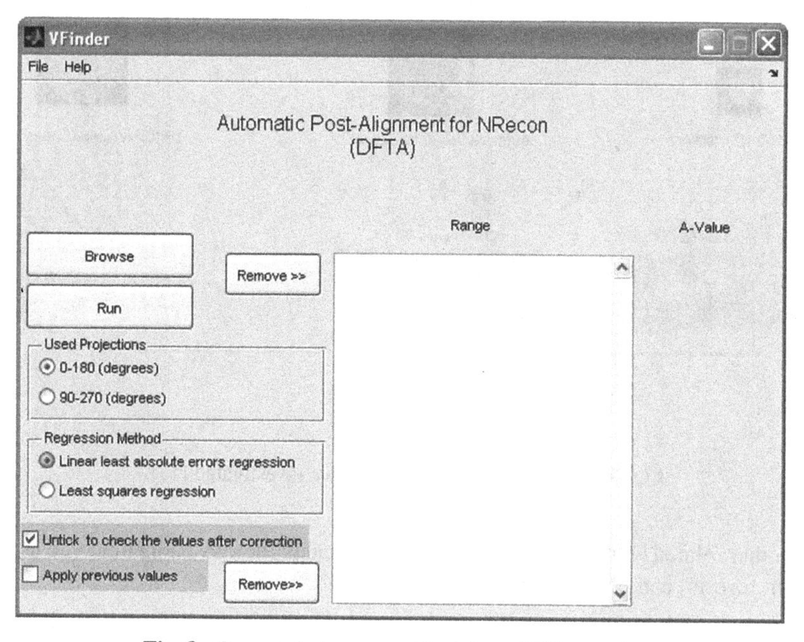

Fig. 8. Our artefacts removal tool from OPT scan data.

Diabetic Retinopathy. Diabetic retinopathy is the regarded as the most common cause of new cases of blindness in people of working age. As such, early diagnosis is the key to slowing down the progression of the disease, thus hopefully preventing blindness. To this end, we divided the fundus image into three different segments, namely, the optic disc, the blood vessels, and the other regions (regions other than blood vessels and optic disk). These regions are then contrasted against the performance of original fundus images. The convolutional neural network as well as transfer deep learning with the state-of-the-art pre-trained models (i.e., AlexNet, GoogleNet, Resnet50, VGG19) were utilized. The results show that the other regions' segment reveals more predictive power than the original fundus image especially when using AlexNet/Resnet50, see Fig. 9 for a generic framework of the experiment (binary classification malignant/non-malignant (benign or healthy)). This could be attributed probably to the fact that complication of this serious metabolic disease is often characterized by the anomaly of hard exudate/secretion substances seen in fundus images.

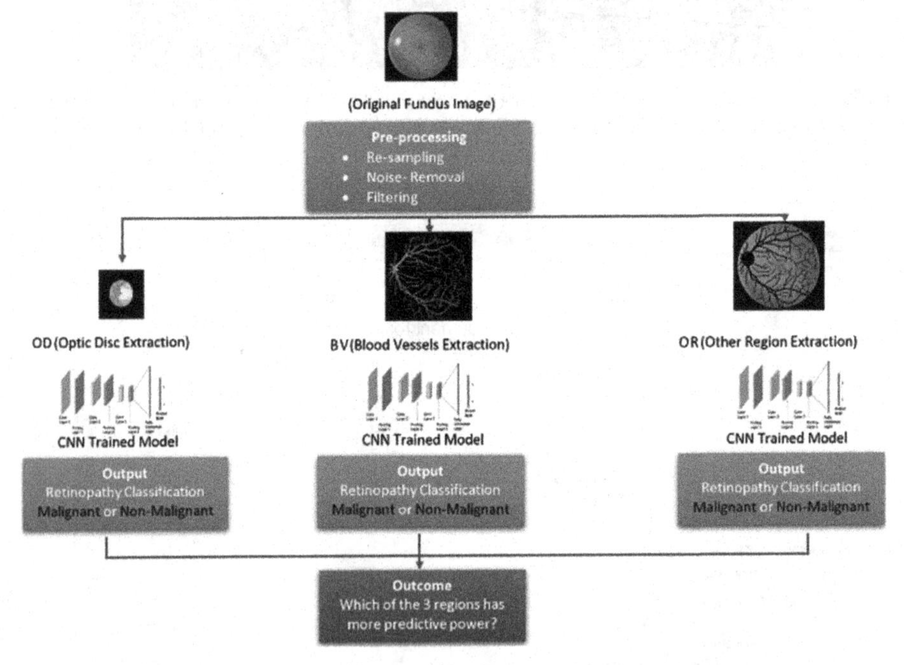

Fig. 9. The three different regions we investigated [17].

Another related work on discrimination of corneal pathology using machine learning (random forests) can be found in [18].

3 Other Potential Areas

There are some other works in which we utilized machine learning. For example, we devised a new way to fuse multi-exposure projections using an algorithm that includes

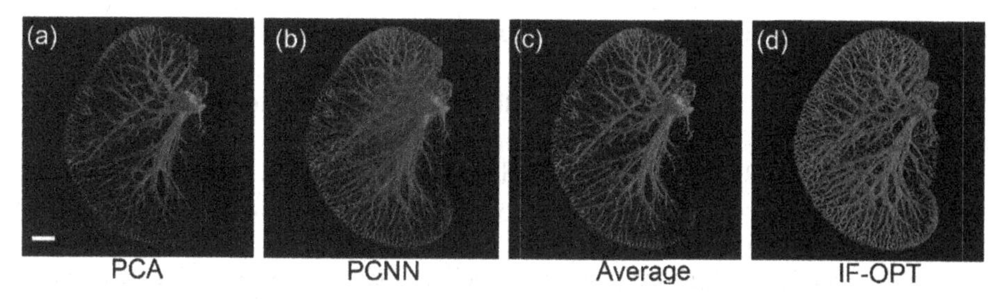

Fig. 10. Biomedical image (i.e., liver of an adult mouse) fusion using different techniques.

principal component analysis (PCA) [19]. The image fusion technique is termed IF-OPT; three exposures were acquired in the following order:

- Low (I0): signal in high intensity areas never become saturated,
- Medium (I1): normal single exposure time setting, and
- High (I2): weakest specific signal clearly visible

The obtained PCA weights for each channel are as follows: 0.29, 0.57, 0.14, for the I0, I1, I2, respectively. The projection images for each data set had been processed with one of the following fusion methods: PCA (principal component analysis), PCNN (pulse coupled neural network) fusing method, Average (arithmetic mean) fusing method, and IF-OPT (proposed) fusing method.

4 Summary

In a nutshell, herein, we summarize the different data analytics and visualization types which we reported in this paper. The summary is illustrated in Table 1.

Table 1. Characteristics of data and approaches reported in this work.

Section	Disease	Data type	ML type	Transparency	Result visualisation
Mimicking Volpara	Breast cancer	FFDM	Supervised learning (random forests)	Yes	Numerical values
Risk prediction	Breast cancer	Variable (age, BMI, parity, image statistics, cancer status, genetic variant)	Logistic and linear regressions	Yes	Numerical values
OPT scan optimization	Diabetes (mice)	2D/3D images	Linear regression/Iterative (EM)	Yes	3D volume visualisation software (e.g., Amira^{TM}, Imaris^{TM}, OptiJ -open source-)
Diabetic retinopathy	Diabetes (Eyes)	Colour fundus images	Deep learning	No	Categorical labels

5 Validation of the AI2VIS4BigData Reference Model

This sub-section links the above research directions (use cases) to the reference model constructed in Reis et al. [20]. The model AI2VIS4BigData is a refined and extended version of the IVIS4BigData reference model which introduces an approach to develop an up-to-date reference model for supporting advanced visual visualisation for Big Data analysis, thus attempting to close the gap in research with regard to information visualization challenges of Big Data analysis as well as context awareness. Figure 11 maps the overall research orientation of this work to the different components of the model.

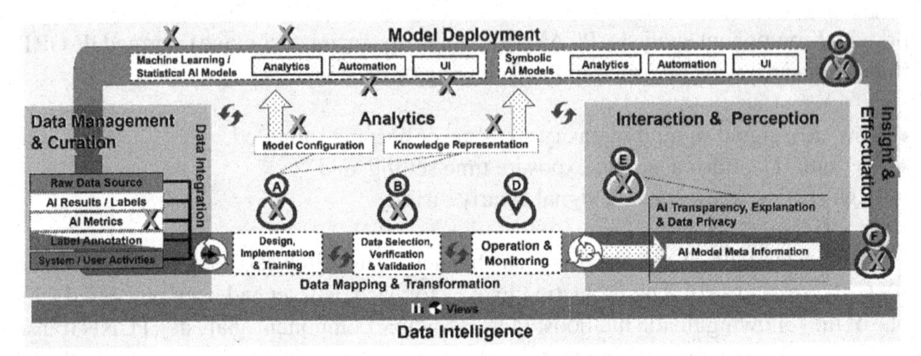

Fig. 11. Mapping the different components of the AI2VIS4BigData model to our research orientation (marked with X), where the items in alphabetic order indicate: Model Designer (A), Domain Expert (B), Model Deployment Engineer (C), Model Operator (D), Model Governance Officer (E) and Model End User (F).

6 Conclusion

This paper exemplifies some of our algorithms/tools that use image analysis coupled with machine learning that could be useful in the process of personalized medicine and of disease progression. Generic workflows are defined in controlled and real-world settings. To illustrate the potential of machine learning in healthcare, we use two cases pertaining to breast cancer and diabetes research. Importantly, we believe that image analysis and deep/machine learning will continue to leverage not only the cancer fighting field but also other disease domains. Finally, we should emphasize that with big data (large sample cohorts) and high-throughput technologies, both image-based and biomarker-based discoveries will manifest a flourishing era.

References

1. Cheddad, A.: "Steganoflage: A New Image Steganography Algorithm", PhD Thesis, Intelligent Systems Research Centre, University of Ulster, UK, September 2009
2. Bailey, D.L., Townsend, D.W., Valk, P.E., Maisey, M.N.: Positron Emission Tomography: Basic Sciences. Springer-Verlag (2005)

3. Berry, E., Bulpitt, A.J.: Fundamentals of MRI: An Interactive Learning Approach. Taylor & Francis, CRC (2008)
4. Bishop, C.: Pattern Recognition and Machine Learning. Springer (2011)
5. Boyd, N., Martin, L., Gunasekara, A., Melnichouk, O., Maudsley, G., et al.: Mammographic density and breast cancer risk: evaluation of a novel method of measuring breast tissue volumes. Cancer Epidemiol. Biomark. Prev. **18**, 1754–1762 (2009)
6. Spjuth, O., Karlsson, A., Clements, M., et al.: E-Science technologies in a workflow for personalized medicine using cancer screening as a case study. J. Am. Med. Inform. Assoc. **24**(5), 950–957 (2017)
7. Byng, J.W., Boyd, N.F., Fishell, E., Jong, R.A., Yaffe, M.J.: The quantitative analysis of mammographic densities. Phys. Med. Biol. **39**(10), 1629–1638 (1994)
8. Jeffreys, M., Harvey, J., Highnam, R.: Comparing a new volumetric breast density method (volpara^{TM}) to cumulus. In: Martí, J., Oliver, A., Freixenet, J., Martí, R. (eds.) IWDM 2010. LNCS, vol. 6136, pp. 408–413. Springer, Heidelberg (2010). https://doi.org/10.1007/978-3-642-13666-5_55
9. van Engeland, S., Snoeren, P.R., Huisman, H., Boetes, C., Karssemeijer, N.: Volumetric breast density estimation from full-field digital mammograms. IEEE Trans. Med. Imaging **25**, 273–282 (2006)
10. Cheddad, A., Czene, K., Eriksson, M., et al.: Area and volumetric density estimation in processed full-field digital mammograms for risk assessment of breast cancer. PLoS ONE **9**(10), 1–10 (2014)
11. Breiman, L.: Random forests. Mach. Learn. **45**, 5–32 (2001)
12. Cheddad, A., Czene, K., Hall, P., Humphreys, K.: Pectoral muscle attenuation as a marker for breast cancer risk in full field digital mammography. Cancer Epidemiol. Biomark. **24**(6), 985–991 (2015)
13. Cheddad, A., Czene, K., Shepherd, J., Li, J., Hall, P., Humphreys, K.: Enhancement of mammographic density measures in breast cancer risk prediction. Cancer Epidemiol. Biomark. Prevent. **23**(7), 1314–1323 (2014)
14. Strand, F., Humphreys, K., Cheddad, A., et al.: Novel mammographic image features differentiate between interval and screen-detected breast cancer: a case-case study. Breast Cancer Res. **18**(1), 100 (2016)
15. Project Final Report [Online]. http://cordis.europa.eu/docs/results/228933/final1-vibrant-executive-summary-final-v2.pdf. Accessed 22 Mar 2020
16. Cheddad, A., Svensson, C., Sharpe, J., et al.: Image processing assisted algorithms for optical projection tomography. IEEE Trans. Med. Imaging **31**(1), 1–15 (2012). PMID: 21768046
17. Qian, W., Cheddad A.: Segmentation-based deep learning fundus image analysis. In: The Proceedings of the 9th International Conference on Image Processing Theory, Tools and Applications IPTA 2019. November 6–9, Istanbul, Turkey (2019)
18. Bustamante, A.A., Cheddad, A., Rodriguez-Garcia A.: Digital Image Processing and Development of Machine Learning Models for the Discrimination of Corneal Pathology: An Experimental Model". Presented at the American Academy of Ophthalmology's annual meeting (AAO 2019), San Francisco, October 12–15
19. Cheddad, A., Nord, C., Hörnblad, A., et al.: Improving signal detection in emission optical projection tomography via single source multi-exposure image fusion. Opt. Express **21**(14), 16584–16604 (2013). PMID: 23938510
20. Reis, T., Bornschlegl, M.X., Hemmje, M.L.: Towards a reference model for artificial intelligence supporting big data analysis. In: Proceedings of the 2020 International Conference on Data Science (ICDATA 2020) (2020)

AI2VIS4BigData: Qualitative Evaluation of an AI-Based Big Data Analysis and Visualization Reference Model

Thoralf Reis(✉), Marco X. Bornschlegl, and Matthias L. Hemmje

Faculty of Mathematics and Computer Science, University of Hagen, 58097 Hagen, Germany
{thoralf.reis,marco-xaver.bornschlegl,matthias.hemmje}@fernuni-hagen.de

Abstract. AI2VIS4BigData is a reference model for Artificial Intelligence (AI) - based Big Data Analysis and Visualization that provides uniform terminology and logical entity-relationships to scientists and professionals working in this application domain. It thereby enables reutilization of concepts and software, prevents reinventing the wheel and facilitates collaboration scenarios. AI2VIS4BigData was systematically derived from two foundation reference models utilizing reasoned assumptions. These assumptions required subjective decisions which were not evaluated right away. This publication targets to change that through presenting two qualitative evaluation approaches that were conducted in the course of an official satellite workshop of an international conference. Selected scientific and industrial experts participated thereby in an expert round table workshop and a survey. The validation results confirm the reference model's practical applicability and legitimate the substantial majority of subjective decisions that were taken in the course of the reference model derivation. This publication concludes with outlining five research fields for future work that comprise the non-validated subjective decisions.

Keywords: AI2VIS4BigData · Evaluation · Reference model · AI · Big data analysis · Visualization

1 Introduction and Motivation

Big Data Analysis, Artificial Intelligence (AI) and Visualization are rather vague yet very popular terms in both scientific and industrial applications [1]. Big Data Analysis describes the exploitation of data for which Doug Laney's data management challenges [2] regarding the data's variety, volume or velocity apply [1]. AI is a collective term for concepts and methods that implement intelligent behavior in machinery and computers [3] which includes, inter alia, the method category of Machine Learning (ML) as well as symbolic learning [4]. Visualization in computer science is closely connected to the terms human-computer interaction, graphics, visual design, psychology, Information Visualization (IVIS) [5] as well as user interfaces. Employing Big Data Analysis, AI, and Visualization together

T. Reis et al. (Eds.): AVI-BDA 2020/ITAVIS 2020, LNCS 12585, pp. 136–162, 2021.
https://doi.org/10.1007/978-3-030-68007-7_9

as a combined application domain enables use cases that could not have been implemented otherwise since they support each other in a symbiotic manner. An example for use cases that benefit from a close connection [3] is the utilization of Big Data Analysis and Visualization by AI user stereotypes in order to investigate data for valuable information and insight that lead to proficient decisions in deriving a set of features, designing the AI model itself and enhancing it over time. Further examples are the utilization of AI to support visual Big Data Analysis through transforming, preparing, and developing the data in terms of its content (e.g. through clustering) [1] as well as the usage of Visualization to meet the growing demand for explainability [6] and transparency [7].

Although AI-based Big Data Analysis and Visualization are trending topics, there was no reference model for this combined application domain until Reis et al. introduced in 2020 the AI2VIS4BigData Reference Model [1]. This reference model's objectives are providing a uniform terminology and comprehension for the different data artifacts, involved user stereotypes as well as their logical relationships in order to ease collaboration and efficient reusability for existing implementations.

The derivation of the AI2VIS4BigData Reference Model in [1] included multiple assumptions and subjective decisions. This paper targets to evaluate these assumptions and decisions with the help of expert feedback and know-how. The evaluation was conducted with selected participants that are experts in the target application domains in an workshop called *"Road Mapping Infrastructures for Artificial Intelligence Supporting Advanced Visual Big Data Analysis"* [8]. The conducted evaluation activities consist of two approaches: An expert round table validation in the course of the workshop and a survey that was completed by every participant prior to the workshop. The workshop was held in June 2020 as an accepted satellite workshop of the International Conference on Advanced Visual Interfaces 2020 (AVI 2020)[1].

Within the remainder of this paper, the AI2VIS4BigData Reference Model, its foundation, elements and subjective decisions in reference model derivation are introduced (Sect. 2), followed by a comprehensive presentation of the conducted expert round table (Sect. 3) and workshop participant survey (Sect. 4). This paper concludes with an initial validation of the user study's result (Sect. 5) and a summary of its contributions as well as an outlook on future research (Sect. 6).

2 AI2VIS4BigData Reference Model

As introduced in [1], the AI2VIS4BigData Reference Model is based on two foundation reference models: the IVIS4BigData Reference Model [9], a reference model for advanced visual Big Data Analysis, and AIGO's AI System Lifecycle [4], a reference model that describes the different stages and activities for the application of AI models. The conducted approach to merge both reference mod-

[1] https://sites.google.com/unisa.it/avi2020/.

els is visualized in Fig. 1. It contains three further ingredients beyond the two reference models: the different types of AI models, the variety of different data manifestations as well as the different user stereotypes involved in AI-based Big Data Analysis and Visualization.

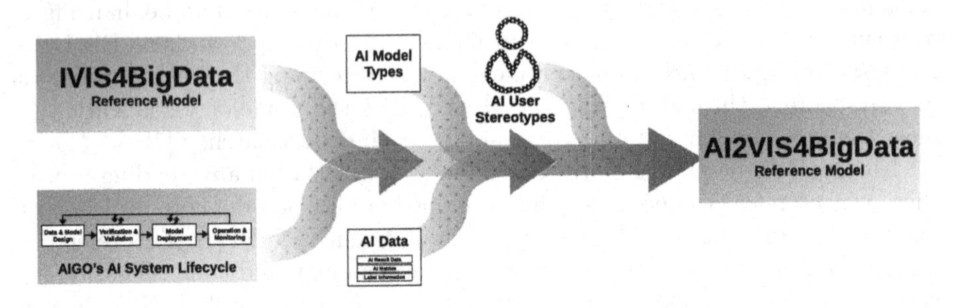

Fig. 1. Visualization of the reference model derivation approach conducted in [1]

The following sections introduce all of these foundation components: the Reference Model IVIS4BigData is introduced in Sect. 2.1, AIGO's AI System Lifecycle in Sect. 2.2, and the different AI model types, AI data as well as AI user stereotypes in Sect. 2.3. Section 2.4 finally presents the resulting AI2VIS4BigData Reference Model together with outlining the assumptions and subjective decisions in reference model design that are subject to the evaluation in this paper.

2.1 IVIS4BigData

In 2016, Bornschlegl et al. introduced in [5] the theoretical reference model Information Visualization for Big Data (IVIS4BigData). This reference model for advanced visual Big Data Analysis *"close[s] the gap in research with regard to Information Visualization challenges of Big Data Analysis as well as context awareness"* [5]. The reference model proved its practical applicability in multiple scientific and industrial use cases like, e.g., in the automotive and robotics application domains [9]. The IVIS4BigData Reference Model is visualized in Fig. 2.

IVIS4BigData contains references to four different, clearly distinguishable user stereotypes. The reason for this explicit display lies in the different organizational and technical knowledge levels of Big Data Analysis user stereotypes [5]: There exist domain experts such as data engineers, data analytics experts, data visualization specialists as well as management-level end user stereotypes [5]. According to Bornschlegl et al., Visualization of information, human interaction, and perception by these different Big Data user stereotypes are pivotal elements for Big Data Analysis [9].

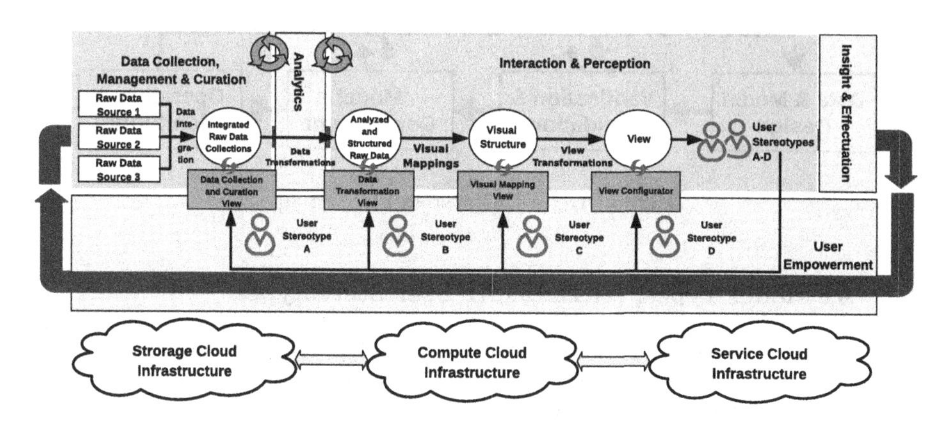

Fig. 2. IVIS4BigData reference model for advanced visual interfaces supporting big data analysis in virtual research environments [5]

The IVIS4BigData Reference Model covers the whole workflow of Big Data Analysis from heterogeneous raw data sources into highly aggregated and processed views that finally enable the different user stereotypes participating in the process to gain insight [5]. In this context, the reference model considers the for this purpose necessary advanced visual user interfaces as well as the underlying data storage, computation, and service infrastructure to be decisive [5].

2.2 AIGO'S AI System Lifecycle

The AI System Lifecycle was presented in 2019 by the AI Group of Experts at the OECD (AIGO) [4]. It covers 4 phases that are visualized in Fig. 3. These phases *"often take place in an iterative manner and are not necessarily sequential"* [4]. The first phase *"Data and Model Design"* marks the starting point of every AI application and consists of planning and designing of all, data collection, data processing as well as model building and interpretation [4]. The thereby generated models are subject to *"Verification and Validation"* [4] in phase two which is carried out by domain experts with sufficient knowledge and expertise to assess the designed AI models and select appropriate data [1]. The thereby developed and refined AI models then are forwarded into an execution environment like, e.g., a cloud system where they are applied in their target use case. This deployment step and the thereby required monitoring activities are summarized in the third phase *"Model Deployment"* [4]. Within the fourth phase *"Operation and Monitoring"*, the productive AI systemas *"recommendations and impacts"* [4] are reviewed and assessed to maintain and if necessary adapt the system [4]. The iterative nature of AI model design (going back and forth through the different phases in order to sharpen and enhance the AI model) is visualized through bidirectional arrows that connect the different phases.

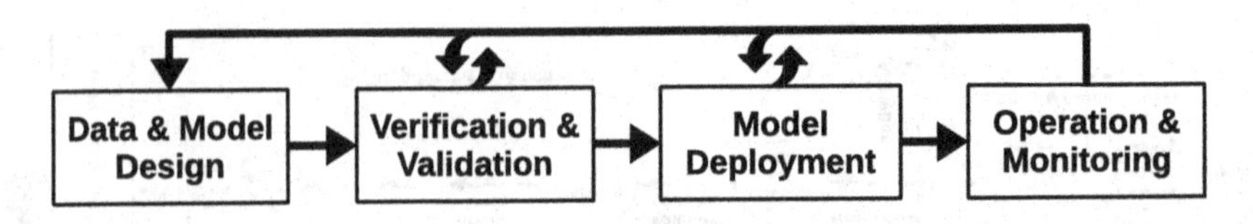

Fig. 3. AIGO's AI system lifecycle [4]

2.3 AI Model Types, AI Data, AI User Stereotypes

The different ingredients utilized to derive the AI2VIS4BigData Reference Model in [1] were comprehensively introduced in [8]. In order to make the evaluations in Sect. 3 and Sect. 4 more comprehensible, a brief explanation is provided as follows:

AI Model Types. There exist various ways to cluster and differentiate AI models from each other [8]. To maintain a reference model that is generalizable and easily understandable, this multi-dimensional problem is reduced to two dimensions for the AI2VIS4BigData Reference Model.

The first dimension are the different existing AI approaches that are summarized within a taxonomy provided by the Internet Policy Research Initiative at MIT (IPRI) [4]. There exist two approach categories for AI models: symbolic and statistical approaches [4]. Symbolic AI strongly depends on model designers with a deep domain knowledge since it requires formalizing intelligent behavior and decision paths within a knowledge base. This knowledge base is then provided to machines and computers which apply the rules and algorithms within the knowledge base on input data in order to deduce conclusions as output [4]. In contrast to these *"human-understandable decision structures"* [4] of symbolic AI, the second category of AI model approaches, statistical AI, utilizes data as foundation for intelligent behavior: statistical techniques and algorithms are implemented by machines and computers to identify patterns within the data and to induce trends from these patterns [4]. Increasing amounts of data in almost all application domains drives the popularity of statistical AI. Since ML *"algorithms are characterized by the ability to learn over time without being explicitly programmed"* [3], ML can be sorted as a subcategory of AI model's statistical approach.

The different application areas within AI-based Big Data Analysis and Visualization serve as second dimension. These application areas were derived in [1] through examination of the purpose AI application. The resulting three categories comprise analytics models, automation models, and User Interface (UI) models [1]. The latter two were motivated through the necessity of bridging the knowledge gap between involved users from different scientific backgrounds (data science as well as AI users) [1]. A task that can be fulfilled with automation and intelligent UI.

AI Data. The different types of AI data were derived in [1] through determining input and output data artifacts of each phase in AIGO's AI System Lifecycle. This derivation resulted in eight different AI data artifacts that are necessary to implement AI-based Big Data Analysis and Visualization. Three of these eight data artifacts can be summarized as being input data: raw data sources (as already introduced in Bornschlegl's IVIS4BigData Reference Model [9]) need to be integrated into the analysis system, system and user activity data are produced while using the system and are required input for the UI and automation AI models and label annotation data (user or system-generated labels that accompany the data) are required for statistical AI models. Two of these eight data artifacts cover AI output data: AI result and label data comprise the categorization, classification or decisions AI models produce based on their input while AI metrics data covers any form of information that indicates how a model performs in terms of resource consumption, time consumption or quality of its output. The remaining three data artifacts are model meta information (data that describes how the models were designed, which data was selected in order to assure compliance and data privacy in legally sensitive application domains), model configuration data (meta information to describe statistical AI models) as well as a knowledge representation (describes the rules, relationships, and algorithms that are modeling the decision structures of symbolic AI [4]).

AI User Stereotypes. The authors of [1] utilize the AI model maturing process to distinguish the different skills that are required in the application of AI-based Big Data Analysis and Visualization. They divide these skill sets into six different user stereotypes. These resulting six user stereotypes are visualized in Fig. 4 and comprise one user stereotype for every AIGO's AI System Lifecycle phase (model designer, domain expert, model deployment engineer, model operator [1]). Further user stereotypes are a model governance officer that assures transparency, explainability, legal compliance as well as data privacy and a model end user stereotype that summarizes the heterogeneous end user group of AI applications (the users who benefit from the AI model's result or that consume its output).

2.4 AI2VIS4BigData Reference Model and Subjective Decisions in Model Derivation

Following the introduced approach, the authors of [1] arrived with the AI2-VIS4BigData Reference Model at a framework, that connects the different existing types of AI models, the multiple manifestations of data involved in AI application as well as the various different AI user stereotypes with each other and links them to the core elements of the underlying reference models IVIS4BigData as well as AIGO's AI System Lifecycle. The resulting reference model not only reveals relationships and interconnections between the different elements but also illustrates chronological orders and logical sequences (e.g. flow of data and causal chains between the elements). AI2VIS4BigData offers applications in the

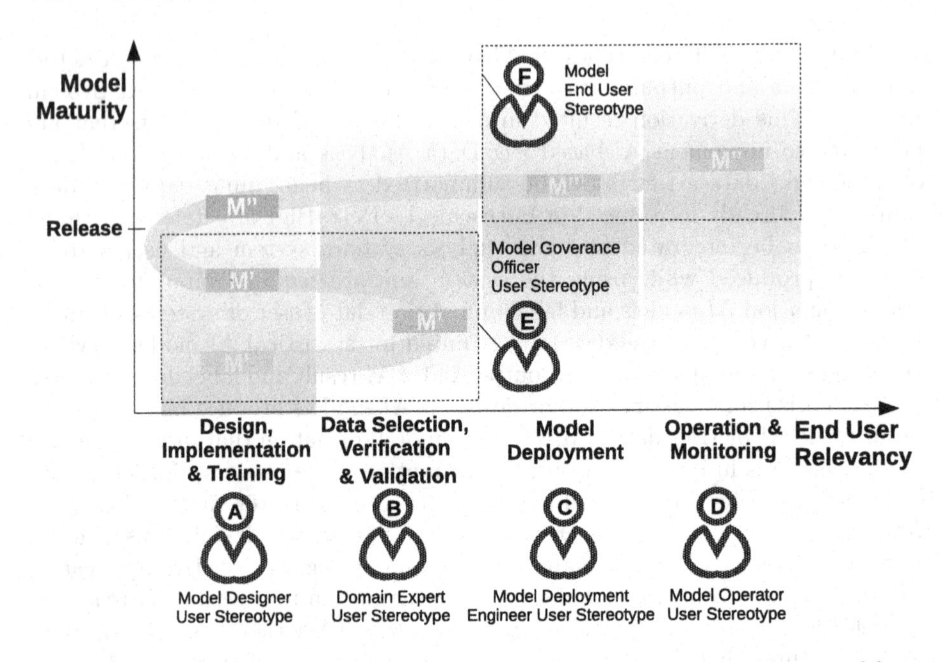

Fig. 4. AI User stereotypes alongside model lifecycle and maturing process [1]

areas of AI-based Big Data Analysis and Visualization the opportunity to reuse established concepts and software and targets to prevent developers from overseeing important aspects and relationships in early project stages (that can only be integrated with high effort in later projects stages). The resulting reference model is visualized in Fig. 5.

To evaluate the AI2VIS4BigData reference model, the methodology in [1] serves as a good starting point. It can be utilized to identify and outline the subjective decisions that were taken in the course of AI2VIS4BigData derivation. Therefore, the following decision groups have to be evaluated:

The first decision group comprises the mapping of the AIGO's AI System Lifecycle [4] phases to IVIS4BigData's processing steps: *"Data and Model Design"*, *"Verification and Validation"* as well as *"Operation and Monitoring"* were mapped to IVIS4BigData *"Analytics"* processing step [1]. Since there exists a matching IVIS4BigData processing step for the *"Model Deployment"* phase according to [1], a new deployment layer was introduced.

The second decision group covers the different decisions that were taken during derivation of the AI model types, AI data and AI user stereotypes (refer to Sect. 2.3): The decisions to cluster AI model types along side the conducted AI approach and the AI model application areas, to identify the different AI data artifacts as well as to differentiate exactly six AI user stereotypes (one per AI System Lifecycle phase and two universal user stereotypes).

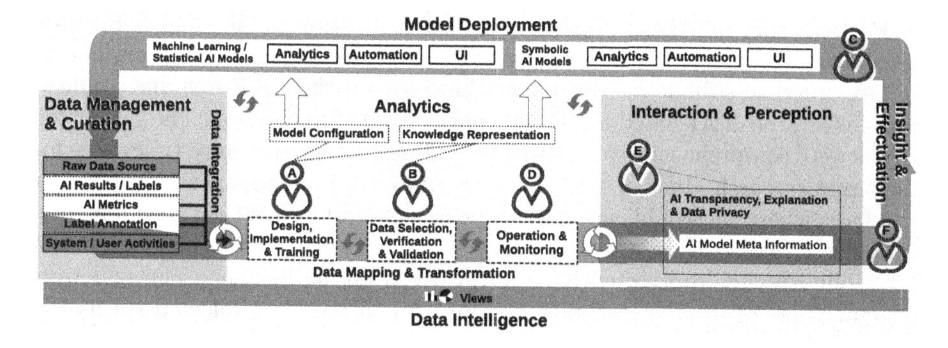

Fig. 5. AI2VIS4BigData: a reference model for artificial intelligence supporting big data analysis [1]

The third decision group contains the decisions that were taken during the mapping of the different artifacts from Sect. 2.3 to the elements of the by then derived reference model. These decisions comprise the mapping of most of the AI data artifacts to *"Data Management and Curation"* layer. Exceptions are the model configuration data and knowledge representation data (both *"Analytics"* layer) as well as the model meta information data (*"Interaction and Perception"* layer). Further decisions were the mapping of the AI user stereotypes to the different reference model elements: While the user stereotypes that were directly derived from AIGO's AI System Lifecycle phases were consequently mapped to the corresponding layer, model governance officer user stereotype was mapped to *"Interaction and Perception"* layer and model end user stereotype was mapped to *"Insight and Effectuation"* layer.

An evaluation of these three decision groups together with an evaluation of the reference model's elements results in an evaluated or falsified reference model. This evaluation is presented in the following two sections.

3 Expert Round Table

Due to the 2020 coronavirus pandemic, the workshop *"Road Mapping Infrastructures for Artificial Intelligence Supporting Advanced Visual Big Data Analysis"* [8] took place virtually. It had the objective to bring together researchers active in the areas of AI-based Big Data Analysis and Visualization to exchange knowledge about their current research activities and evaluate how the AI2VIS4BigData reference model can be applied to them in order to achieve a road map for both, research activities and potential collaborations. This roadmap can support the acceleration in research activities by means of transforming, enriching, and deploying AI models and algorithms as well as intelligent advanced visual user interfaces supporting creation, configuration, management, and usage of distributed Big Data Analysis.

Participating in the workshop was open to the public and interested researchers and practitioners were invited via a *"call for paper"*[2]. All applicants were required to submit a short paper that covered their research and applications in the area of AI-based Big Data Analysis and Visualization. The submitted papers were comprehensively reviewed regarding content-relevance (relevance for the target research areas of AI, Big Data Analysis, and Advanced Visual User Interfaces where each publication should cover at least two of the three domains) as well as formal criteria (e.g. language quality). The review was conducted in a single-blind review process with three reviewers per submission. The reviewers were members of an international program committee of 14 selected specialists from 9 different universities in six different European countries. The submissions were rated with three categories: positive (to be accepted), negative (to be rejected), and neutral. Only submissions that received a positive rating by the majority of its reviewers were accepted.

Overall, eight submissions were accepted by the program committee: one submission in the research field of metagenomics [10], four submissions that covered topics around health care and medical applications, one submission in the economical application domain of stock market analysis, one submission introducing visualization methods for AI and one submission that introduces AI2VIS4BigData reference model [8]. The eight workshop participants were affiliated with six different universities in five different European countries.

3.1 Method

The virtual workshop was implemented as a focus event (expert round table) [11] which was exclusively open to authors of accepted papers as well as the international program committee. The focus event was structured in three sessions. In the first session, the authors introduced their accepted research papers in 15-min voice-over-powerpoint presentations. The second session was composed of a presentation of the AI2VIS4BigData reference model followed by a comprehensive Q&A. The third session comprised the actual reference model validation.

The validation of the AI2VIS4BigData reference model was prepared in advance by the authors by filling an evaluation template based on their paper. The template consisted of five pages. In the first three pages, the authors were required to mark the AI models, AI data and AI user stereotypes that they rated to be relevant to their research. The fourth page of the template showed the complete AI2VIS4BigData reference model and the authors were required to tag the elements their research could be integrated into. The last page was empty and provided the authors with the possibility to creatively describe their research infrastructure methodology, pipeline, architecture or use case if AI2VIS4BigData would exist. Each author presented their own template within the workshop's third session before all workshop participants discussed the remarks and findings.

[2] https://easychair.org/cfp/AVI2020AIBigData.

3.2 Results

The presentation of the validation templates of every author during the expert round table workshop revealed that all of the described research within the accepted papers can be integrated into the AI2VIS4BigData reference model. Although most of the authors selected only a subset of the reference model's AI model types, AI data, and AI user stereotypes to be relevant for their study, all of the existing artifacts were selected by at least one participant. Beyond the mere validation of applicability of the reference model, four explicit findings were mentioned by the authors in the course of the workshop:

1. The reference model shall cover and emphasize the important aspect of data privacy which is not only because of the GDPR becoming more and more important.
2. The term "Label Information" is misleading. It shall describe the data artifact of a class or label that accompanies the features during AI model training and that is often determined through a human user conducting the so called "labeling". It can be mixed up with the actual result of the AI model application, the "AI Result Data".
3. The term "User Interactions" is misleading. It shall describe the data artifact that is generated during using and controlling the Big Data Analysis and AI system and is fed back for further applications (e.g. as input for an UI model). It can be mixed up with data from Raw Data Sources which can also originate from user interactions (e.g. Twitter usage data).
4. The Visualization aspect of the reference model is not significant and could be emphasized.

4 Workshop Participant Survey

To systematically evaluate every component of AI2VIS4BigData Reference Model and every decision in its design, all authors of accepted workshop papers were required to participate in a workshop participant survey. In order to prevent any bias through listening to the answers of other workshop participants, the authors were asked to fill out an online questionnaire[3] in advance to the workshop. Since *"survey results depend crucially on the questionnaire"* [12], the following subsection introduces the methodology and the resulting questionnaire.

4.1 Method

The online questionnaire was structured in 7 sections containing overall 56 questions. The majority of the questions were closed ones with a few open questions to *"add richness to survey results that is difficult, if not impossible, to achieve with closed questions"* [12]. Questions with rating scales used 5 points and thereby followed best practices [12].

[3] https://forms.gle/YZ3bmsuL1MX6pYJJ9.

The overall structure of the questionnaire was built to commence with general questions such as demographics or questions related to the research activities of the participants. The second section contained questions regarding the underlying IVIS4BigData Reference Model [9] as well as AIGO's AI System Lifecycle [4]. These questions were accompanied by a short textual and graphical introduction in case the participant was not familiar with them. The third section targeted to evaluate the AI2VIS4BigData design decisions and its elements. The last questionnaire section went beyond the reference model validation in order to prepare future work such as a reference implementation through asking the participants about insights regarding their perceived challenges as well as their utilized technologies.

4.2 Results

The results of the workshop participant survey are presented within this section. The survey was completed by all seven accepted authors of the workshop. These authors are scientists with research institutes in Italy (2), Germany (2), Ireland (1), Sweden (1) and the United Kingdom (1) with self-assessed expertise in AI (6), Big Data Analysis and visual analytics (3) and Visualization (2) with different domain specializations such as genetics, cardiology, and Natural Language Processing (NLP).

Demographics and Research Area and Activities. The survey participants hold degrees as M.Sc. (4), PhD (1), and full professors (2). They contributed to between 1 and 3 (4), 16 (1), 60 (1), or 240 publications (1). The research groups of the participants were either small with 1 to 5 members (4) or medium-sized with 5 to 10 members (3). The educational levels of these members comprise non-graduated and graduated students (28.6%), PhD students (100%), PhDs (85.7%), and professors (42,9%).

The participants describe their target industry sector to be healthcare (2), education (2), manufacturing, and natural resources (1), finance (1), and agriculture & environmental (1). The average participant spends 42.1% of his/her time with AI, 28.87% with Big Data Analysis, and 29.03% with Visualization. The time share of each participant is visualized in Fig. 6.

Asked whether seven different application scenarios combining AI, Big Data Analysis, and Visualization are relevant to their respective research activities, the participants answered on a 5-point scale from *"Strongly Agree"* to *"Strongly Disagree"* as displayed in Table 1. The result can be summarized as an approval of the practical relevance of the different application scenarios interconnecting AI, Big Data Analysis, and Visualization since every application scenario received a positive rating by the majority of the participants. The open question for further relevant application scenarios was answered with *"Emotional Monitoring"*, *"Robotics and Cyber Security"*, *"Multimodal Communication Sources"*, and *"Applying AI to improve interaction with visualization (e.g. anticipate user click)"*.

Table 1. Relevance assessment for application scenarios in the participant's research

Application scenario	Research relevance assessment				
	Strongly agree	Agree	Neutral	Disagree	Strongly disagree
Applying AI to ease Big Data exploration (e.g. to programmatically identify outliers)	1	5	1	0	0
Applying Visualization to ease Big Data exploration (e.g. to visually identify outliers)	2	4	1	0	0
Applying Big Data to design AI models (e.g. adjust weights of a neural network)	1	3	2	1	0
Applying Visualization to design AI models (e.g. visualize algorithm connections and information flow)	3	3	1	0	0
Applying AI and Big Data to ease Visualization and UI comprehension (e.g. through intelligent UI that explains and highlights useful tools)	3	3	0	1	0
Applying AI and Big Data to automate repetitive user or system activities (e.g. perform a normalization step that is always executed by the user in a certain setup automatically)	2	4	1	0	0
Applying AI to integrate different sources of Big Data (e.g. merging their different formats)	3	4	0	0	0

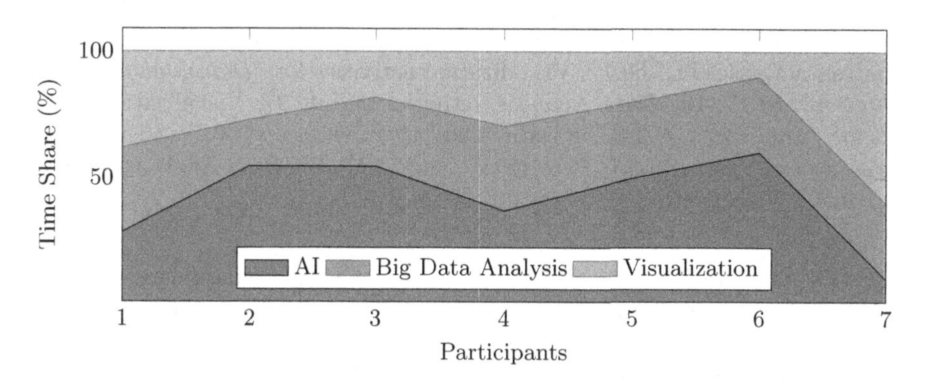

Fig. 6. Distribution of Time Spent for the AI, Big Data Analysis, and Visualization

IVIS4BigData. AI2VIS4BigData's foundation Reference Model IVIS4BigData was assessed through four closed questions that followed a brief description. The overall applicability of IVIS4BigData to the participants' research activities was agreed by 71.4%, declined by 0%, while 28.6% remained unsure. Asked whether they associate the four processing steps of IVIS4BigData with the research domain of AI, the participants answered as follows: 57,1% associated *"Data Management & Curation"* with AI, 85.7% associated *"Analytics"* with AI, 71.4% associated *"Interaction & Perception"* with AI, and 100% associated *"Data Intelligence"* with AI. The answers to the question whether they regularly conduct activities in these four IVIS4BigData processing steps are visualized in Fig. 7.

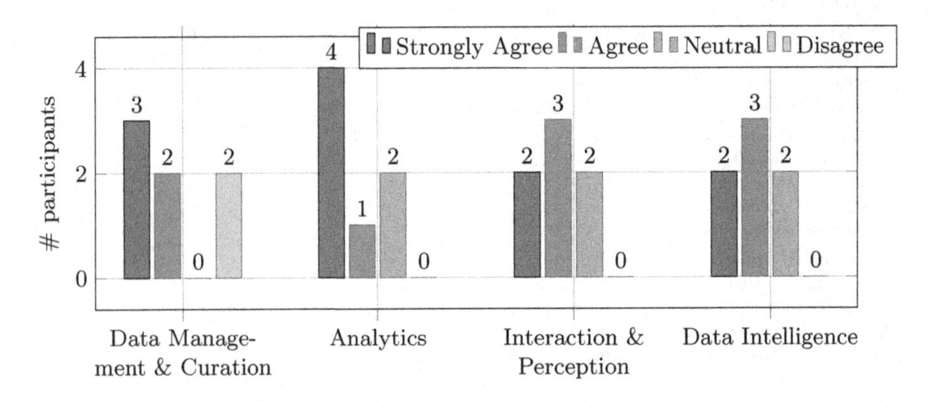

Fig. 7. Assessment of regularly conducted activities per IVIS4BigData processing step

The assessment of the time being spent for either Big Data Analysis or Visualization revealed very heterogeneous results yet averaged to 39.3% Big Data Analysis activities and 60.7% Visualization activities for *"Data Management & Curation"*, 57.1% Big Data Analysis activities and 42.9% Visualization activities for *"Analytics"*, 39.3% Big Data Analysis activities and 60.7% Visualization activities for *"Interaction & Perception"*, and 53.6% Big Data Analysis activities and 46.4% Visualization activities for *"Data Intelligence"*.

AIGO's AI Lifecycle. AI2VIS4BigData's second underlying reference model, AIGO's AI System Lifecycle, was approved to be applicable to the participants' research activities by 57.1% and rated to maybe be applicable by 42.9%. The participants associated the lifecycle phases with Big Data Analysis and Visualization as follows: *"Data & Model Design"* was associated by 42.8% with Visualization and by 100% with Big Data Analysis, *"Verification & Validation"* was associated by 42.8% with Visualization and by 100% with Big Data Analysis, *"Model Deployment"* was associated by 42.8% with Visualization and by 71.4% with Big Data Analysis, and *"Operation & Monitoring"* was associated by 71.4% with Visualization and by 57.1% with Big Data Analysis. The answers to the question whether they regularly conduct activities in these four lifecycle phases are visualized in Fig. 8.

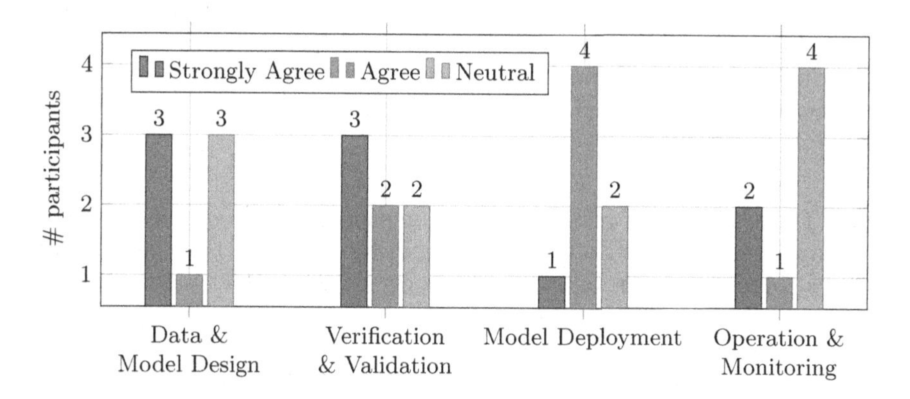

Fig. 8. Assessment of regularly conducted activities per AI system lifecycle phase

In order to evaluate the combination of IVIS4BigData Reference Model and AIGO's AI System Lifecycle, the participants were asked which IVIS4BigData processing steps and AI System Lifecycle phases they associate with each other. The result is visualized in Fig. 9.

AI Models. In order to evaluate whether the AI models that were utilized to derive the AI2VIS4BigData reference model are relevant to the practical research activities of the selected experts participating in the workshop, the questionnaire asked the participants how often they utilize the different AI approaches symbolic AI and ML or statistical AI in reality. Furthermore, the participants were asked to rate on a five point scale from *"Always"* to *"Never"* how frequently analytics

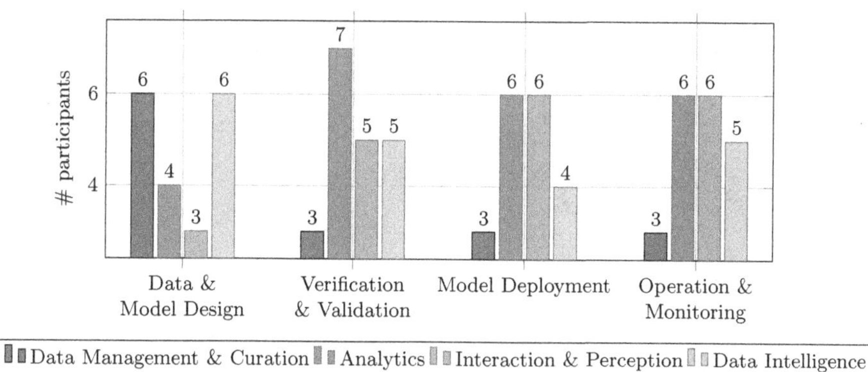

Fig. 9. Associations of IVIS4BigData processing step and AI system lifecycle phases

models (e.g. to preprocess data), UI models (e.g. to predict UI activities), and automation models (e.g. to automate repetitive tasks) are used in the course of their research activities. The answers to both questions are visualized in Fig. 10.

For the purpose of assessing whether the reference model is missing important AI model types, an open question asked the participants to name further ones. The participants namend the AI model types *"Predictive Models"*, *"AI models for signal processing"* as well as *"interactive AI models for Image classification and video classification"*.

Data. The evaluation of relevant data commenced with asking the participants for data content formats that are relevant in the course of their research. The feedback comprised unstructured text like, e.g., ASCII (71.4%), structured text like, e.g., XML (28.6%), video data (57.1%), audio data (28.6%), biometric data like, e.g., DNA sequences (57.1%), analog and digital signals like, e.g., sensor measurements (28.6%) and medical images or scans (14.3%). In order to assess the practical relevance of AI2VIS4BigData's data artifacts, the survey participants were asked multiple questions regarding the relevance of each data artifact in context of their daily research activities regarding Big Data Analysis, AI, and Visualization. The rating was conducted on a five point scale from *"Strongly Agree"* to *"Strongly Disagree"*. To make the result more comprehensible, this rating was translated in the course of questionnaire evaluation to a relevance score that was calculated as follows: The five point scale was translated to a value range from +2 to −2 and all values of the seven questionnaire feedback were summed up. The resulting qualitative evaluation of the data artifacts' practical relevance is visualized in Fig. 11.

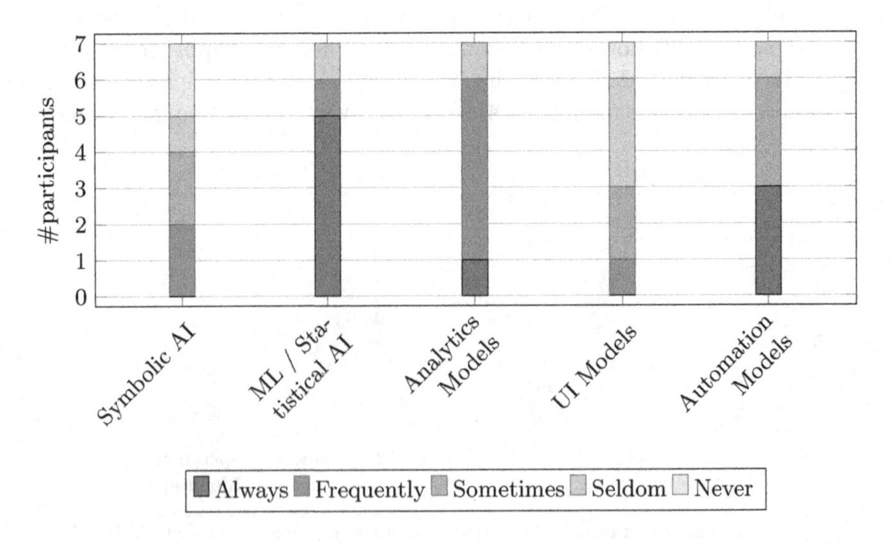

Fig. 10. Assessment of practical relevance of different AI model types

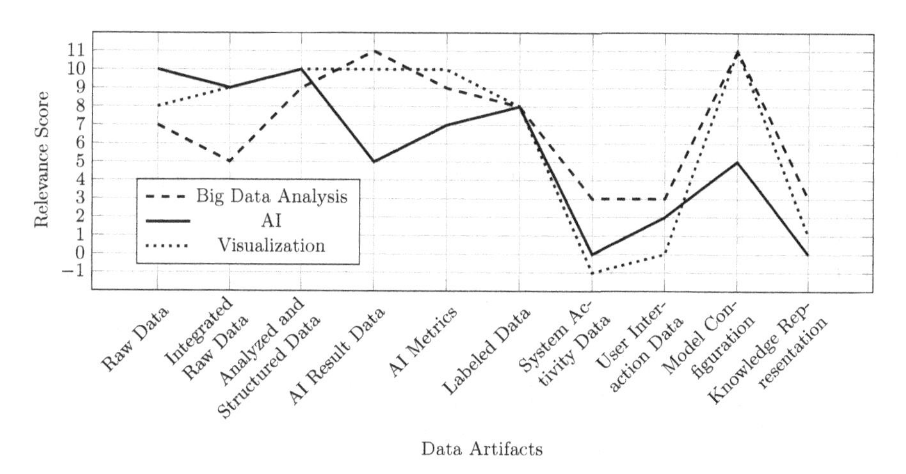

Fig. 11. Qualitative evaluation of the data artifacts' practical relevance

A further question targeted to evaluate which of the IVIS4BigData processing steps *"Data Management & Curation"*, *"Analytics"*, *"Interaction & Perception"*, and *"Data Intelligence"* the participants associate with the respective data artifacts. Every participant was allowed to assign a single data artifact to no, some or all processing steps. The resulting association votes are visualized in Fig. 12. The maximum number of votes per processing step and data artifact is seven (the number of survey participants) while a single data artifact could theoretically be associated with 28 association votes (four times seven).

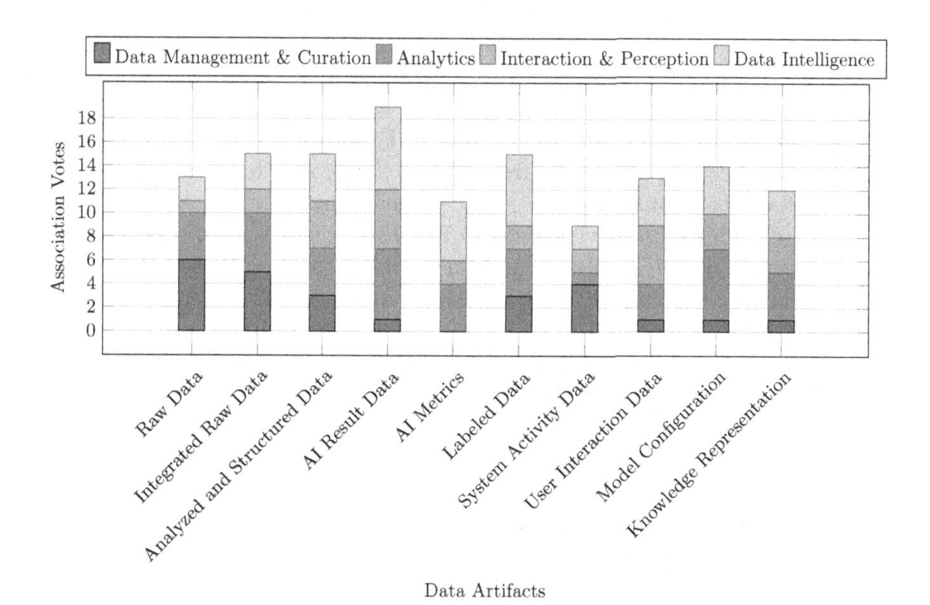

Fig. 12. Associations of IVIS4BigData Processing Step and Data Artifacts

User Stereotypes. To assess whether the six AI2VIS4BigData user stereotypes are complete and if they were associated with the right reference model elements, the questionnaire contained for this purpose overall seven questions structured into three categories: The first category targets to establish fundamental concepts like, e.g., the target audience. The second category covers the evaluation of the user stereotypes completeness. This is conducted through assessing the relevance and application domain association of all AI2VIS4BigData (AI) and IVIS4BigData user stereotypes (Big Data Analysis and Visualization) as well as through conducting a user stereotype mapping for all AI activities. The third category targets to evaluate the association of the identified user stereotypes within the reference model itself.

To learn more about the survey participants' development target audience, the questionnaire contained the question what educational background the users have that will interact with the outcome, system, or framework of their respective research activities. According to the survey feedback, the target audience consists of users with academical background (42.9%), users with technical background (28.6%), users of all skill-levels (14.3%) as well as *"naive"* users (14.3%). To find out whether the activities in the participants' research could be associated with clearly distinguishable user stereotypes, the participants were asked to provide feedback on a three point scale (*"Agree"*, *"Neutral"*, *"Disagree"*) whether they agree that there are these clearly distinguishable user stereotypes in all combinations of two of AI, Big Data Analysis, and Visualization. The existence of clearly distinguishable user stereotypes was approved by 71.4%, disapproved by none and neutrally assessed by 28.6% for Big Data Analysis and Visualization, was approved by 57.1%, disapproved by none and neutrally assessed by 42.9% for Big Data Analysis and AI, and was approved by 71.4%, disapproved by none and neutrally assessed by 28.6% for AI and Visualization.

In order to assess the legitimacy of the AI2VIS4BigData user stereotypes, the survey participants were provided with an complete list of all AI2VIS4BigData and IVIS4BigData user stereotypes and were asked whether these user stereotypes are relevant for their practical research. Following the approach presented in the Data subsection, the rating from *"Strongly Agree"* to *"Strongly Disagree"* was converted into a number from +2 to −2 and summed up to serve as a *"Relevance Score"*. This score is visualized in Fig. 13 and serves as an indicator for a user stereotypes' practical relevance. As a second step, the survey asked its participants whether they would associate the respective user stereotype with Big Data Analysis, AI, or Visualization. The total number of selections per application domain is also visualized in Fig. 13 as association score.

Another approach to identify, if there are any user stereotypes missing or if the defined ones are not clearly distinguishable from each other, is to assess whether the survey participants can unambiguously map the different activities that are conducted in the course of AI application to the six different AI user stereotypes. The result of this assessment is summarized in Table 2. It displays per AI activity the number of associations of the respective AI user stereotype (zero if not mentioned, seven associations as maximum per pair).

Table 2. Number of associations between AI user stereotypes to AI activities

AI activity	Associated AI user stereotypes					
	Model designer	Domain expert	Model deployment engineer	Model operator (MLOps)	Model governance officer	Model end user
Algorithm selection	3	3	3	0	1	2
Data selection	2	4	1	1	3	3
Data preprocessing	2	2	0	2	2	2
Algorithm parametrization	3	3	2	0	0	2
Knowledge and rule definition (Symbolic AI)	5	5	3	2	2	2
Workflow definition	3	2	3	1	1	1
Evaluation method selection	2	5	1	0	1	2
Evaluation method parametrization	3	2	2	0	0	1
Runtime environment configuration	2	1	4	1	0	2
Data labeling	2	3	0	2	2	1
Model training	4	1	1	2	1	1
Model testing	1	2	3	1	0	3
AI metrics assessment	4	4	1	1	0	1
Monitoring model execution	2	1	3	2	1	2
Monitoring model design	4	2	1	2	3	1
Releasing model	0	1	4	2	2	1
Deploying model	1	1	5	2	1	2
Applying model	1	2	3	2	0	2
Configuring model execution	2	2	3	2	0	1

The third category of user stereotype evaluation targets to assess the underlying mapping decisions of AI2VIS4BigData. For this purpose, two survey questions addressed the association of the six AI user stereotypes with AIGO's AI System Lifecycle phases (Fig. 14) and IVIS4BigData's processing steps (Fig. 15).

Challenges and Technologies. Relevant challenges in practical research that need to be addressed by AI2VIS4BigData Reference Model as well as technology preferences and choices of the survey participants are valuable insights that support specifying the theoretical concepts of the Reference Model into a architecture and enable proof-of-concept implementations. Consequently the survey contains questions for both categories.

The evaluation of challenges consisted of three questions. Two closed questions assessed the likeliness and the association AI, Big Data Analysis, and Visualization of nine challenges that were derived from state of the art. The result of these two questions is visualized in Fig. 16. It contains a *"Likeliness Score"* that transfers the five point rating scale from *"Extremely Likely"* to *"Extremely*

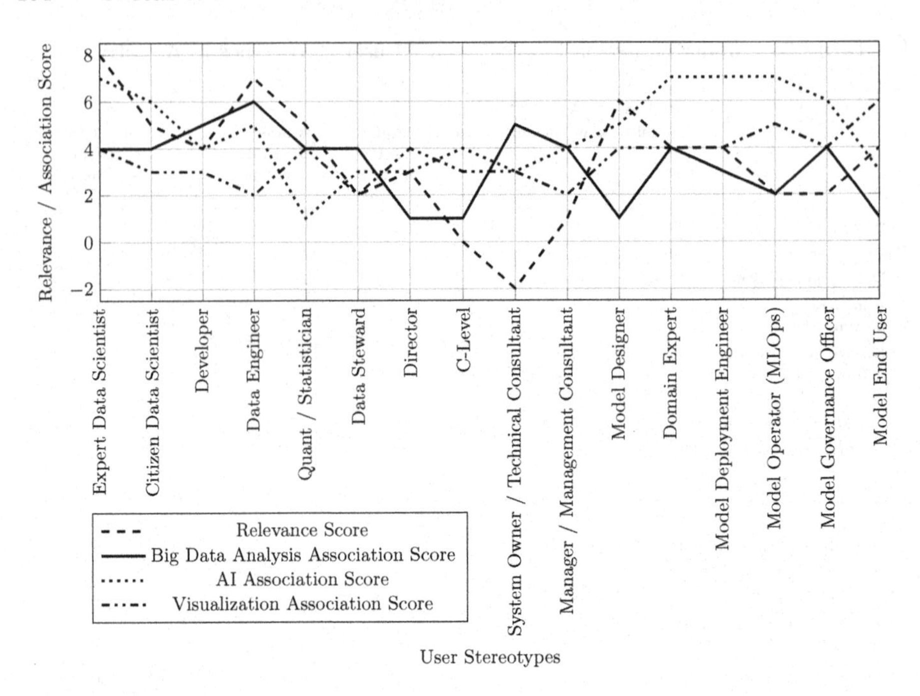

Fig. 13. User stereotype evaluation: practical relevance and domain association

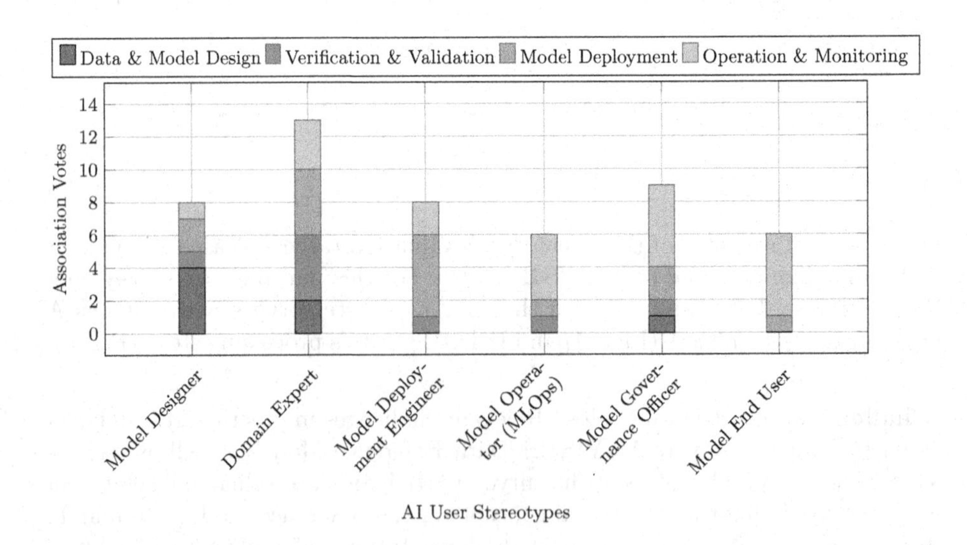

Fig. 14. Associations of AIGO's AI system lifecycle phases and AI user stereotypes

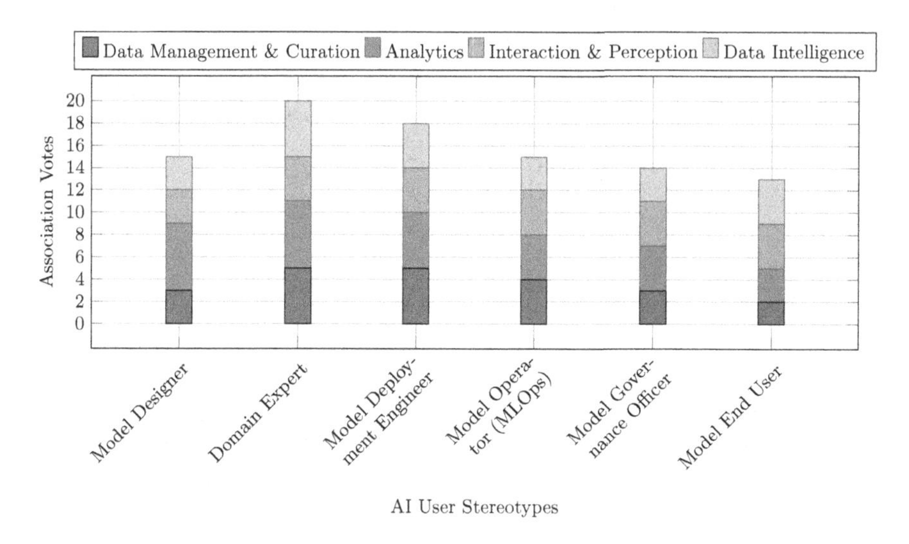

Fig. 15. Associations of IVIS4BigData processing step and AI user stereotypes

Unlikely" into numeric values from +2 to −1 and a *"Association Score"*, a concept and methodology that was already introduced in user stereotype subsection. The third question was an open one that asked the survey participants for further challenges that are relevant to their research activities. The feedback comprises *"lack of sufficient training data"*, *"data heterogeneity"*, and *"high dimensionality"*.

A prototype reference implementation of the AI2VIS4BigData Reference Model strongly depends on decisions regarding technologies such as programming languages and architectures. These decisions lead to pronounced capabilities and restrictions for various aspects like, e.g., performance or user-friendliness. Assessing the taken decisions of multiple experts in AI-based Big Data Analysis and Visualization can ease implementation design or at least focus the decision making for it. Consequently, the survey was utilized to ask the participants what type of platforms and software they utilize in their research activities. 57.1% of the participants answered to use solely open-source platforms and software while 42.9% used a combination of open-source as well as commercial platforms and software. All participants that utilized open-source platforms stated to use Google's Tensor Flow[4] while the participants used various different commercial platforms with Microsoft's Azure Machine Learning[5] being the most popular one (57.1%). Further mentioned commercial platforms were Mathworks

[4] https://www.tensorflow.org/.
[5] https://azure.microsoft.com/en-us/services/machine-learning/.

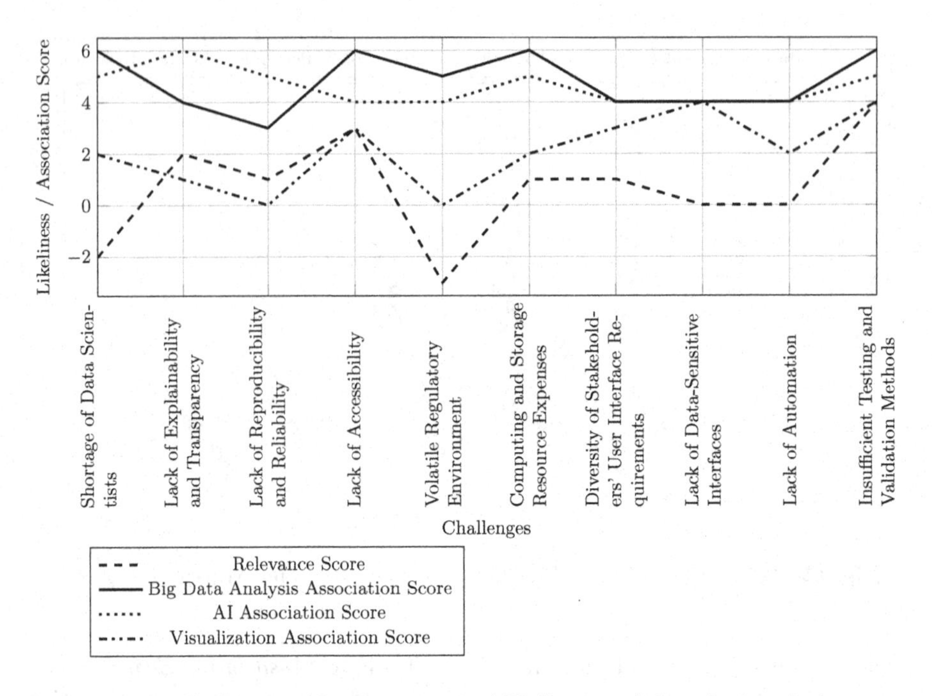

Fig. 16. Challenge evaluation: practical likeliness and domain association

(MATLAB, Simulink)[6], Google AI platform[7] with services like, e.g., AutoML, IBM Watson Studio[8] (each 28,6%) as well as Databricks[9] (14.3%).

The utilized open-source software for AI comprised MLib (Apache Spark)[10] with 42.9% followed by Weka[11] with 28.6%. Further AI software with 14.3% utilization rate each were Mahout (Apache Hadoop)[12], Image J[13] in combination with PHP MySQL, Keras[14] and python[15] libraries such as LIME. The most-popular software for Big Data Analysis were NoSQL databases (42.9%), Apache Spark[16] (28.6%), Apache Hadoop[17], and Apache Kafka[18] (both 14.3%). D3.js was with 42.9% the most-popular open-source software for Visualization followed

[6] https://www.mathworks.com/.
[7] https://cloud.google.com/ai-platform.
[8] https://www.ibm.com/uk-en/cloud/watson-studio.
[9] https://databricks.com/.
[10] https://spark.apache.org/mllib/.
[11] https://www.cs.waikato.ac.nz/ml/weka/.
[12] https://mahout.apache.org/.
[13] https://imagej.nih.gov/ij/.
[14] https://keras.io/.
[15] https://www.python.org/.
[16] https://spark.apache.org/.
[17] https://hadoop.apache.org/.
[18] https://kafka.apache.org/.

by Ggplot2 with 28.6%. Further Visualization software with 14.3% utilization rate each were Plotly[19], R[20], MATLAB, ImageJ, Java[21], C3.js[22], and Dart[23].

A further question was, where the participants execute their software. While 71.2% execute it on-premise, 28.8% utilize a hybrid combination of on-premise and cloud execution with AWS[24], Azure[25], Google Cloud[26], oVirt[27], and other virtual machines as cloud services.

Although the survey participants applied multiple programming languages, all of them utilized python in their research projects. Further popular programming languages were R (57.1%), Java, and SQL (both 42.9%). Other answers comprised JavaScript [28], MATLAB, PHP[29], C++[30] (14.3% each).

5 Validation and Limitations

This publication presents two evaluation approaches that were conducted with the help of participants of an AVI conference workshop in June 2020. One evaluation approach, the expert round table (Sect. 3), targeted to validate the applicability of the AI2VIS4BigData Reference Model in the practical research and work of the workshop participants. A workshop participant survey (Sect. 4), the second evaluation approach, aimed to investigate whether the subjective decisions that were taken in the course of deriving the reference model, comply with the experiences of experts in the field of AI-based Big Data Analysis and Visualization.

Expert Round Table Validation. The conducted expert round table revealed that the research activities of the workshop participants could either be completely integrated into AI2VIS4BigData Reference Model or could at least benefit from applying it to selected activities in their research. This was shown through both, the presented validation templates that confirmed every reference model element as well as the contributions and discussions in the workshop itself. Three of the four explicit findings were addressed through adding an explicit remark on data privacy to the model governance officer's focus (1), renaming the introduced label information data from [1] to label annotation data (2), and merging user interaction data and system activity data from [1] into system/user activity

[19] https://plotly.com/.
[20] https://www.r-project.org/.
[21] https://www.java.com/.
[22] https://c3js.org/.
[23] https://api.dart.dev.
[24] https://aws.amazon.com/.
[25] https://azure.microsoft.com/.
[26] https://cloud.google.com/.
[27] https://www.ovirt.org/.
[28] https://www.javascript.com/.
[29] https://www.php.net/.
[30] https://isocpp.org/.

data (3). No immediate measure was taken for the fourth finding that will be closely monitored in future AI2VIS4BigData research.

Workshop Participant Survey Validation. The subjective decisions that need to be validated are introduced in Sect. 2.4. They are structured into three decision groups. All three decision groups were covered by several survey questions.

The first decision group consists of the multiple decisions that were taken in mapping of the AIGO's AI System Lifecycle phases to IVIS4BigData's processing steps. Before assessing the mapping itself, the survey revealed that the majority of the workshop participants who all utilize AI, Big Data Analysis, and Visualization (refer to Fig. 6) confirm the applicability of both reference models and regularly conduct activities within the reference model's processing steps (refer to Fig. 7) and phases (refer to Fig. 8). The result of the mapping evaluation itself is visualized in Fig. 9. It shows that most participants map data and model design phase to the *"Data Management & Curation"* and *"Data Intelligence"* processing steps. This implies the necessity of revision. The mapping of the verification and validation phase to *"Analytics"* processing step was clearly validated (100% approval rate). The mapping of operation and monitoring phase to *"Analytics"* processing step was approved as well although a mapping to *"Interaction & Perception"* received the same approval rate (85.7%). The statement that there exists no exact mapping for the model deployment phase was falsified: 85.7% mapped it to *"Analytics"* as well as *"Interaction & Perception"* processing step. Although the original reasoning was falsified, the AI2VIS4BigData's model deployment layer can be kept as a separate layer on top of these two processing steps to visualize its content-related proximity.

The second decision group covers the decisions that were taken when defining or selecting the different manifestations of the AI model types, AI user stereotypes as well as AI data artifacts. The assessment of the conducted AI approaches in Fig. 10 reveals that ML and statistical AI is very popular among the survey participants while symbolic AI received a worse practical relevance rating. Nevertheless, more than half of the participants utilize symbolic AI always or frequently. Consequently both AI approaches are legit ingredients of the AI2VIS4BigData Reference Model. The two AI model application areas of analytics and automation received very high relevance ratings and thus are justified. Even if the UI models received clearly fewer approval (42.9% utilize them frequently or sometimes), this relevance rate still legitimizes use of this application for deriving an AI model type. Nevertheless the UI models need to be closely monitored in future research together with the additionally mentioned AI models types like, e.g., the predictive models. Several data artifacts were assessed regarding their relevance in the practical research application of the survey participants. The result is visualized in Fig. 11. The raw data sources of AI2VIS4BigData were assessed for validation purposes in more detail utilizing the IVIS4BigData data artifacts raw data, integrated raw data, and analyzed/structured raw data which this data artifact bundles. The relevance for

AI of all data artifacts was validated through high relevance scores for almost all data artifacts. Exceptions are the system activity data (0), user interaction data (2) and knowledge representation (0). While the former two data artifacts' low relevance score can be explained by the rather low popularity of UI models among the workshop participants (as shown earlier), the low relevance score for the knowledge representation can be explained through the low popularity of symbolic AI. Nevertheless, no given data artifact received a negative relevance score which leads to no immediate reference model adaption necessity under the explained circumstances. In order to identify all relevant AI user stereotypes and validate the ones that are selected for AI2VIS4BigData, all participants were asked whether they agreed that there exist clearly distinguished user stereotypes between all combinations of two out of three of AI, Big Data Analysis, and Visualization. While the majority of all survey participants agreed with all three combinations, the user stereotypes of AI and Big Data Analysis received with 57.1% the lowest approval rating. This implies that there might be several user stereotypes that are relevant for both application domains. As Fig. 13 shows, the AI user stereotypes of AI2VIS4BigData were all validated positively with a relevance score of two or higher and an AI association score of three or higher. Further candidates for being additional AI user stereotypes can be derived from having also a relevance score of two or higher and an AI association score of three or higher. These user stereotypes are expert and the citizen data scientist, developer as well as manager and director. Assuming that an AI user stereotype is missing, an AI activity is expected to receive a very low association score (the survey participants do not find a good match within the existing user stereotypes). Table 2 provides therefore an indication of the completeness of the six AI user stereotypes and potential responsibilities for the identified five new user stereotypes since it displays the various activities for applying AI together with the association score per AI user stereotype. As a result, all activities received an association score of three or higher and can thereby be considered to be validated. An exception is the *"Data Preprocessing"* activity: The survey participants clearly were not able to decide which user stereotype is conducting this activity (five user stereotypes received an association score of only two).

The third decision group consists of all decisions regarding the mapping of the previously introduced AI data artifacts and AI user stereotypes to the different layers of AI2VIS4BigData Reference Model. For this purpose, the survey asked the participants which IVIS4BigData processing steps they would associate with what data artifacts. The result is visualized in Fig. 12. It confirms the mapping of raw data sources and system activity data to *"Data Management & Curation"* processing step as well as model configuration and knowledge representation data to *"Analytics"* processing step. It also reveals that the survey participants would rather map the AI result and label data, AI metrics, and label annotation data to the two processing steps *"Analytics"* and *"Data Intelligence"* as well as the user interaction data to *"Interaction & Perception"* processing step. The mapping of the AI user stereotypes to both, AIGO's AI System Lifecycle phases as well as IVIS4BigData's processing steps is evaluated within the Figs. 14 and 15.

The result confirms the mapping of the model designer, domain expert, model deployment engineer, model operator, and end user stereotypes to their respective lifecycle phase and processing step as the majority of survey participants decided to map them accordingly (on par with another phase or processing step at least). The model governance officer user stereotype's mapping to *"Interaction & Perception"* processing step was also confirmed, yet it contrast to Fig. 4, the majority of the survey participants mapped this user stereotype to *"Operation & Monitoring"* lifecycle phase.

The challenges and technology that have been evaluated in the course of the survey can't be utilized to validate the reference model at the moment since it still is described on an abstract level. Nevertheless, they prepare the further specification and development focus of the AI2VIS4BigData Reference Model. Regarding the challenges, they outline that the top five challenges in AI and Big Data Analysis comprise a shortage of data scientists, a lack of explainability and transparency, a lack of accessibility, computing and storage resource expenses as well as insufficient testing and validation methods (refer to Fig. 16). The technology evaluation suggests that a future reference implementation of AI2VIS4BigData shall be based on open-source platforms and software, support both, on-premise and hybrid deployment scenarios and shall support a variety of different libraries and programming languages (with python and R being the most-relevant ones).

Limitations. The generalizability of the results of the two AI2VIS4BigData validation approaches, the expert round table as well as the workshop participant survey strongly depends on representative demographics of the workshop participants. An important limiting factor that needs to be mentioned is therefore the rather small number of seven participants. Especially, since the participants have not been selected to maximize representativity but based on qualitative aspects of their submitted work that was reviewed by an international program committee. All of the participants have a high educational background (M.Sc. at least) and are affiliated with European research institutions (geographical bias). There was no workshop participant that works in a larger research group with more than 10 members or that focuses on the industry sectors of banking and securities, communications, media, services, retail, or transportation.

6 Conclusion and Outlook

This paper qualitatively evaluated the AI2VIS4BigData Reference Model with the support of selected experts that participated in an official satellite workshop of the AVI2020 conference. For this purpose, two different validation approaches were applied with an expert round table validation to validate the practical applicability of the reference model itself and a workshop participant survey to assess the reference model's elements and their alignment in more detail.

This paper briefly introduced the AI2VIS4BigData Reference Model and its components and revealed the subjective decisions that were taken during its derivation in [1]. Furthermore, it explains the conducted validation approaches, their constraints such as the workshop setup as well as their results. These results are then utilized to carry out the qualitative evaluation itself.

The results of the evaluation revealed that all workshop participants approved the general applicability of the AI2VIS4BigData Reference Model and confirmed the majority of the subjective decisions that were taken in the course of its creation. Nevertheless, this evaluation disclosed that some of its elements or the alignment of them needs to be assessed and potentially revised in future work. As an outlook, this future work needs to include the examination the following validation results:

1. Emphasizing the importance of Visualization for the reference model (e.g. through additional elements or layers)
2. Revising the mapping of *"Data & Model Design"* lifecycle phase
3. Monitoring the practical relevance of UI models
4. Assessing the common user stereotypes with Big Data Analysis as AI user stereotype candidates (e.g. developer or management user stereotypes)
5. Revising the mapping of AI data artifacts based on the participants' feedback

This examination potentially leads to a revised version of the AI2VIS4BigData Reference Model and thereby lays the foundation for future specification activities such as a reference implementation.

References

1. Reis, T., Bornschlegl, M.X., Hemmje, M.L.: Towards a reference model for artificial intelligence supporting big data analysis. In: Proceedings of the 2020 International Conference on Data Science (ICDATA 2020) (2020, to appear)
2. Laney, D.: 3D data management: controlling data volume, velocity, and variety. Technical report, META Group (2001)
3. ISO. ISO/IEC JTC 1/SC 42 Artificial Intelligence (2018). https://isotc.iso.org/livelink/livelink/open/jtc1sc42
4. OECD. Artificial Intelligence in Society (2019)
5. Bornschlegl, M.X., et al.: *IVIS4BigData*: a reference model for advanced visual interfaces supporting big data analysis in virtual research environments. In: Bornschlegl, M.X., Engel, F.C., Bond, R., Hemmje, M.L. (eds.) AVI-BDA 2016. LNCS, vol. 10084, pp. 1–18. Springer, Cham (2016). https://doi.org/10.1007/978-3-319-50070-6_1
6. Barredo Arrieta, A., et al.: Explainable Artificial Intelligence (XAI): concepts, taxonomies, opportunities and challenges toward responsible AI. Inf. Fus. **58**, 82–115 (2020)
7. Krensky, P., et al.: Critical Capabilities for Data Science and Machine Learning Platforms. Gartner Inc., vol. G00391146 (2020)
8. Reis, T.M., Bornschlegl, X., Hemmje, M.L.: AI2VIS4BigData: qualitative evaluation of a big data analysis, AI, and visualization reference model. In: Lecture Notes in Computer Science. LNCS, vol. 12585 (2020, to appear)

9. Bornschlegl, M.X.: Advanced visual interfaces supporting distributed cloud-based big data analysis. Dissertation, University of Hagen (2019)
10. Krause, T., Andrade, B., Afli, H., Wang, H., Zheng, H., Hemmje, M.: Understanding the role of (advanced) machine learning in metagenomic workflows. Lecture Notes in Computer Science, LNCS, vol. 12585 (2020, to appear)
11. Bornschlegl, M.X.: *IVIS4BigData*: qualitative evaluation of an information visualization reference model supporting big data analysis in virtual research environments. In: Bornschlegl, M.X., Engel, F.C., Bond, R., Hemmje, M.L. (eds.) AVI-BDA 2016. LNCS, vol. 10084, pp. 127–142. Springer, Cham (2016). https://doi.org/10.1007/978-3-319-50070-6_10
12. Krosnick, J.A.: Questionnaire design. In: Vannette, D., Krosnick, J. (eds.) The Palgrave Handbook of Survey Research, pp. 439–455. Springer, Cham (2018)

Progressive Visualization of Epidemiological Models for COVID-19 Visual Analysis

Marco Angelini and Giorgio Cazzetta(✉)

Sapienza University of Rome, Rome, Italy
{angelini,cazzetta}@diag.uniroma1.it

Abstract. COVID-19 data analysis has become a prominent activity in the last year. The use of different models for predicting the spread of the disease, while providing very useful insights on the epidemics, are not inherently designed for interactive analysis, with time for a single computation ranging in the tens of seconds. In order to overcome this limitation, this paper proposes three techniques for progressive visualization of *Susceptible-Infectious-Recovered* (SIR) models data, that govern the trade-off between time and quality of the intermediate results. The techniques are quantitatively evaluated showing promising results.

Keywords: Progressive visual analytics · Epidemiological models · Interactive exploration · Susceptible-Infectious-Recovered Model

1 Introduction

Data analysis of COVID-19 has been a prominent activity since its early detection, with efforts ranging in various activities, from monitoring the infection cases during time, analyzing medical properties of the virus, providing risk indicators, usually split by various countries in the world. Among them, an interesting task has been the one to predict the evolution of the infection, with proposals ranging from machine learning and artificial intelligence approaches [1], to several models coming from epidemiology domain. While those models help in controlling the evolution of the infection and represent valid instruments in supporting decision making, they usually ask the right parameterization and customization in order to provide valuable and reliable results. This parameterization, even for simple models, requires to explore the results in order to understand their fit to the problem at hand. At the same time, the results of these models, even when correctly parameterized, are often used to monitor the predicted trends of the infection and compare them, or fit them with real data collected from hospitals and medical centers. However, the computation and rendering time of the models for monitoring activities usually contrast with the time constraints needed to support the interactive visual exploration, usually requiring tens of seconds for a single run. Among the several existing models, this paper focuses on the

T. Reis et al. (Eds.): AVI-BDA 2020/ITAVIS 2020, LNCS 12585, pp. 163–173, 2021.
https://doi.org/10.1007/978-3-030-68007-7_10

Susceptible-Infectious-Recovered (SIR) models family. These models exploit the theory by Kermack and McKendrick [2] to model the spread of a disease in a population. While these models are quite fast to compute, the fit of their results with respect to collected data can require time to be produced, and the parameterization of the model can require to explore the results of the different runs produced. In order to allow interactive exploration of the parameterization space and to support monitoring activities of the models results in real-time this paper proposes a solution, based on Progressive Visual Analytics discipline [3,4] that focuses on the progressive visualization of the results of the SIR models. The contributions are:

- the study of the SIR models, providing an iterative version able to produce intermediate results from the model with converging quality to exact result;
- a set of three strategies for governing the progressive visualization of the SIR models results, diminishing the required rendering time by optimizing the intermediate results to render;
- a quantitative evaluation conducted on the Italian regions data, showing the benefits of applying the proposed techniques, in terms of better support to interactive analysis of the results.

The rest of the paper is organized as follows: in Sect. 2 existing proposals are reviewed, while in Sect. 3 a general description of the SIR model and its variations is proposed. Section 4 presents the proposed techniques and the implemented prototype, evaluated then in Sect. 5. Section 6 concludes the paper.

2 Related Work

Several works exist that use visualization techniques applied to COVID-19 data. Dey et al. [5] proposed an environment to explore data concerning the COVID-19 in order to better understand trends and evolution of the epidemics. Marcílio-jr et al. [6] proposed a new visual analytic tool that uses k-nearest neighbours of cities to mimic regions and allows analysis of COVID-19 dissemination based on the comparison of a city under consideration and its neighbourhood. Differently from our approach, no prediction models are used in these works, with the main aims being the visualization of actually collected cases and/or the similarity among them.

Maciejewski et al. proposed PanViz [7], a visual analytic toolkit for analyzing the effect of decision measures implemented during a simulated pandemic influenza scenario. However, they do not cope with the problem of computing results of the models in a time compatible with human interaction, but they focus specifically on visualization of the effects that decision making (e.g. quarantine an area, limit movements) have on the disease spread. The work by Chen et al. [8] reports an analysis of prediction models applied to COVID-19 that exploits s SIR model. However, no considerations are made on enabling interactive parameterization and response time compatible with interactive visual analysis, as our work does. Finally, Ramanathan et al. [9] proposed a visual analysis environment of the parameterization space for SIR models. However, they focus on supporting, not in real-time, the parameterization of the models, while no discussion is present in allowing a real-time rendering of the results useful for interactive analysis.

Progressive Visual Analytics (PVA in what follows) is a novel discipline that aims at making interactive the visualization and analysis of problems requiring long computational time, through the production of intermediate partial results with a controlled level of quality and converging toward the exact result. As reported in the review by Angelini et al. [10], it can also be applied to produce visual results compatible with Human time constants [11] (e.g. an update of the visualization every 3 s to guarantee the flow of analysis and avoid User attention disruption) to support the Visual Analytics cycle. While several proposals exist in the PVA field that apply the discipline to specific domain problems (e.g. Turkay et al. [12] for credit card transactions analysis) or techniques (e.g. Pezzotti et al. [13] for progressive t-sne), to the best of authors' knowledge no contribution exists that apply PVA to epidemiological models. This paper proposes a solution for both keeping analysis of SIR models interactive and for allowing an exploration of their parameterization space, exploiting the progressive visualization part of PVA.

3 Epidemiological Models Background

Several compartmental models exist whose purpose is to simplify the mathematical modelling of the spread of infectious diseases. In an epidemiological model the population is assigned to compartments; for example, in the simple SIR Model the population is divided between Susceptible (S), Infectious (I), or Recovered (R). People may progress between compartments following a flow from S to R passing from I, formalizing the mathematical model through a system of differential equations.

This kind of models are very useful to predict things such as how a disease spreads, or the total number of infected persons, and could be an effective tool to help public health interventions. The SIR model is one of the simplest compartmental models and it can be easily extended by considering more intermediate states between S and R, and more complex flows between them.

In this work a more complex model is leveraged and it is fine-tuned with parameters that steer the transitions through the several stages of the model. The model schema is represented in Fig. 1 in which:

- **N**: total population
- $\mathbf{S(t)}$: number of susceptible individuals at time t
- $\mathbf{E(t)}$: number of exposed individuals at time t
- $\mathbf{I(t)}$: number of infected individuals at time t
- $\mathbf{C(t)}$: number of critical individuals at time t
- $\mathbf{R(t)}$: number of recovered individuals at time t
- $\mathbf{D(t)}$: number of dead individuals at time t

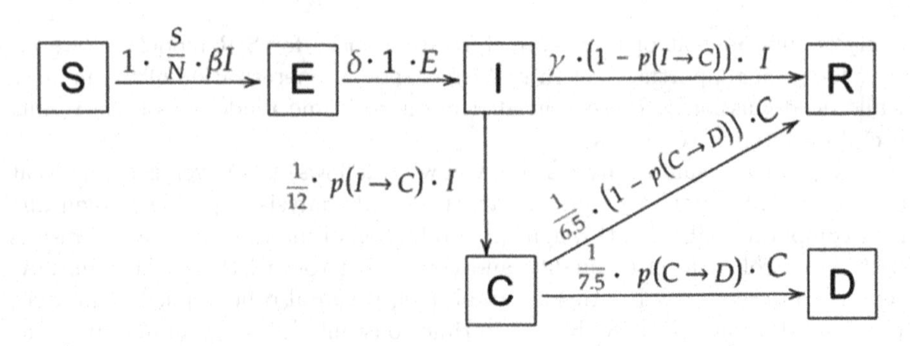

Fig. 1. Model schema [14]

- $\boldsymbol{\beta}$: expected amount of people an infected infects per day
- $\boldsymbol{\delta}$: proportion of infected recovering per day
- $\mathbf{P(I \to C)}$: probability of going from infected to critical
- $\mathbf{P(C \to D)}$: probability of going from critical to dead

The system extracts day by day the transitions of the population from one stage to another via transfer functions. In particular people in S (Susceptible) can transit to E (Exposed) with a rate that depends by β parameter, people from E can transit to I (Infected) with a rate depending on δ parameter, people from I can transit to C (Critical) with a specific probability (P(I $\to$ C), or R (Recovered) with the complementary probability (1- P(I $\to$ C). Once people is in C, they can arrive in D (Dead) with the specific probability P(C $\to$ D) or in R with probability (1 $-$ P(I $\to$ C)).

The parameters of the transfer functions are both the result of a fine-tuning of the model, starting from examples existing in the literature (for example δ = 1/9), or derived from statistically collected data on real cases.

In order to validate the model results and obtaining more reliable predictions, usually a curve fitting technique is applied to model outputs, in order to fit the resulting curves to real collected cases. We fit the model outputs using the deads curve, since it can be considered of better quality and more representative of real trends than the infected and the recovered curves, since a more accurate count of the dead rather than of the sick and consequently of the recovered is supposed to be done, due to the large number of asymptomatic and the insufficient number of swabs performed.

It is important to note that curve fitting methods in general do not guarantee to find a global minimum and that initial guesses for the parameters are crucial in order to avoid long and/or not converging fitting. The fitting operation is a long activity that can require tens of seconds to complete. Once the fitting has been carried out it is possible to generate the model that allows to predict the behavior of the curves for each single component of the model.

4 Progressive Visualization Technique

In this section we present the proposed techniques and compare them with the monolithic case. Further on, the system developed to support the analysis of the various techniques will be presented.

In the monolithic case, in order to have the curves predicted by the SIR model the user has to wait a computation time that, for some regions, lasts well over 20 s; this delay mainly depends on the fitting function and on the number of iterations needed to fit the real data. We developed a variation in the model fitter that allows us to obtain the predicted model after every iteration of the fitting step, allowing to greatly reduce the production of visual results. It additionally exploits the characteristic that after each fitting step we are able to construct a complete prediction, even with different quality with respect to the final one. Three solutions have been designed to reduce the user's waiting and inactivity time of the monolithic case:

- **naive progressive visualization**, in which the prediction curves resulting from all iterations of the fitting phase are rendered;
- **high-variation progressive visualization**, in which only curves that have undergone a significant change with respect to the previous iteration are rendered;
- **smart progressive visualization** in which the above mentioned curves are represented in a second progression that affects the number of visualized points of the curve with respect to the quality of each intermediate result.

The **naive progressive visualization** is trivial to implement. It allows to have the rendering of curves starting from the first iteration without waiting a long time compared to the monolithic case. However, a large number of curves will be represented to the user, with many of them having a low quality (representing values too immature to be considered close to the final solution, considered as the optimal solution). It could be possible even to have sequences of very similar trends in which the changes between one and the other would be unnoticeable to the user and therefore unnecessary.

Starting from these considerations, the **high-variation progressive visualization** has the task of reducing the number of unnecessary renderings from the user point of view. Root-mean-square error (RMSE) is used to measure the differences between predicted curves and real curves data (0 if the curves are equal and increasing values for more different curves). The rendering for iteration i will be executed if the variation between $rmse_i$ and $rmse_{i-1}$ exceeds a threshold level chosen by the user (adaptive threshold could be considered in a future work), as shown in Algorithm 1.

A solution like the previous one does not take into account the quality of the progression, in particular it only renders iterations if there is sufficient variation in the quality of the fitting with the previous iteration. In this way, the number of iterations to render will be heavily decreased, keeping intact the quality. However, low quality curves, particularly at the early stages of the progression, will

Algorithm 1. high-variation solution pseudo-code

$C_i \leftarrow curvePredictedIteration_i$
$C_{i-1} \leftarrow curvePredictedIteration_{i-1}$
$C_{i-2} \leftarrow curvePredictedIteration_{i-2}$
$rmse_i \leftarrow RMSE(C_i, C_{i-1})$
$rmse_{i-1} \leftarrow RMSE(C_{i-1}, C_{i-2})$
$variation \leftarrow \Delta rmse_i, rmse_{i-1}$
if $variation > threshold$ **then**
  $renderIteration_i$
end if

still be visualized. The **smart progressive visualization** tries to make a step further, reducing the number of iterations to be rendered to the only ones that increase the quality of the rendering. It maps the number of instants to represent a curve to a liner scale of quality that have as extremes the minimum quality (maximum error, iteration 0) and the maximum theoretical quality ($rmse = 0$). The more is the quality of a curve, the more number of instants will be rendered. If the quality fluctuates between different iterations, the number of points to be rendered will stay fixed, in order to avoid visual ripples. Algorithm 2 shows in detail how the solution works.

Algorithm 2. progressive solution pseudo-code

$C_i \leftarrow curvePredictedIteration_i$
$C_{i-1} \leftarrow curvePredictedIteration_{i-1}$
$C_r \leftarrow curveRealData$
$rmse_i \leftarrow RMSE(C_i, C_r)$
$rmse_{i-1} \leftarrow RMSE(C_{i-1}, C_r)$
$maxError \leftarrow RMSE_0$
$variation \leftarrow \Delta rmse_i, maxError$
if $variation > threshold$ **then**
  $renderIteration_i$
  $stopProgression$
else
  if $rmse_i < rmse_{i-1}$ **then**
    $renderIterationWithPointProportionalToQuality$
  end if
end if

The three solutions have been implemented in a prototype environment consisting of a Python back-end part for the SIR model computation and a D3.js [15] front-end part for the rendering. An overview of the system is shown in Fig. 2 where a linechart with six curves is represented, three continuous colour curves representing the value over the time for the real death, real infected, and real recovered data, and three dotted colour curves representing the corresponding predicted trends. On the top part the user can choose the Italian region on which the prediction is performed, the progressive visualization technique to apply and the corresponding threshold parameters. Three labels shows for each technique the id of the actual iteration, the total number of fitting iterations for the specific region and the number of rendered iterations for the selected solution.

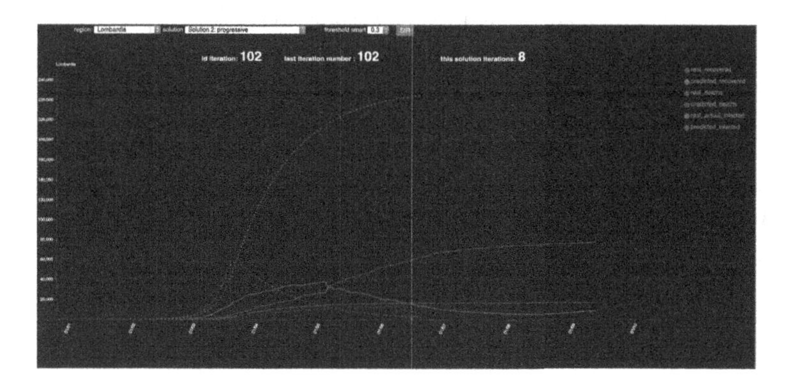

Fig. 2. Intermediate rendering for the smart progressive visualization technique, where only a interval of time instants is represented for the predicted infected curve.

While in Fig. 2 an intermediate rendering for the smart progressive visualization technique is represented, in Fig. 3 the sequence of three different renderings is represented for the Lombardia region. The first and second renders represent only a sub-part of the predicted infected curve; this means that they are not stable with respect to the input threshold value (0.3 in this case). The second follows the first in sequence since its quality is better than the first, so it represents a bigger time interval for the predicted infected curve. The last one represents the whole prediction time interval, so it is stable regarding the threshold value and it is the last rendering of the process, obtained sooner (savings 100 iterations) with respect to the monolithic case. A video demonstration is available at this link https://youtu.be/o7IhWtFkRvY.

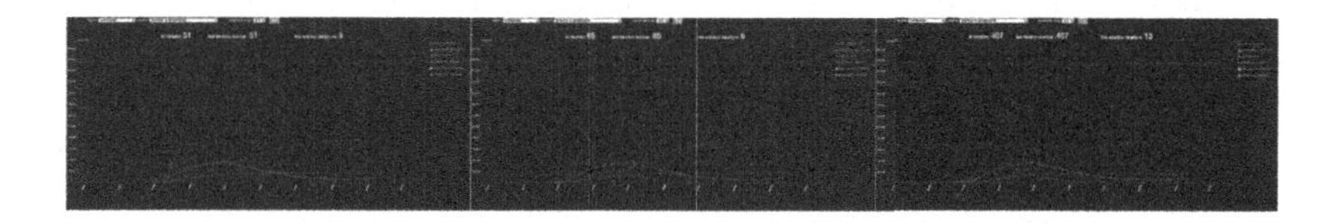

Fig. 3. Sequence of 3 different stages of the smart progressive visualization technique.

5 Evaluation

In the first part of this section results on the fitting function of the model are discussed with respect to the dataset of the Italian regions. In the second part the evaluation of the proposed techniques is discussed considering the time to compute the different renderings, their quality and the reduction of number of renderings for each solution. Curve fitting is the process of constructing a curve or a mathematical function, which has the best correspondence to a series of assigned points. In the model of this work it performs several iterations using the least square minimization as fitting method, trying to adjust the numerical values for the model so that it most closely matches the real data. We first computed the needed number of function evaluations (*nfeval* in what follows) to fitting the model to the real Italian regions data. In Fig. 4a the barchart represents the *nfeval* variation for all the Italian regions for a specific day. It can be seen that there is high variability in the results (considering for example Bolzano region with less than 100 and Trento with more than 1100 iterations).

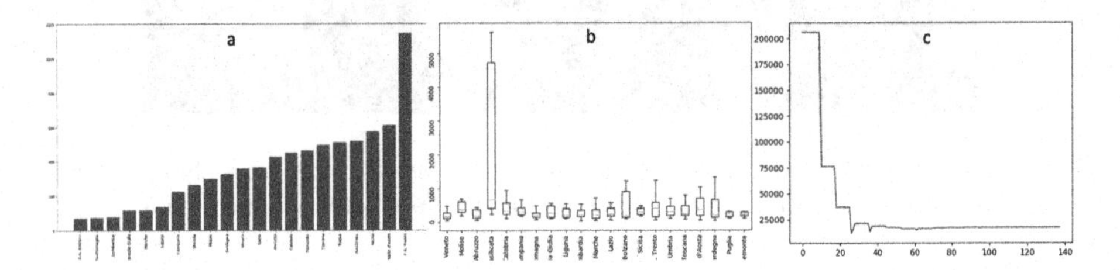

Fig. 4. a) The barchart shows the number of function evaluations (*nfeval*) for each Italian region; it follows that the distribution is highly variable (comparing Bolzano and Trento regions for example). (b) Each boxplot represents the *nfeval* distribution for each region over time: the distribution is computed measuring the *nfeval* values for each fitting function for different time instants with a frequency of 10 days. (c) Root mean square error between R curve predicted for each fitting iteration and the R real data for the Liguria region

As second experiment we measured the *nfeval* variation over time. In particular the *nfeval* is measured for different time instants with a frequency of 10 days (first *nfeval* computed 10 days after the beginning of the epidemics, the second after 20 days, and so on). In Fig. 4b, 21 boxplots are represented, one for each region; each boxplot represents the *nfeval* distribution for the specific region over the sampled data; boxplots do not include outliers. The large variation for the *nfeval* is not only between regions but depends also from the time instants on which it is sampled. For a specific region the *nfeval* can assume a value far from the median of the distribution (Basilicata region assumes value (5500) so far to it median (about 700)). It confirms that on average a high number of iterations must be considered in the monolithic case, resulting in high response times.

To measure the quality of the fitting for each iteration the root mean squared error (RMSE) between the predicted curves obtained for each fitting iteration and the corresponding real data are computed. In Fig. 4c the RMSE for the Liguria region is represented. Similar to other regions, the obtained curve shows a trend that is mostly monotonic decreasing, indicating that the more iterations are computed, the better quality is obtained for the prediction. Additionally, the trend shows that the optimal result is computed quite fast (iteration 40 out of 140) and that the remaining iterations do not differ sensibly to it. While not a general property for all the trends, it remains valid on average and can be tuned for window-based approaches with the right extent of the window.

In what follows, the different techniques proposed to represent the SIR model are compared. Table 1 shows for each approach the time for the first rendering and the number of renderings for each approach for a specific case study of the Lombardia region.

Table 1. First time rendering and number of renderings for all the proposed techniques

Solutions	Measures	
	Time for first rendering	Number of rendering
Monolithic	13.075 s	1
Naive	0.091 s	492
High variation (t = 10)	0.632 s	58
Progressive (t = 0.3)	1.631 s	13

Compared to the monolithic case, the naive progressive visualization allows the user to have a first view right away (0.091 s), without making the user waits until the end of the process of the monolithic case (13.075 s). The high-variation progressive visualization reduces the number of rendering of the naive from 492 to 58 (88% improvement). In this case the first rendering is rendered slightly later (0.632 s compared to 0.091 s), but still in interactive time (less than a second). At the same time it has a better quality since, with a 36% lower RMSE with respect to the first rendering of naive solution. The smart progressive visualization further reduces the number of renderings to 13 (77% lower than high-variation solution), with the first rendering computed after 1.631 s, it has a quality of first rendering marginally better (10%) considering the high-variation solution, but it represents only a limited interval of prediction. However, after 5 and 10 s renders, it assumes quality of the rendering of the 57% and 61% better than naive progressive visualization, while high-variation solution has a comparable quality (10% worse) for the same intervals. Additionally, smart progressive visualization presents a smoother unfolding of the curves with much less variations.

6 Conclusions and Future Works

In this paper we explored techniques for allowing a progressive visualization of the results coming from SIR models, controlling their quality during the progression and allowing an interactive analysis of their results. The three proposed techniques have been evaluated and shows interactive time rendering and good quality bounds. These characteristics are useful to allow an exploration of parameterization space in real-time and/or the monitoring and what-if analysis of different mitigation actions for limiting the spread of COVID-19 in terms of effects on the prediction. Future works includes a more robust evaluation of the three techniques in terms of the trade-off between time and quality of the result, the further refinement of the *progressive* technique to better support a fluid rendering of the curves, and the development of an environment that exploits these techniques for predictive visual analytics of COVID-19 data.

References

1. Ito, R., Iwano, S., Naganawa, S.: A review on the use of artificial intelligence for medical imaging of the lungs of patients with coronavirus disease 2019. Diagnostic and Interventional Radiology. Ankara, Turkey (2020)
2. Kermack, W.O., McKendrick, A.G.: A contribution to the mathematical theory of epidemics. Proc. R. Soc. London A Math. Phys. Eng. Sci. **115**(772), 700–721 (1927)
3. Stolper, C.D., Perer, A., Gotz, D.: Progressive visual analytics: user-driven visual exploration of in-progress analytics. IEEE Trans. Visual Comput. Graphics **20**(12), 1653–1662 (2014)
4. Fekete, J., Primet, R.: Progressive analytics: a computation paradigm for exploratory data analysis. CoRR, vol. abs/1607.05162 (2016)
5. Dey, S.K., Rahman, M.M., Siddiqi, U.R., Howlader, A.: Analyzing the epidemiological outbreak of COVID-19: a visual exploratory data analysis approach. J. Med. Virol. **92**(6), 632–638 (2020)
6. Marcílio-Jr, W.E., Eler, D.M., Garcia, R.E., Correia, R.C.M., Rodrigues, R.M.B.: Visual analytics of COVID-19 dissemination in São Paulo state, Brazil (2020)
7. Maciejewski, R., et al.: A pandemic influenza modeling and visualization tool. J. Vis. Lang. Comput. **22**(4), 268–278 (2011). Part Special Issue on Challenging Problems in Geovisual Analytics
8. Chen, B., et al.: Visual data analysis and simulation prediction for COVID-19. arXiv preprint arXiv:2002.07096 (2020)
9. Ramanathan, A., Steed, C.A., Pullum, L.L.: Verification of compartmental epidemiological models using metamorphic testing, model checking and visual analytics. In: 2012 ASE/IEEE International Conference on BioMedical Computing (BioMedCom), pp. 68–73 (2012)
10. Angelini, M., Santucci, G., Schumann, H., Schulz, H.-J.: A review and characterization of progressive visual analytics. Informatics **5**, 31 (2018)
11. Card, S.K., Robertson, G.G., Mackinlay, J.D.: The information visualizer, an information workspace. In: Proceedings of the SIGCHI Conference on Human Factors in Computing Systems, CHI 1991, New York, NY, USA, pp. 181–186, Association for Computing Machinery (1991)
12. Turkay, C., Kaya, E., Balcisoy, S., Hauser, H.: Designing progressive and interactive analytics processes for high-dimensional data analysis. IEEE Trans. Visual Comput. Graphics **23**(1), 131–140 (2017)
13. Pezzotti, N., Lelieveldt, B.P.F., Maaten, L.v.d., Höllt, T., Eisemann, E., Vilanova, A.: Approximated and user steerable TSNE for progressive visual analytics. IEEE Trans. Visual Comput. Graphics **23**(7), 1739–1752 (2017)

14. Henri, F.: Infectious disease modelling: fit your model to coronavirus data, April 2020. https://towardsdatascience.com/infectious-disease-modelling-fit-your-model-to-coronavirus-data-2568e672dbc7
15. Bostock, M., Ogievetsky, V., Heer, J.: D^3 data-driven documents. IEEE Trans. Visual Comput. Graphics **17**(12), 2301–2309 (2011)

An Experience on Cooperative Development of Interactive Visualizations for the Analysis of Urban Data

Paolo Buono[1(✉)], Maria Costabile[1], Alessandra Legretto[1], and Palmalisa Marra[2]

[1] Università Degli Studi di Bari Aldo Moro, Via Orabona 4, Bari, Italy
{paolo.buono,maria.costabile,alessandra.legretto}@uniba.it
[2] Links Management and Technology S.P.A., Via R. Scotellaro 55, Lecce, Italy
palmalisa.marra@linksmt.it

Abstract. Digital technologies and social networks offer several possibilities for improving the quality of life in Smart Cities. Citizens are willing to contribute to the efficiency of services that Smart Cities offer by reporting through different channels, such as phone/fax, front office, website, mobile app, sensors, several problems they observe in the city. This paper contributes to the advancement of the practice of HCI by describing an experience carried out with the employees of a municipality about the identification and implementation of interactive visualizations, in order to support them in the management of urban issues reported by citizens. The performed experience was inspired by the Cooperative Method Development (CMD), that emphasizes a strong collaboration between IT researchers and experts in a work practice, working side by side and being focused on the practitioners' problems, in order to identify critical aspects and possible improvements that lead to the design and development of new software artifacts. The municipality employees greatly appreciated their active involvement in the overall CMD process, as well as the improvements on data analysis, thanks to the developed interactive visualizations that enable them to detect trends, anomalies and significant facts in the management of urban issues.

Keywords: Practice of Human-Computer interaction · Visual Analytics · Data analysis · Smart cities

1 Introduction and Motivation

More and more city administrations solicit citizens to provide indications about various problems occurring in the city. They offer different channels, such as phone/fax, front office, web-site, mobile app, through which a citizen may report a description of the type of problem (e.g. "broken or faulty street lights"), its gravity and location, in order to allow municipality employees to faster solve the problem. Often, in smart cities, sensors directly provide measures of a monitored aspect; for example, sensors that monitor weather conditions and pollution are placed in specific locations to provide data about

T. Reis et al. (Eds.): AVI-BDA 2020/ITAVIS 2020, LNCS 12585, pp. 174–183, 2021.
https://doi.org/10.1007/978-3-030-68007-7_11

the evolution of the observed phenomenon. Citizens themselves can be seen as complex sensors that contribute with their individual measurements according to their subjective sensations, current perceptions or personal observations (e.g., see [1–3]).

In recent years the mobile device is becoming the privileged means to report problems. With a single "button press" by the user, the municipality employees get the photo of the problem, its precise location, the sender's contact details, and other data that become immediately available in the municipality system. The citizen has the satisfaction of contributing to improve the city quality and perceives that there are more chances that the issue will be solved faster. Thus, citizen participation is a win-win condition for providing better services in the city.

The authors of this paper are part of the research team that has been working in a project of a municipality whose overall aim is to implement an effective approach of citizen participation in order to provide more efficient and satisfactory services to their citizens. It is a wide project with several specific objectives. The experience described in this paper focuses on the conception of ideas, design and development of interactive visualizations to support municipality employees in the critical analysis of urban data. These activities were carried out based on a strong collaboration with the municipality stakeholders using a qualitative research approach, including interviews and focus group, as prescribed by the Cooperative Method Development (CMD) proposed by Dittrich et al. [4] and used in various research projects with companies, like those in [5, 6]. The active involvement of the practitioners in the overall CMD process, including the fact that they could directly evaluate the obtained improvements, was instrumental in emphasizing the value of the developed interactive visualizations for supporting the analysis of urban data.

The contribution of this paper is two-fold. First, the presented experience confirms the value of CMD approach and ethnographically-inspired research that bring in-depth understanding of the socio-technological realities surrounding a work practice [7, 8], in order to support designers in creating software artifacts that better shape user experiences. Second, it provides evidence on the value of information visualization techniques to support the analysis of big data produced in smart cities. The positive outcomes of this experience should encourage other researchers to adopt similar approaches for effective technology transfer.

The paper organization is the following. Section 2 describes the CMD-based approach to create interactive visualizations that support the analysis of urban data. Section 3 briefly illustrates the dataset used in the examples provided in this paper. Section 4 describes some of the implemented interactive visualizations. Section 5 concludes the paper and highlights future work.

2 Developing Interactive Visualizations According to CMD

CMD requires the cooperation between researchers and practitioners to carry out qualitative empirical research, in order to identify critical aspects and possible improvements in processes and software artifacts related to some activities in a certain work practice, to implement these improvements and to evaluate them [4].

Originated in fields such as psychology and social sciences, qualitative research keeps increasing in human-computer interaction and software engineering, since it is an effective way to explore the in-situ practice of interest [9]. Quantitative methods were often claimed to be better than qualitative ones, since the latter rely on subjective interpretation. Several studies have shown that careful qualitative researchers may analyze data and present results in ways that ensure the necessary objectivity and soundness. Moreover, qualitative research is more flexible and gives the possibility to involve practitioners in the process, enabling researchers to discuss and evaluate with practitioners the possible improvements of their practices. Understanding the social side of a software project helps to select and develop methods and tools that better support the addressed work practice [7]. Practitioners can actively participate in the whole research process addressing their problems and discussing them with researchers. Thus, qualitative research is very appropriate in the cooperation with companies and organizations.

The CMD approach "combines qualitative social science fieldwork with the problem-oriented method, technique and process improvement" [4]. CMD actually proposes an evolutionary cycle, which consists of three phases that can be repeatedly applied in the same context:

1 – Understand Practice: qualitative empirical investigation into the problem domain is performed, in order to understand existing practices and to identify problematic aspects from the practitioners' point of view.
2 – Deliberate Improvements: the results of the first phase are used as an input for the design of possible improvements, e.g., new software artifacts. This is done in cooperation between researchers and the involved practitioners.
3 – Implement and Observe Improvements: the improvements are implemented, and researchers observe practitioners performing their activities after the improvements. The results are evaluated together with the involved practitioners.

In the experience we are describing, phase 1 consisted of several meetings among researchers and the municipality stakeholders, which also included interviews and focus groups, during which it came out that the city control staff is very much interested in the quality of the processes they perform to solve the problems presented by the citizen. In particular, they want to analyze how much time such processes take, in order to understand the reasons why solving a certain type of problems might take too long; addressing such reasons will permit them to reduce the process time, thus providing a better service to the citizens. Practitioners showed the data visualizations they used, which are based on very common techniques, such as histograms, bar charts and maps. These techniques can visualize at most three attributes of the available data. For instance, a histogram represents the time reference (years) along the x axis and the number of reports received by citizens on the y axis, showing, for each year, five close bars, each for one of the five areas in which the city is divided (each area is called "municipio" in Italian). The researchers pointed out that, due to the multidimensional nature of the data, more powerful visualizations could be adopted, capable to provide more insights on the data.

This led to phase 2, where the researchers illustrated some multidimensional visualization techniques that would allow the practitioners to interact with the data in order to better analyze them. These techniques were proposed by the researchers on the basis of their academic knowledge, but the discussion about which method should be selected and how it should be applied involved the practitioners very much. Many different and powerful visualization techniques are available in the literature. Annual conferences on Information Visualization and Visual Analytics keep providing a lot of references. Several books are also published on these research areas (e.g. [10–12]). The choice of a proper visualization technique depends very much on the type of data as well as on the goals of the analysis, i.e. on what the municipality control staff wants to understand and get from the data. Thus, interviews and focus groups were held in order to discuss such issues with various municipality stakeholders and different visualizations techniques that could provide significant alternatives were analyzed. Effective visualizations should indeed, facilitate the interpretation of the data related to the provisioning of urban services by highlighting trends and significant facts.

As the successive phase 3, the researchers implemented prototypes of these techniques, applied them to some of the available urban data and showed the results to practitioners. Further informal discussions, interviews, focus groups and tests with the municipality employees by using the thinking aloud protocol [13] were conducted, in order to evaluate the developed prototypes.

In order to conduct good investigations, different perspectives should be compared. Thus, the final proposal was to provide different and powerful visualizations, in order to allow the municipality experts to perform exploratory visual analyses to amplify their cognition.

In this paper we present two of such visualizations. Some of the implemented techniques are not novel, they are based on well-known techniques that are here applied to the dataset of urban data and resulted very effective. This is the case of the Treemap

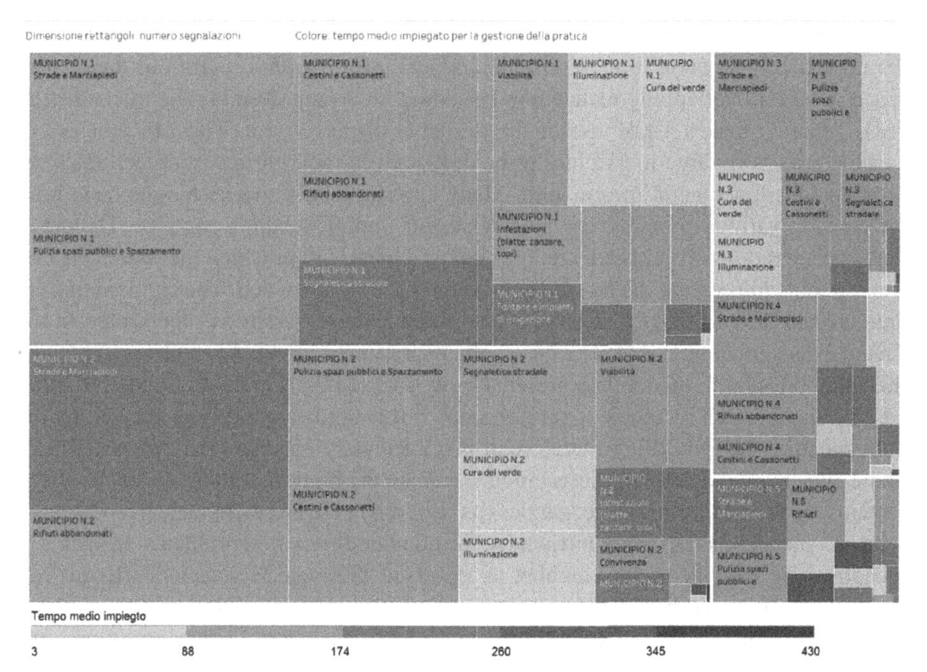

Fig. 1. The Treemap shows the different types of issues of the five city areas (MUNICIPIO 1,…, MUNICIPIO 5). The color represents the average time spent to manage and solve issues of the specific type. The color is darker when the average time increases. (Color figure online)

shown in Fig. 1, while the other visualization described in Sect. 4 is new, even if inspired by existing techniques.

3 Dataset

The dataset considered in the examples shown in this paper is composed of 14643 instances of urban issues, each one describing a problem occurring in the city, as reported by a citizen through a mobile app. Each instance is characterized by the following very typical attributes of this domain: problem id; title and description (written by the citizen); type; location; area (municipio) in which the problem occurs; date and time of problem reporting; date and time in which the process to solve the reported issue ended; note sent by the municipality employees to the citizen to communicate the end of the process. The time (in days) spent to process the reported issue is computed as the difference between the date in which the process ended and the date in which the problem was reported.

4 The Implemented Interactive Visualizations

This section describes three of the interactive visualizations that were conceived, designed, developed and evaluated in an evolutionary cycle, according to the CMD described in Sects. 2. Their goal is to improve the activities performed by the municipality employees in the analysis of multidimensional of urban data. The visualizations were initially created using Tableau [1], then they were developed in Kibana [2] using Vega and Vega lite [3] plugins.

The first visualization applies the Treemap technique introduced by Ben Schneiderman [14]. It is useful to represent hierarchical information. It partitions the display space into non-overlapping rectangular bounding boxes representing the tree structure [15]. Treemap makes 100% use of the available display space. This efficient use of space allows very large hierarchies to be displayed in their entirety and facilitates the presentation of semantic information. Many applications of this technique have been proposed in various domains, e.g. stock exchange, public health, insurance. The urban data considered in this research are modeled as a hierarchy in which the root is the city and the root children are the five areas in which the city is divided. The children of each area are the different types of issues. This three-level hierarchy is represented in the Treemap as shown in Fig. 1. The city is the overall map, divided in five rectangles by the white lines, each rectangle represents a city area (MUNICIPIO 1, …, MUNICIPIO 5). The size of each rectangle is proportional to the number of reports received by the corresponding MUNICIPIO; therefore, it is immediately observed that MUNICIPIO 1 and 2, which are the two largest rectangles, contain the highest number of reports. Each rectangle is divided in further rectangles (its children in the hierarchy), each represents a type of issue and its size is proportional to the number of reported problems. In each city area, the type with the highest number of reports is "Strade e Marciapiedi" (Roads and pavements), followed by "Pulizia spazi pubblici e Spazzamento" (Public spaces cleaning), "Segnaletica stradale" (Road signs), and others. The color of a rectangle represents

[1] https://www.tableau.com.

[2] https://www.elastic.co/kibana

[3] https://vega.github.io.

the average time to solve the problems of that type. The darker the color, the longer the time spent. For example, by looking at the rectangles labeled "Strade e Marciapiedi" in MUNICIPIO 1 and in MUNICIPIO 2, it is evident that they present an almost similar number of problems, but the darker color of the rectangle in MUNICIPIO 2 indicates that the process of solving the problems takes, on average, a longer time. This was immediately recognized by the municipality employees as soon as we illustrated how the Treemap works. They provided a very positive feedback, acknowledging the usefulness of Treemap as a tool that shows in a single view the main evidences they were looking for, i.e. the type of problems processed in longer time, indicated by the darker rectangles.

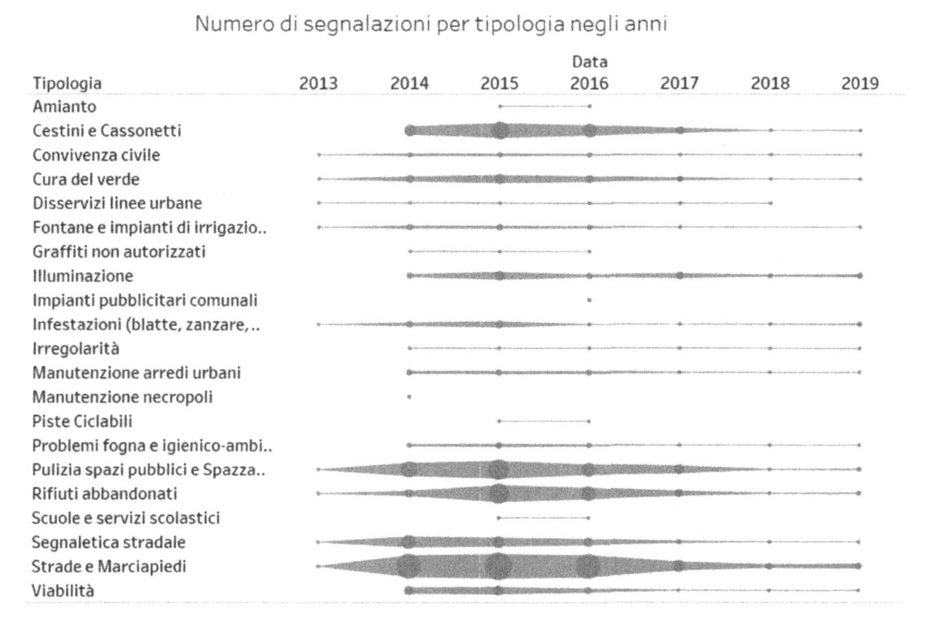

Fig. 2. This visualization shows the trend of the different types of reported problems during the years 2013–2019. The types of problems are listed in the left column "Tipologia".

Another need of the municipality employees is to analyze how the number of problems varies over the years. In order to include temporal information, a flow diagram, shown in Fig. 2, has been implemented. The years from 2013 to 2019 are shown on the columns, the types of problems are shown on the rows. For each type of problem and for each year, it is shown a circle whose size is proportional to the number of reported problems. A band connecting consecutive circles on a row shows the trend over time. An interesting indication emerging from this visualization is that, since 2017 the number of reported problems decreases considerably. This is in part due to the better work performed by the city government in the last years. However, the municipality employees are investigating more deeply on this, in order to better understand the possible causes.

With respect to Fig. 2, the municipality employees want to visualize other attributes, such as the average time spent to solve problems and the city areas in which the problems occur. They also prefer a more detailed view over time, i.e. referring to months rather than years. A new visualization technique has been created to satisfy these requirements.

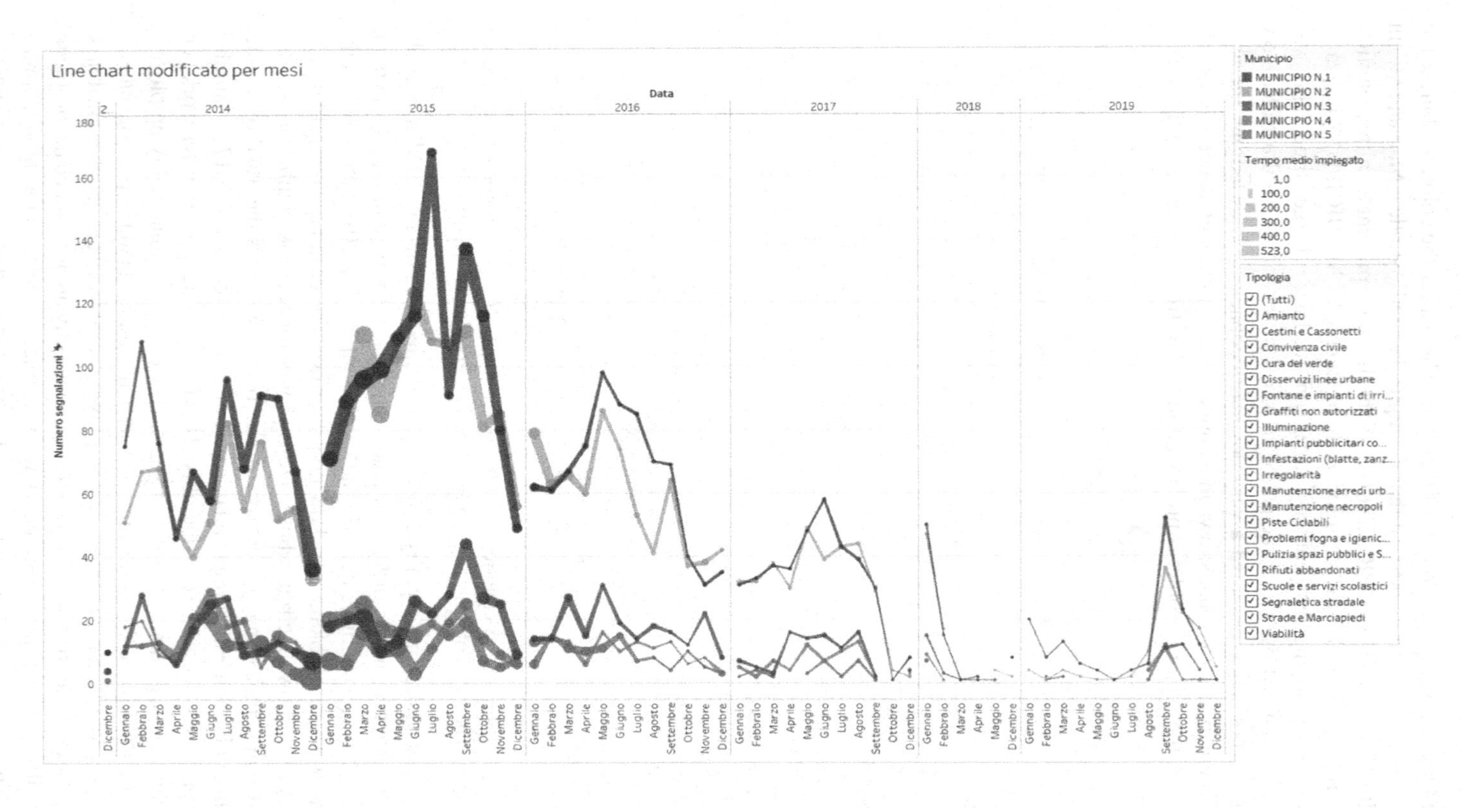

Fig. 3. A visualization in which, for each year, lines connecting 12 nodes (each node is a month) are shown in a color indicating the city area (see legend at the top of the left panel). The size of each node is proportional to the average time to process issues.

5 Conclusions

This paper reports an experience carried out with the employees of a municipality to identify and implement techniques and tools that might improve the analysis and the management of urban issues reported by citizens. The experience was based on a qualitative research approach, as suggested by the Cooperative Method Development (CMD) proposed by Dittrich et al. and adopted in several research projects [4]; it confirmed the value of ethnographically inspired research.

Based on this experience, we strongly encourage other researchers to adopt a similar approach in order to effectively transfer innovation to the daily practices of various application domains (see, e.g., the case in [5]). Indeed, this experience is a further demonstration of the value of CMD, which goes well beyond Human-Centred Design. It emphasizes a strong collaboration between IT researchers and practitioners, working side by side and being focused on the practitioners' problems, not only in the design-evaluation cycle but even before, i.e. starting from the analysis of the critical aspects of the procedures adopted in a certain practice and the identification of possible improvements, from which ideas on the design of new software artifacts come out, which are then prototyped and evaluated up to the development of the final artifact. The CMD approach guides the researchers in addressing questions such as: How do practitioners carry out their daily work? What are the methods they use? What are the improvements we get by integrating a specific method? In this way, researchers and practitioners can identify, manage and improve critical aspects of relevant processes in a work practice.

The municipality stakeholders greatly appreciated their active involvement. The participatory meetings and focus groups represented a novelty with respect to their usual involvement in other projects; they realized how much useful information about the project was provided by the different stakeholders expressing their own point of view. Another important benefit is that, working very closely with the researcher in the design of new solutions for their problems, users are more prone to accept these solutions and use the resulting system with more satisfaction (Fig. 3).

The qualitative empirical investigation, performed during the several meetings of researchers and other stakeholders in the early stage of the project, was the key of the success of the overall experience. The performed activities are very close to those of the Emphaty stage of the Design Thinking model (see, e.g. [16]), which in the last years has triggered increasing interest among software development organizations, in order to improve design and innovation processes and to provide better experiences to end users. Empathy is not only the first one of the five stages of Design Thinking but, in our opinion, it is the fundamental one because designers get very much in contact with users while performing user research, and this is instrumental to gain real insights into users' needs and expectations.

As further contribution, this paper provides more evidence that information visualization techniques are very valuable in supporting the analysis of big data that are processed in smart cities, in order to provide better services to the citizens. The municipality employees acknowledged the power of the implemented visualizations to highlight the situations of the different city areas and the different types of problems reported by citizens. They liked the interactivity of the visualizations, which allow them to see the data from different perspectives and make sense of the data.

The collaboration with the municipality employees continues and we are working together to other visualization techniques, in particular to some that may show data to a daily level of granularity. However, a more challenging future work is on incorporating Visual Analytics in this project. Specifically, we are going to use predictive models that may provide estimations of the required time to solve the different issues. This estimation is useful for both citizens and municipality employees. The idea is to allow the decision maker to compare different predictive models and to choose the best one for the data of interest. To this aim, we are planning to adopt an approach similar to the one presented in [17]. Further directions are planned for this work. One might be to adopt advanced interaction techniques to perform cooperative analysis. The approach proposed in [18] uses spatially-aware cross-devices interaction to exploit the presence of multiple devices, in order to combine them and create a multi-user interface. Another direction is to adopt other qualitative methods, borrowed from the software engineering to apply in the context of visualization [19].

Currently the dashboard is dynamic but has a little personalization. More attention will be devoted to provide the user with the ability personalize and evolve their own software environments [20].

References

1. Buono, P., Costabile, M.F.: Insights on the development of visual tools for analysis of pollution data. In: Proceedings: DMS 2012 – 18th International Conference on Distributed Multimedia Systems (2012)
2. Goodchild, M.F.: Citizens as sensors: the world of volunteered geography. GeoJournal **69**(4), 211–221 (2007). https://doi.org/10.1007/s10708-007-9111-y
3. Resch, B.: People as sensors and collective sensing-contextual observations complementing geo-sensor network measurements. In: Krisp, J. (eds.) Progress in Location-Based Services. Lecture Notes in Geoinformation and Cartography. Springer, Berlin, Heidelberg (2013) https://doi.org/10.1007/978-3-642-34203-5_22
4. Dittrich, Y., Rönkkö, K., Eriksson, J., Hansson, C., Lindeberg, O.: Cooperative method development. Empir. Softw. Eng. **13**(3), 231–260 (2008). https://doi.org/10.1007/s10664-007-9057-1
5. Ardito, C., Buono, P., Caivano, D., Costabile, M.F., Lanzilotti, R.: Investigating and promoting UX practice in industry: an experimental study. Int. J. Hum Comput Stud. **72**(6), 542–551 (2014). https://doi.org/10.1016/j.ijhcs.2013.10.004
6. Ardito, C., Buono, P., Caivano, D., Costabile, M.F., Lanzilotti, R., Dittrich, Y.: Human-centered design in industry: lessons from the trenches. Computer (Long. Beach. Calif) **47**(12), 86–89 (2014). https://doi.org/10.1109/mc.2014.355
7. Dittrich, Y., John, M., Singer, J., Tessem, B.: Editorial: for the special issue on qualitative software engineering research. Inf. Softw. Technol. **49**(6), 531–539 (2007). https://doi.org/10.1016/j.infsof.2007.02.009
8. Sharp, H., deSouza, C., Dittrich, Y.: Using ethnographic methods in software engineering research. In: Proceedings of the 32nd ACM/IEEE International Conference on Software Engineering-Volume 2, pp. 491–492 (2010)
9. Seaman, C.B.: Qualitative methods in empirical studies of software engineering. IEEE Trans. Softw. Eng. **25**(4), 557–572 (1999). https://doi.org/10.1109/32.799955
10. Tukey, J.W.: Exploratory Data Analysis. Addison-Wesley (1977)

11. Card, S.K., Mackinlay, J.D., Shneiderman, B.: Using vision to think. In: Readings in Information Visualization: Using Vision to Think, San Francisco, CA, USA: Morgan Kaufmann Publishers Inc., pp. 579–581 (1999)
12. Ward, M., Grinstein, G., Keim, D.: Interactive Data Visualization: Foundations, Techniques, and Applications. A. K. Peters Ltd, USA (2010)
13. Nielsen, J.: Usability Engineering. Academic Press, New York (1993)
14. Shneiderman, B.: Tree visualization with tree-maps: 2-d space-filling approach. ACM Trans. Graph. **11**(1), 92–99 (1992)
15. Bederson, B.B., Shneiderman, B., Wattenberg, M.: Ordered and quantum treemaps: making effective use of 2D space to display hierarchies. ACM Trans. Graph. **21**(4), 833–854 (2002)
16. Fabri, M.: Thinking with a new purpose: lessons learned from teaching design thinking skills to creative technology students. In: Marcus, A. (ed.) DUXU 2015. LNCS, vol. 9186, pp. 32–43. Springer, Cham (2015). https://doi.org/10.1007/978-3-319-20886-2_4
17. Buono, P., Legretto, A., Bertini, E., Costabile, M.F.: Visual techniques to compare predictive models. In: Proceedings of the 13th Biannual Conference of the Italian SIGCHI Chapter: Designing the next interaction, pp. 1–5 (2019)
18. Desolda, G., Ardito, C., Jetter, H.C., Lanzilotti, R.: Exploring spatially-aware cross-device interaction techniques for mobile collaborative sensemaking. Int. J. Hum. Comput. Stud. **122**, 1–20 (2019) ISSN 1071-5819 https://doi.org/10.1016/j.ijhcs.2018.08.006
19. Ardimento, P., Baldassarre, M.T., Caivano, D., Visaggio, G.: Multiview framework for goal oriented measurement plan design. In: Bomarius, F., Iida, H. (eds.) PROFES 2004. LNCS, vol. 3009, pp. 159–173. Springer, Heidelberg (2004). https://doi.org/10.1007/978-3-540-24659-6_12
20. Costabile, M.F., Fogli, D., Lanzilotti, R., Mussio, P., Piccinno, A.: Supporting work practice through end-user development environments. J. Organ. End User Comput. **18**(4), 43–65 (2006). https://doi.org/10.4018/joeuc.2006100103

Explaining AI Through Critical Reflection Artifacts

On the Role of Communication Design Within XAI

Beatrice Gobbo(✉)

Design Department - DensityDesign Research Lab, Politecnico Di Milano, Milan, Italy
beatrice.gobbo@polimi.it

Abstract. Artificial intelligence algorithms – and data that feed them – are increasingly imbued with agency and impact and are empowered to make decisions in our lives in a wide variety of domains: from search engines, information filtering, political campaigns, health to the prediction of criminal recidivism or loan repayment. Indeed, algorithms are difficult to understand, and explaining "how they exercise their power and influence" and how a given input (whether or not consciously released) is transformed into an output. In the computer science field, techniques of *explainable artificial intelligence (XAI)* have been developed for disclosing and studying algorithmic models, using data visualization as visual language to let experts explore their inner workings. However, current research on *machine learning explainability* empowers the creators of machine learning models but is not addressing the needs of people affected by them. This paper leverages on communication and information design methods (or competences) to expand the explainable machine learning field of action towards the general public.

Keywords: Explainable AI · Communication design · Data visualization

1 Introduction

The increasing use of *artificial intelligence* in people's everyday life has raised the need for solutions aimed to reveal the work done by machine learning when transforming a given input into an output, especially when the latter is perceived as wrong or biased. Indeed, in the social science field, they [1] talked about *algorithm drama* referring to the role of algorithms in public life, highlighting the lack of clarity for the public in regard to how them assert their power and influence [2]. In the computer science field, they are trying to develop more and more precise XAI techniques for examining and studying machine learning models at different degrees of sophistication with purposes that range from improving performance to debugging them. However, the current status of the research on machine learning *explainability* is still empowering the creators of machine learning models but is not informing the people affected by them [3, 4]. Data visualization and interactive interfaces are even used for teaching naïve users how

The term *artifact* is intended as a man-made object.

T. Reis et al. (Eds.): AVI-BDA 2020/ITAVIS 2020, LNCS 12585, pp. 184–188, 2021.
https://doi.org/10.1007/978-3-030-68007-7_12

ML models react to different data inputs [5]. The act of making something understandable and informative entails a process that reveals an underlying phenomenon, which is related both with the ability to visually communicate information and with the aptitude of end users to interpret the decision taken by the [6] model. Starting from the assumption that there are *no standard methods* for visually communicating, by the means of data visualization and diagrams, algorithmic decisions to the *affected* general audience [7], both the communication design and the computer science community would benefit from the introduction of methods for visually communicating algorithmic decisions to the affected general audience for the design of emerging data experiences.

2 Reaching the General Audience

The aim of information design is to interpret and translate information into analogical and/or digital artifacts [8]. In 2011, Moere and Purchase [9], talking about the role of information visualization in design studies, argued that visualization of data with personal relevance could help non-expert users in reaching reflective insights. Highlighting data with personal relevance by the means of data visualization does activate users' critical thinking [8] about the objectivity of machine learning models, pushing them in reaching reflective insights. Indeed, promoting algorithmic transparency, awareness and accountability at all levels has become an important challenge in terms of governance. However, given that the transparency, accountability and explainability of AI towards the lay public is considered problematic [10], it's important to take into account that the level of details proposed to users must be calibrated according to their ability and attitude to understand. Even looking at purely computer-based researches, the complexity of the desired explanation changes depending on the end user and the purpose of the application: the message can be communicated using metaphorical narratives for reducing the complexity of the vocabulary [11, 12], as well as explanations can be generated through different types of media, such as visualization and verbalization [13].

In the information design field, it is not uncommon to find projects that try to explain the mechanisms of AI algorithms and, as mentioned before, the ways in which the message is built and communicated are various: the explanation is never *unto itself*, but is always included and inferable from the demonstration of how the algorithm produces a certain output. Thus, the role of the communication designer is understood as that of the translator, who operates a continuous process of mediation between the starting and finishing system [8], employing a combination of media and languages suitable for understanding. Data visualizations, diagrams, illustration, animations, videos, games, performances are the tools that in communication design could be combined to bring the general user closer to the understanding of the algorithmic model, to understand why a decision has been taken and to act critically in the society.

2.1 Critical Reflection Artifacts

This position paper wants to list which criteria should be considered when the communication designer produces an artifact with the intention of making AI algorithms more transparent and understandable by a general user.

- **Language:** the visual and verbal language employed, depending on the combination of media used to visually represent an explanation.
- **Approach:** the approach used for presenting the artifact.
- **Aim:** the type of effect that the artifact must have on the user.

From those criteria emerges that, when it comes to communication and information design, using the term *explanation* is limiting for addressing the general public. Thus, the communication and information designer plays an essential role in interpreting and translating information by reformulating and transmuting contents from one shape to another. Digital artifacts designed to explain why (and how) an AI system produces a certain output can be generally intended as *critical reflection artifacts* [14]. Narrowing down, the aforementioned critical reflection artifacts can be organized according to the above criteria (*Language, Approach, Aim*) in the following six groups. See Fig. 1.

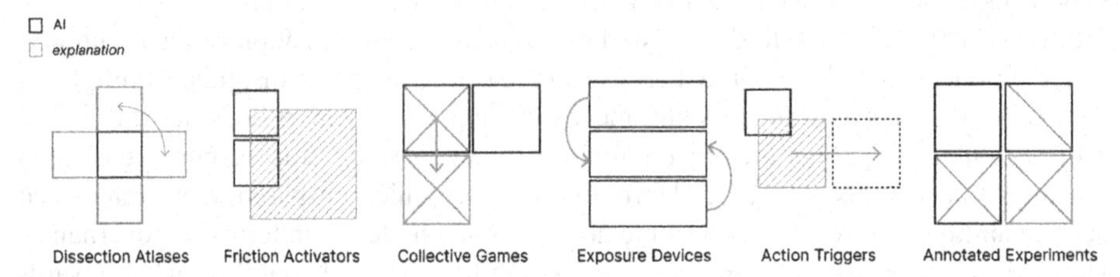

Fig. 1. A synthetic and visual showcase of the critical reflection artifacts. Black lines summarie the black/opaque model while the blue ones highlight the different approaches used to design *critical reflection artifacts.*

- **Dissection Atlases**

Language: data visualization, diagrams with annotations, lines of code. *Approach*: those artifacts open and dissect the "*black box*", focusing on visually representing the process in which data input and output. *Aim*: the overall view is that of a complex but usable set of content, with the aim of providing an atlas that requires a slow reading for understanding the process [15, 16].

- **Friction Activators**

Language: real-time videos, snapshots without extensive descriptions. *Approach*: those artifacts show the effect that AI has on real life as a visual filter. *Aim*: those types of artifacts push the user to slow down and to think. The absence of extensive descriptions leaves users free to reflect and find connections between AI and reality [17, 18].

- **Collective Games**

Language: interactive digital games, diagrams and text. *Approach*: the functioning of the algorithm(s) is discernible from the game mechanisms and is partially unveiled at the end using diagrams and illustrations. *Aim*: after a seemingly playful experience, users come to an explanation section showcasing the actions performed by the user and how AI has interpreted them [19, 20].

- **Exposure Devices**

Language: static or interactive visualizations. *Approach*: those types of communication artifacts showcase and visualize contents generated by artificial intelligence as they are, translating them in diagrams and abstract visual models. *Aim*: users can see the history of generated contents, filter and analyze them to understand the relation between their profile, choices and contents provided by an AI system [21, 22].

- **Action Triggers**

Language: videos (documentary-films, trailers, Instagram stories), annotations, data visualization and illustrations. *Approach*: those type of artifacts can also be understood as campaigns of social activism. Video documentaries and animated graphics tell personal stories of users and explain limitations and overuses of the technology. *Aim*: those type of artifacts directly pushes users to act critically in society as form of activism [23].

- **Annotated Experiments**

Language: pre-recorded input/output videos, diagrams and interactive visualization explaining technical details, explanatory text. *Approach*: the shape of these artifacts appears like a logbook/tutorial during the application of one or more algorithmic models. *Aim*: those artifacts give users the hands-on knowledge for reproducing the same experiments [24].

3 Discussion

This paper argues for adopting information visualization and communication design strategies when dealing with AI explanations addressed to a general audience. By mapping three criteria it is possible to expand the definition of "*explanation*" that becomes a critical reflection artifact. The combination of different media and languages, combined with data visualization, could help non-expert users in reaching reflective insights, enhancing the informative and critical role of the use of visualization. This research is onerous and challenging, and much interdisciplinary work can still be done to understand the level of complexity that artifacts must have.

References

1. Diakopoulos, N.: Algorithmic accountability: journalistic investigation of computational power structures. Digit. J. **3**(3), 398–415 (2015)
2. Gillespie, T.: The Relevance of Algorithms. Media Technol., no. Light 1999, pp. 167–194 (2014)

3. Abadi, M., et al.: TensorFlow: large-scale machine learning on heterogeneous distributed systems. arXiv preprint arXiv:1603.04467 (2016)
4. Strobelt, H., Gehrmann, S., Behrisch, M., Perer, A., Pfister, H., Rush, A.M.: Seq2Seq-Vis: a visual debugging tool for sequence-to-sequence models. IEEE Trans. Vis. Comput. Graph. **25**(1), 353–363 (2018)
5. Barron, W.: Teachable Machine Tutorial: Bananameter. *Medium*, Sep
6. Ziewitz, M.: Governing algorithms: myth, mess, and methods. Sci. Technol. Hum. Values **41**(1), 3–16 (2016)
7. Correll, M.: Ethical dimensions of visualization research. In: Proceedings of the 2019 CHI Conference on Human Factors in Computing Systems, pp. 1–13 (2019)
8. Baule, G., Caratti, E.: Towards translation design a new paradigm for design research. Futur. Think., pp. 1–14 2016
9. Vande Moere, A., Purchase, H.: On the role of design in information visualization. Inf. Vis. **10**(4), 356–371 (2011)
10. Kolkman, D.: The (in) credibility of algorithmic models to non- experts. Inf. Commun. Soc. **4462**, 1–17 (2020)
11. Jentner, W., Sevastjanova, R., Stoffel, F., Keim, D.A., Bernard, J., El-Assady, M.: Minions, sheep, and fruits: metaphorical narratives to explain artificial intelligence and build trust. In: Workshop on Visualization for AI Explainability at IEEE (2018)
12. El-Assady, M., Jentner, W., Kehlbeck, R., Schlegel, U.: Towards XAI : structuring the processes of explanations. (2019)
13. Sevastjanova, R., et al.: Going beyond visualization: verbalization as complementary medium to explain machine learning models. In: Workshop on Visualization for AI Explainability at IEEE VIS (2018)
14. Zingale, S.: Interpretazione e progetto. semiotica dell'inventiva (2012)
15. Crawford, K., Joler, V.: Anatomy of an AI system
16. Share Lab: The Human Fabric of the Facebook Pyramid. https://labs.rs/en/category/facebook-research/
17. Atken, M.: Gloomy Sunday. (2017). http://www.memo.tv/works/gloomy-sunday/
18. Atken, M.: Optimising for beauty (2017). http://www.memo.tv/works/optimising-for-beauty/
19. Google Creative Lab: Quick, Draw (2017). https://experiments.withgoogle.com/quick-draw
20. Google AI: Semantris (2018). https://experiments.withgoogle.com/semantris
21. Invernizzi, M., Ciuccarelli, P.: Visual monitoring of complex algorithms. In: 2CO Communication Complexity Contribution from 2017 Tenerife Conference, pp. 115–120 (2020)
22. Beaman, H., Campagna, T., Mniestri, A. Rossetti, G., Wang, X., Durand, R.: Tracking gender bias in amazon search results (2020)
23. Buolamwini, J., Gebru, T.: Gender shades: intersectional accuracy disparities in commercial gender classificatio. In: Conference on Fairness, Accountability and Transparency, pp. 77–91 (2017)
24. Cattaneo, A., et al.: DeepfakeLab (2020) https://deepfakelab.theglassroom.org

Information Visualization and Visual Analytics at IVU Lab

Paolo Buono(✉)

Dipartimento di Informatica, Università Degli Studi di Bari Aldo Moro,
Via E. Orabona, 4, Bari, Italy
paolo.buono@uniba.it
http://ivu.di.uniba.it/people/buono.htm

Abstract. This paper summarizes some works performed in Information Visualization and Visual Analytics in the last two decades at the IVU Lab (Interaction, Visualization and Usability and UX Laboratory) of the University of Bari Aldo Moro. This Lab has a long tradition in HCI. At the IVU Lab, Paolo Buono is the coordinator of the Information Visualization and Visual Analytics activities and he (co)authored the publications that resulted from the research on this topic.

Keywords: InfoVis · Data analysis · Predictive Visual Analytics

1 Introduction

The work performed at IVU Lab on Information Visualization (InfoVis) and Visual Analytics (VA) is mainly motivated by the increasing need, in many fields, of tools that help people to make rapid and effective decisions. Presenting data through proper visualizations has a great potential of improving their understandability, as well as their analysis, but requires a lot of work when data amount is huge (Big Data) and/or change dynamically. In the following, some of the works performed at IVU Lab are briefly reported. Figure 1 shows some of the visualization techniques that were developed.

"Visual analytics combines automated analysis techniques with interactive visualizations for an effective understanding, reasoning and decision making on the basis of very large and complex data sets" [18]. The main focus at IVU Lab is on the human side of the data analysis. Effective interactive visualizations enhance the innate human ability to visually perceive patterns and trends to effectively understand, reason and make decisions. The techniques and tools we develop aim at enabling effective data navigation and interpretation, preserving user control, thus enabling users to discover interesting or unusual patterns,

http://ivu.di.uniba.it.

T. Reis et al. (Eds.): AVI-BDA 2020/ITAVIS 2020, LNCS 12585, pp. 189–194, 2021.
https://doi.org/10.1007/978-3-030-68007-7_13

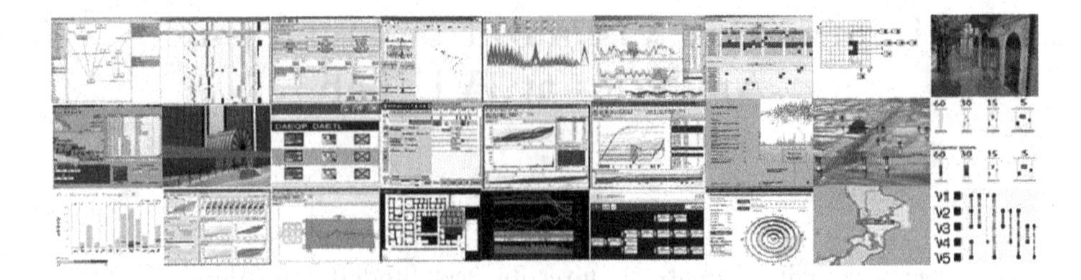

Fig. 1. Visualizations techniques developed at IVU Lab.

even without the need to know in advance what kind of phenomena should be observed.

2 Visual Analytics

VA often involves Data Mining (DM) methods to process data in order to reduce the complexity and size of big data before presenting them to the user. A challenge faced at IVU Lab has been the visualization of the results of DM methods, such as Association Rules and Clustering. In most cases, DM methods produce thousands **Association Rules** that the user must analyze. We provided a visual strategy that exploits a combination of graph-based and parallel coordinates techniques to visually present the results of association rule mining algorithms [3]. Data miners get an overview of the rule set they are interacting with and can deeper investigate inside a specific set of rules. The developed tools were embedded in a framework for data analysis, called DAE [8], which was developed within the scope of the FairsNet EU Project. Some DM methods produce Multilevel Association Rules that introduce further complexity, related to the level of abstraction of the rules. A solution that allows the navigation across two dimensions: a) the abstraction levels and b) rule granularity levels were presented in [2]. An association rule can be visually encoded as antecedent and consequent, each of them is a node composed of a set of atomic values, the relation between such nodes can be represented as graphs, so the visualization is based on the classic node-link approach, while other graph visualization techniques are proposed in the literature. At IVU Lab, in collaboration with foreign colleagues, in particular J.-D. Fekete and C. Plaisant, we are investigating on novel approaches for **visualizing dynamic hypergraphs**, which pose very challenging issues, such as the visualization of network topology changes over time, providing techniques and tools to enable users to detect patterns and inconsistencies [20]. This research has been appreciated by the community. In particular, two further papers report how to visualize dynamic hypergraphs, using the PAOHVis technique, in an ordered, clean and understandable way, that avoids intersections and allow to see the topology evolution over time [21]. The Digital Humanities users we interacted with, during the development of the PAOHVis technique needed to label data and reorganize them, possibly in clusters. We then realized an enhancement of the PAOHVis tool that allows users to cluster data according to a mixed-initiative approach, where, in accordance with the VA strategy, the human and the machine are interleaved in the analysis. The approach is called PK-Clustering and visualizes all clustering algorithm results on the screen, by allowing the user to select which algorithm best fit the data at hand [19].

Other significant activities have been performed with environment experts to identify interactive visual tools suitable for their purposes [9]. We exploited KNIME to visually **model the process and transform the data** in the format they need. In the context of air quality monitoring, we developed a system that allows decision makers to monitor the state of **air quality** [1]. Recently, an ongoing work is proposing a novel user interface to analyze pollution data by first applying **clustering** algorithm, then visualizing data and clustering results on a geographic map using different visualization techniques.

A study addressing **big data** has been made, by analyzing one year of highway traffic data, characterized by an elevated number of vehicles traveling on the highway and the temporal aspect [12]. Moreover, we started a collaboration with a company (Links SpA) and Enrico Bertini (New York University) in the **Predictive Visual Analytics** field. We developed an interactive visual tool that allows for an easy comparison of multiple prediction models, in order to select the one that best fit the data under investigation [16]. With the company, we aim to transfer knowledge to Public Administration (PA) employees, to allow them choosing adequate visualization tools, in order to rapidly perform complex analyses. Related to this, we also focused on supporting the work of PA evaluators when performing usability tests to evaluate websites [7].

3 Time Series

The work on Time Series started at the Human-Computer Interaction Lab (HCIL) of the University of Maryland, coordinated by Ben Shneiderman. A first paper that reviews the state of the art on **time series visualization**, focuses on techniques that enable users to visually and interactively query time series [6]. The developed tool, TimeSearcher, allows people to explore multidimensional data using synchronized tables and graphs; it includes mechanisms to get overviews of data as well as details, to filter in order to reduce the scope of the search, to select patterns and find similar occurrences, etc. Search algorithms allows for easy comparison. Since time series, often describe a phenomenon, which can be repetitive and can, thus, be predicted, an obvious extension of TimeSearcher is towards predictions. Therefore, a subsequent work on time series was performed to define a data driven **forecasting method** and an interface called Similarity-Based Forecasting (SBF) that displays graphically, as a river plot, statistical information about the SBF subset [13]. A forecasting preview interface allows users to interactively explore alternative pattern matching parameters and see multiple forecasts simultaneously. Time series are typically visualized as line chart and linear timeline. But there are alternatives that in some case can be more effective. We proposed a **novel circular visualization technique** to analyze domestic energy consumption [4]. This technique was also used in different domains, for example when quantifying self (see [17]) is relevant [5], and also to support **awareness in distributed teams** by exploiting collaborative traces of team members [10]. The circular visualization has several advantages: in particular, in the latter case, it makes easy to identify the time zones where different people work.

4 Other Topics and Research Directions

IVU members developed a visual technique and a tool for video summarization to analyze long videos and identify interesting scenes. Compared to the literature, the analysis mainly relies on humans' interaction, since the tool allows users to quickly perform complex queries by simply selecting relevant parts of a video through point&click [11,14]. A similar approach has been adopted also to extract video sequences in surgery videos [11]. A study that falls in cybersecurity visualization was conducted to understand how to visualize possible threats in android mobile apps [15]. Mobile applications are now widely distributed, they can be a source of a wealth of data revealing many personal data of their owner. Cybersecurity visualization is one of emerging areas where it is worth spending efforts to make more comprehensible and robust systems. Other directions could be towards the visualization of evolution of relationships among people, which has been recently found very relevant since the COVID disease has appeared.

Acknowledgements. The author wishes to thank the member of IVU Lab for the fruitful discussions and the continuous collaboration over time that led to successful work and many interesting insights.

References

1. Andriani, E., Brattoli, M., Buono, P., De Gennaro, G., De Gennaro, L., Mazzone, A.: A gis tool for atmospheric emission management in south of italy. Fresen. Environ. Bull. **21**(11A), 3325–3329 (2012)
2. Appice, A., Buono, P.: Analyzing multi-level spatial association rules through a graph-based visualization. In: Ali, M., Esposito, F. (eds.) IEA/AIE 2005. LNCS (LNAI), vol. 3533, pp. 448–458. Springer, Heidelberg (2005). https://doi.org/10.1007/11504894_63
3. Bruzzese, D., Buono, P.: Combining visual techniques for association rules exploration. In: Proceedings of the Working Conference on Advanced Visual Interfaces, pp. 381–384 (2004). https://doi.org/10.1145/989863.989930
4. Buono, P.: A low cost system for home energy consumption awareness. In: Am I 2015 - CEUR Workshop Proceedings. vol. 1528. CEUR (2015). http://ceur-ws.org/Vol-1528/paper9.pdf

5. Buono, P.: A circular visualization technique for collaboration and quantifying self. In: Proceedings of the Workshop on Advanced Visual Interfaces AVI. vol. 07–10-June-2016, pp. 348–349 (2016). https://doi.org/10.1145/2909132.2926091
6. Buono, P., Aris, A., Plaisant, C., Khella, A., Shneiderman, B.: Interactive pattern search in time series. In: Visualization and Data Analysis 2005. International Society for Optics and Photonics, vol. 5669, pp. 175-186 (2005). https://doi.org/10.1117/12.587537
7. Buono, P., Caivano, D., Costabile, M.F., Desolda, G., Lanzilotti, R.: Towards the detection of ux smells: the support of visualizations. IEEE Access **8**, 6901–6914 (2020). https://doi.org/10.1109/ACCESS.2019.2961768
8. Buono, P., Costabile, M.F.: Visualizing association rules in a framework for visual data mining. In: Hemmje, M., Niederée, C., Risse, T. (eds.) From Integrated Publication and Information Systems to Information and Knowledge Environments. LNCS, vol. 3379, pp. 221–231. Springer, Heidelberg (2005). https://doi.org/10.1007/978-3-540-31842-2_22
9. Buono, P., Costabile, M.: Insights on the development of visual tools for analysis of pollution data. In: DMS, pp. 54–59 (2012)
10. Buono, P., Costabile, M., Lanzilotti, R.: A circular visualization of people's activities in distributed teams. J. Visual Lang. Comput. **25**(6), 903–911 (2014). https://doi.org/10.1016/j.jvlc.2014.10.025
11. Buono, P., Desolda, G., Lanzilotti, R.: Scenes extraction from videos of telementored surgeries. In: DMS, pp. 106–111 (2013)
12. Buono, P., Legretto, A., Ferilli, S., Angelastro, S.: A visual analytic approach to analyze highway vehicular traffic. In: 22nd International Conference Information Visualisation (IV), pp. 204–209 (2018). https://doi.org/10.1109/iV.2018.00044
13. Buono, P., et al.: Similarity-based forecasting with simultaneous previews: a river plot interface for time series forecasting. In: 11th International Conference Information Visualization (IV2007), pp. 191–196 (2007). https://doi.org/10.1109/IV.2007.101
14. Buono, P., Simeone, A.: Video abstraction and detection of anomalies by tracking movements. In: Proceedings of the International Conference on Advanced Visual Interfaces, pp. 249–252 (2010). https://doi.org/10.1145/1842993.1843036
15. Buono, P., Carella, P.: Towards secure mobile learning. visual discovery of malware patterns in android apps. In: Banissi, E., et al. (eds.) 23rd International Conference on Information Visualisation, IV 2019, Paris, France, Part I. July 2–5, 2019, pp. 364–369. IEEE (2019). https://doi.org/10.1109/IV.2019.00068
16. Buono, P., Legretto, A., Bertini, E., Costabile, M.F.: Visual techniques to compare predictive models. In: Proceedings of HCItaly 2019. CHItaly 2019, Association for Computing Machinery, New York, NY, USA (2019). https://doi.org/10.1145/3351995.3352035
17. Hilviu, D., Rapp, A.: Narrating the quantified self. In: Adjunct Proceedings of the ACM International Joint Conference on Pervasive and Ubiquitous Computing and International Symposium on Wearable Computers. UbiComp/ISWC'15 Adjunct, ACM, New York, NY, USA, pp. 1051–1056 (2015). https://doi.org/10.1145/2800835.2800959
18. Keim, D., Andrienko, G., Fekete, J.-D., Görg, C., Kohlhammer, J., Melançon, G.: Visual analytics: definition, process, and challenges. In: Kerren, A., Stasko, J.T., Fekete, J.-D., North, C. (eds.) Information Visualization. LNCS, vol. 4950, pp. 154–175. Springer, Heidelberg (2008). https://doi.org/10.1007/978-3-540-70956-5_7

19. Pister, A., Buono, P., Fekete, J.-D., Plaisant, C., Valdivia, P.: Integrating prior knowledge in mixed-initiative social network clustering. In: IEEE Transactions on Visualization and Computer Graphics (2020). https://doi.org/10.1109/TVCG.2020.3030347
20. Valdivia, P., Buono, P., Fekete, J.D.: Hypenet: visualizing dynamic hypergraphs. In: Puig, A.P., Isenberg, T. (eds.) EuroVis 2017 - Posters. The Eurographics Association (2017). https://doi.org/10.2312/eurp.20171162
21. Valdivia, P., Buono, P., Plaisant, C., Dufournaud, N., Fekete, J.-D.: Analyzing dynamic hypergraphs with parallel aggregated ordered hypergraph visualization. IEEE Trans. Vis. Comput. Graph. **27**(1), 1–13 (2021). https://doi.org/10.1109/TVCG.2019.2933196

Visual Analytics for Financial Crime Detection at the University of Perugia

Emilio Di Giacomo, Walter Didimo, Luca Grilli, Giuseppe Liotta, and Fabrizio Montecchiani(✉)

Dipartimento di Ingegneria, Università Degli Studi di Perugia, Perugia, Italy
{emilio.giacomo,walter.didimo,luca.grilli,giuseppe.liotta, fabrizio.montecchiani}@unipg.it

Abstract. This paper describes the research activity on financial crime detection developed by the computer engineering group at the University of Perugia. The presented research aims at designing and experimenting advanced visual interfaces to support financial crime detection, with a focus on tax evasion discovery. The activity of the group on this topic, which has been ongoing for ten years now, involves institutional and industrial collaborations and already led to system prototypes in use at different institutions. The scientific relevance of the research is witnessed by several publications in top-tier international journals and conferences.

1 Research Context and Motivation

Financial crimes represent a major problem of many governments and are often related to organized crimes like terrorism and narcotics trafficking. Tax noncompliance and money laundering are among the most common types of financial crimes. They are based on relevant volumes of financial transactions to conceal the identity, the source, or the destination of illegally gained money. For instance, the estimated amount of money laundered globally in one year is 2 trillion in current US dollars [16]. The major challenge for tax administrations and financial intelligence units (the main financial subjects fighting against such crimes) is to deal with the volume and the complexity of the collected data.

In particular, tax noncompliance is a financial crime that represents a serious economic problem for many countries. It consists of a range of activities, such as tax evasion and tax avoidance, that undermine the government's tax system. As a consequence, a fundamental goal is to reduce the so-called tax gap, that is, the difference between the tax amount that should be collected and the actually collected amount. For example, in Europe, the estimated VAT (Value Added Tax) gap for the year 2016 amounted to 147 billion Euros [2]. Among the European countries, Italy has a severe tax gap, which is estimated at over 97 billion Euros per year in the period 2013–2015 [12]. To deal with this phenomenon, many tax administrations are experimenting novel solutions that exploit advanced data

Research partially supported by Dip. Ingegneria Univ. Perugia, RICBA19FM: "Modelli, algoritmi e sistemi per la visualizzazione di grafi e reti".

T. Reis et al. (Eds.): AVI-BDA 2020/ITAVIS 2020, LNCS 12585, pp. 195–200, 2021.
https://doi.org/10.1007/978-3-030-68007-7_14

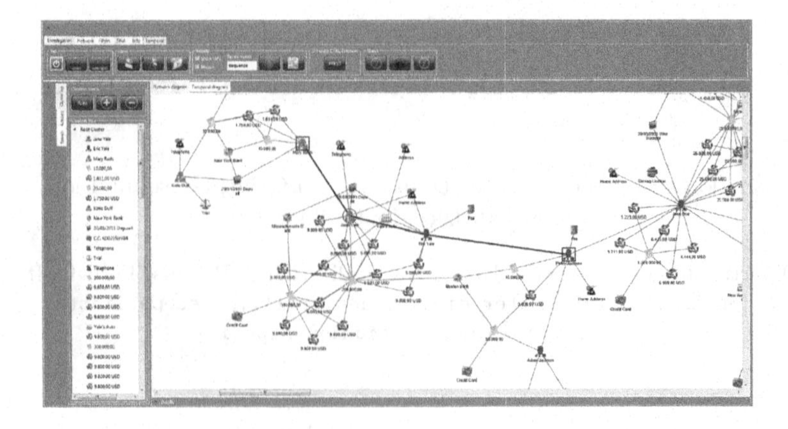

Fig. 1. A snapshot of the VISFAN system, originally published in [10].

analytics techniques [13–15]. In particular, the Italian Revenue Agency (Agenzia delle Entrate) has put in place various strategies to reduce the tax gap. A key one is building an effective law enforcement policy based on an accurate assessment of the so-called tax risk of the taxpayers. The main purpose of the tax risk assessment is to identify those taxpayers who are more likely to be involved in relevant tax evasion activities, which will subject to fiscal audits.

In this scenario, investigation and assessment activities can strongly benefit from network-based analysis, where financial operators are seen as actors that relate to each other within an interdependent system. The importance of analyzing economic transactions over a network of subjects rather than focusing on individual entities has been recently emphasized in [3]. Moreoever, it is widely accepted that the exploration of such networks in order to discover criminal patterns strongly benefits from a strict integration of social network analysis and visualization tools (see, e.g., [8,17,18]). Our goal is to exploit network visualization methods and visual analytics tools in order to design advanced systems that support the analyst in complex investigation scenarios.

2 Main Research Activities

Visual Analysis of Financial Activity Networks. About ten years ago, our research group started a collaboration with the Financial Intelligence Agency (AIF) of the San Marino Republic. The result of this collaboration has been the design of a system, called VISFAN, for the visual analysis of financial activity networks; see Fig. 1 for a snapshot of the system interface. The system allows either the analysis of data within the same financial institution (bank, money service businesses, insurance agency, etc.) or the analysis of suspicious transaction data collected by FIUs from different financial subjects. To this aim, VISFAN adopts different models to deal with the different types and sizes of the networked data sets managed in these two scenarios. On the other hand, unified algorithms and interaction paradigms are provided for fundamental analysis features, such as clustering, automatic graph drawing and centrality indexes. After the development of a first prototype, the system has been further engineered and become a commercial product. It is currently adopted by AIF, which gave us positive feedback about its usefulness.

We refer the interested reader to the related publications for a more complete description of our research [4,9–11].

Visual Analytics for Tax Risk Assessment. A more recent key collaboration with the Italian Revenue Agency (IRV) allowed us to further develop our research in the field of financial crime detection, with a focus on tax evasion discovery. In cooperation with IRV, we developed a new system called TAXNET. It supports the work of tax officers through a set of functions that combine a powerful visual language with network visualization techniques. The system models the data as a unified network, whose nodes represent taxpayers and whose edges are different types of economic and social relationships between them. The user can visually define classes of suspicious patterns, based both on topological properties and on node/edge attributes. TAXNET exploits effective graph pattern matching techniques to efficiently extract subgraphs that correspond to one or more suspicious patterns, it provides facilities to conveniently merge the results, and it implements new ad-hoc centrality indexes to rank taxpayers based on their fiscal risk. The system also offers visual tools to interact with those subgraphs that match a desired pattern, so to get more details or to filter out less relevant information. To efficiently execute graph pattern matching routines on large networks, data are conveniently stored in a graph database instead of a traditional relational database. After the positive results of preliminary experiments conducted on a restricted set of real data, IRV is engineering and scaling the system to work on larger datasets. The experimental data suggest that using TAXNET can reduce the time needed to execute fundamental analysis tasks, it can facilitate the retrieval of suspicious patterns, and it can increase the reliability of the results.

As a follow-up of the aforementioned research activity, we worked on two main directions: extending our model to temporal networks with dynamic attributes and extending our analytics tools to better support the decision making process. Concerning the second direction, we designed a novel approach, called MALDIVE (MAtch, Learn, DIffuse, and VisualizE), that combines different data mining and data analytics methods, such as graph pattern matching, social network analysis, machine learning, information diffusion, and network visualization. The main goal of such new approach is to keep under control the decision-making process of the public administration. It allows public officers to better analyze and validate the results provided by automatic classification techniques. The approach is based on the conceptual pipeline shown in Fig. 2, which can be summarized as follows. We first construct a social network where taxpayers are interconnected by various types of relationships and we define suspicious graph patterns that represent risky schemes on this network. Such patterns are

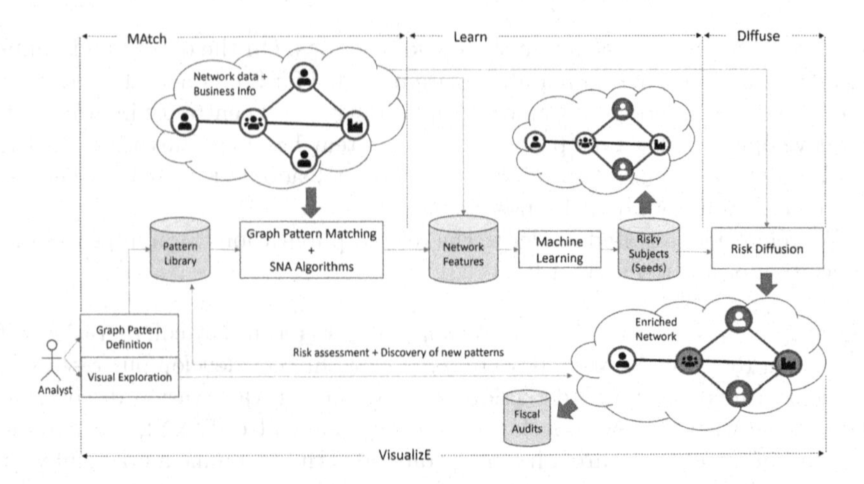

Fig. 2. A high-level scheme of the MALDIVE approach for the tax risk assessment of taxpayers, originally published in [6]. It follows a pipeline that combines various data mining and analytics methods in order to support a human decision-maker.

stored in a pattern library and matched in the social network in order to retrieve risky subjects. Based on this social network and on the matched results, we compute both classical social network analysis (SNA) indexes and domain-specific indexes to highlight the most relevant actors. Next, we make use of a tax risk forecasting model in which machine learning algorithms are trained not only on standard business features of the taxpayers but also considering their social network indexes computed in the previous phase. The forecasting model is trained on the basis of the outcome of previous fiscal audits and it turns out to be quite effective on identifying the most risky taxpayers. We then apply an information diffusion method to propagate the fiscal risk in the taxpayer social network. The diffusion process is based on a stochastic model that simulates the spread of an information over an underlying network. In the last phase, the social network, suitably enriched with the fiscal risk scores computed in the previous steps, is the input of a network visualization interface. The purpose of this last phase is to support the analyst in validating the fiscal risk scores assigned by the previous phases. Thanks to a visual exploration of the social network, the analyst can better assess the real risk profile of taxpayers, thus carrying out a more effective selection of tax audits.

We refer the interested reader to the related publications for a more complete description of our research [1,5–7].

3 Future Research Directions

Some of the future activities that we plan to conduct in order to further develop our research on network visualization and visual analytics for financial crime detection are: (i) Establishing new collaborations with institutions and industries at both national and international level, so to expand the scope of our systems; (ii) Designing new visualization models and interaction paradigms that best fit the investigation process scenario; (iii) Implementing new tools for extracting and processing data from diverse sources (e.g., the dark web).

References

1. Angori, L., Didimo, W., Montecchiani, F., Pagliuca, D., Tappini, A.: ChordLink: a new hybrid visualization model. In: Archambault, D., Tóth, C.D. (eds.) GD 2019. LNCS, vol. 11904, pp. 276–290. Springer, Cham (2019). https://doi.org/10.1007/978-3-030-35802-0_22
2. CASE Research: Study and reports on the vat gap in the eu-28 member states: 2018 finalreport (2018). https://ec.europa.eu/taxation_customs/sites/taxation/files/2018_vat_gap_report_en.pdf
3. Council of the European Union: 9046/16. VAT Action Plan. Towards a single EU VAT area (2016). http://data.consilium.europa.eu/doc/document/ST-9046-2016-INIT/en/pdf
4. Di Giacomo, E., Didimo, W., Liotta, G., Palladino, P.: Visual analysis of financial crimes: [system paper]. In: Proceedings of the International Conference on Advanced Visual Interfaces, pp. 393–394. ACM (2010)
5. Didimo, W., Giamminonni, L., Liotta, G., Montecchiani, F., Pagliuca, D.: A visual analytics system to support tax evasion discovery. Decis. Support Syst. **110**, 71–83 (2018)
6. Didimo, W., Grilli, L., Liotta, G., Menconi, L., Montecchiani, F., Pagliuca, D.: Combining network visualization and data mining for tax risk assessment. IEEE Access **8**, 16073–16086 (2020)
7. Didimo, W., Grilli, L., Liotta, G., Montecchiani, F., Pagliuca, D.: Visual querying and analysis of temporal fiscal networks. Inf. Sci. **505**, 406–421 (2019)
8. Didimo, W., Liotta, G.: Mining Graph Data, chap. Graph Visualization and Data Mining, pp. 35–64. Wiley (2007)
9. Didimo, W., Liotta, G., Montecchiani, F.: Vis4aui: visual analysis of banking activity networks. In: GRAPP/IVAPP, pp. 799–802 (2012)
10. Didimo, W., Liotta, G., Montecchiani, F.: Network visualization for financial crime detection. J. Vis. Lang. Comput. **25**(4), 433–451 (2014)
11. Didimo, W., Liotta, G., Montecchiani, F., Palladino, P.: An advanced network visualization system for financial crime detection. In: IEEE Pacific visualization symposium, pp. 203–210. IEEE(2011)
12. Italian Government, Ministry of Economy and Finance: Relazione sull'economia non osservata e sull'evasione fiscale e contributiva anno 2018 (2018). http://www.mef.gov.it/documenti-allegati/2018/A6_-_Relazione_evasione_fiscale_e_contributiva.pdf
13. OECD: Advanced Analytics for Better Tax Administration. OECD Publishing, Paris (2016). https://doi.org/10.1787/9789264256453-en
14. OECD: The Changing Tax Compliance Environment and the Role of Audit. OECD Publishing, Paris (2017). https://doi.org/10.1787/9789264282186-en
15. Pijnenburg, M., Kowalczyk, W., van der Hel-van Dijk, E., et al.: A roadmap for analytics in taxpayer supervision. Electron. J. e-Government **15**, 14 (2017)
16. United Nations: Money-laundering and globalization. http://www.unodc.org/unodc/en/money-laundering/globalization.html

17. Westphal, C.: Data Mining for Intelligence, Fraud, & Criminal Detection. CRC Press (2009)
18. Xu, J., Chen, H.: Criminal network analysis and visualization. Commun. ACM **48**(6), 101–107 (2005)

Author Index

Author Index

Printed in the United States
By Bookmasters